THE
DESTINY
BOOK

REDISCOVERING THE MOTHER OF SPIRITUALITY

HELENA LIND

Foreword
GREGORY V. DIEHL

Library of Congress Control Number: 2023914798

ISBN-13: 978-1-945884-80-1 (paperback)
ISBN-13: 978-1-945884-81-8 (hardcover)
ISBN-13: 978-1-945884-82-5 (ebook)

First edition, published by Identity Publications.
Editor: Gregory V. Diehl

Cover Ornament: Ladies Who Destine, 2023, inspired by classic Greco-Roman Goddesses, Helena Lind with LensGo beta.

Autodesk Sketchbook pencil drawing, a 2023 interpretation of Ananke and the Moirai by Edmond Lechevallier-Chevignard, 1857, La Magasin Pittoresque. Original is in the Public Domain. https://commons.wikimedia.org/wiki/File:Ananka_i_Mojre.JPG

The Destiny. 2020. Painting by and Copyright Rebecca Stockburn in design cooperation with and for Helena Lind's publications and media.

Book Cover by MiblArt, Ternopil, Ukraine

Contents

Author's Note

Due to the dynamic nature of the Internet, any URLs or web addresses, or links stated in this book are subject to change and/or may have been changed since this book was published; hence, they may not always be valid.

Some of the Gutenberg Project and other links listed in the back matter may not work in all countries due to local copyright laws.

Most specific names and terms were anglicized.

I am trying to avoid the use of excess timeline details, dates, numbers, etc., wherever possible since this is not a scholarly or pontificating work but a rather easy reintroduction of the history and lasting significance of the metaphysical order of cosmic and human Destiny to entertain and spark curiosity.

Furthermore, I predominantly write in the collective form to ward off pronoun pile-ups. I dislike indoctrination, so I include my readers in the only way synonymous with how *we*, as humanity, would work best—together, in concert.

Dedication

To my loved ones, near and far, human and feline, on all levels of existence, and especially to Paul for his unwavering understanding.

Foreword

Many people say they have a book in them. Someday, they'll get around to writing it. But more often than not, that book never materializes and makes its way into the public light.

Independent thinker and creator Helena Lind, though, had indeed been working on a viable book concept for many years. It would culminate her lifetime of experience, inquiry, and contemplation into a dynamic subject of grand scale: destiny. At last, she invites us to reflect on the interplay between choice and fate, agency and determinism, and the human quest for meaning in an unpredictable universe—without prescribing any particular dogmatic and limiting view. Instead, she sparks contemplation, curiosity, and a deeper appreciation for how we have come to view the forces that have potentially always been influencing human lives.

The desire to understand how people see their place in the world has been one of the primary driving factors in my life, too. It has motivated my lifestyle choices and informed everything I've written or had a hand in publishing. The release of this book brings clarity to this supremely important topic, and I am tremendously glad to have had the opportunity to play a part in it.

As history shows, there has never been a time that freethinkers, and even whole societies, have not grappled with the implications of fate, free will, and why things happen the way they do. In one form or another, people have always felt something greater than themselves that influences the progression of the cosmos and their place within it. The book you are reading explores these multifaceted conceptions of destiny from throughout history—the cultural, religious, and philosophical underpinnings that have shaped our collective understanding of the "big picture." It illuminates ancient beliefs about predetermined cosmic order, myths of gods and goddesses, and modern, scientifically informed interpretations of life, the universe, and everything.

The Destiny Book shows how this universal idea has always been with us. Though conceptions of overarching cosmic order evolve, adapt, and transform along with human consciousness, certain themes and principles seem to recur wherever and whenever we look for them—and so, we stand to learn from them. The lingering awareness of where things *are* going, where they *ought to* go, or perhaps even where they *must* go still makes the world go 'round.

We all sometimes look at the world around us dissatisfied. We feel called to do something to improve it and move it closer to how we think it should be. We are always moving toward a personal conception of what is right and necessary, even if most of us avoid too much scrutinzing about it. One way or another, we adhere to a narrative that grants order and a sense of purpose to everything.

Left unexamined, our underlying metaphysical beliefs can become dangerous things. We can't really know who we are and what we are capable of unless we are willing to assess the lens through which we look at life. We might start to believe that going against the narrative that we have accepted is to go against existence itself: what Helena calls a dogmatic, thus faux, destiny—and so, others must be made to act against their will according to what we believe.

I know many readers will understand when I say that I have always felt pulled toward certain fundamental ideals. With experience, I embraced them as an inescapable part of who I was and increasingly necessary to uphold in the world. They represented what I would always seek to do and become: my personal destiny. I could never say with certainty what would happen in my future—only what I would always choose to pursue as long as I could, as a seed sprouts into a tree given conditions that allow it.

The Destiny Book shows us how to question the standards through which we evaluate the meaning of our actions and everything seemingly good or bad that happens to us. Helena's heroic effort gives us a generous helping of how human thought has evolved in this domain over the centuries. By understanding why we believe what we do about the universe, we will come to understand ourselves considerably better, too.

This first volume constitutes the introduction, the companion to the documented backstory of a larger and integrated modern take on human destiny. Readers will surely look forward to Helena expanding on it in her upcoming work in the *Destinosophy* series. I am grateful to have helped bring it out to the world.

By Gregory V. Diehl—author, publisher, and mentor

Preface

Inspired by lifelong awareness and the disruptive events of 1992, I first envisaged and even working-titled *The Destiny Book* after having been told that I'd reached the dead-end street in most, or as some professionals claimed, in all possible ways. Challenging years of phoenixing followed, reliably accompanied by a steady comparison of roadmaps, fitting in the labor of love on this ancient showrunner's story whenever possible. Result: an informal perspective of a worldview-shaping paradigm through my affectionate lens, my prism of interpretation, and the first of several nonfiction and fiction concepts on our sublime topic.

Ideally, the reader finds this publication a ticket to rediscover one of life's greatest enigmas, an introduction to some of the many facets of a de facto pièce de résistance, and, not too boring 411 to my upcoming publications and world events, especially the catharsis that awaits humanity. I created it as an accessible, relatable essence of some of the most relevant mythologies and tenets of this arcane entity spanning several millennia. Take it as a curiosity-provoker, an invitation to think anew, a collection of keywords to tickle interest, and a gentle nudge to hop on a swift quest to discover the many aspects of the lode star we call Destiny. Due to my talking point's unlimited vastness, this little book can only be a teaser to an infinite movie. Yet, this first stepping stone may already help to dust off some often overly simplistic, if not reductionist, ideas encircling this *primus inter pares*—the first among all otherwise equal metaphysical phenomena.

And I am here to make that clear.

Introduction

The most beautiful experience we can have is the mysterious. It is the fundamental emotion which stands at the cradle of true art and true science. Whoever does not know it and can no longer wonder, no longer marvel, is as good as dead.

— ALBERT EINSTEIN

Before anyone asks: I don't *believe* in Destiny in the typical way, as in believing in a theology or ideology conceived and accepted upon cultural or social agreement or via "persuasion." Because Destiny is neither. My unbridled consciousness and intuitive cognition of a trailblazing, religion-independent yet spiritual cosmic paradigm inspires uncounted millions worldwide to acknowledge its relevance from the moment go! As a testament to my first-hand experience with this grand enigma, I created this book as a shareable quintessence of Destiny's amazing backstory. I call it long-term personal awareness; others may consider it to be an act of faith or confirmation bias. We're all right. Whatever works best works best.

Destiny is a complex and polarizing topic preloaded with ancient, seminal meaning and unending popularity. And like all worthwhile movers and shakers, it triggers a healthy amount of prejudice, derision, and even antagonism. Not for nothing, since this arcane fountainhead of abstract phenomena transcends cosmogonies, mythologies, deities, and faith systems. Naturally, it entices strong opinions about deterministic influences on well-cultured ideas of human moral responsibility versus a more or less decreed existence and world. The thought goes that if external Destiny is predominantly in charge of it all, we cannot be held accountable for ethical and material trespassing of rules and laws. And that, in tandem with the resulting scarcity of freedom, isn't all too compatible with the governing agenda. Therefore, skeptics feel deeply objecting to absurd transcendental ideations, including the slightest inkling of being guided, let alone determined, for that must be impossible. In contrast, others may criticize that divine Destiny is solely enacted by almighty God instead of an impersonal seminal principle that, bar a few ancient exceptions, hardly ever required systemic dogma, organized worship, or submissive prayers because of the absence of a point. Because petitioning for a change of plan or fortunes to a faceless paradigm doesn't feel right enough, nor does it make much sense to us anthropomorphizing[1] mortals. And that's why a synergetic dialogue is ruled out unless humanoid form, emotion, mentality, and hierarchy are applied. Which we did. Aplenty. Even to Destiny.

Nonetheless, this conundrum flows forever forward without God(s) and codified beliefs. Our cookie crumbles just as it does, or rather, it is kept from negatively disintegrating more often than not, sadly rarely recognized yet. Do we ever even pause, think and let alone acknowledge that of all the many facts not in our favor (and in view of the multitude of possibilities that can go wrong for our fragile setup), so far not as much as easily could happen is actually occurring? Even though it may appear very different to those afflicted by what occurs?

Whether we revere our own liberty or God(s), benevolent worldviews are rightly highly respected since they provide helpful notions to foster all-important equilibrium. Reality is what we experience and how. There is no *one way* to feel, opine, and do things anyway. Thankfully, Destiny isn't an ideological or religious premise where critics or contenders may be at risk of becoming a target for zealous scorn and limitations to their physical existence. In contrast, everything is quite easy here.

Our formative concept of Destiny has stood the test of time and remains incredibly and increasingly popular because it just *is* the natural umbrella concept staying religiously neutral and independent for the ages. As the antithesis of entropy, its invisible sway on humanity inspired leading codes and creeds that adopted Destiny's characteristics to better equip their celestial personalities.

The direction, balance, and order-inducing notions of our chaos-taming *éminence grise*, prevalent throughout most, if not all, great civilizations, are arguably the mother, foundation, precursors, surefire blueprint, and ignitor of the faiths [2] we cherish, question, or reject today and, especially, tomorrow.

We behold the vertex, i.e., pinnacle, the original mover resulting in the creation of human outlook and religion, our Mothership in the universe. A fun testament to this is that our splendid, established religions rushed to "adopt" Destiny to supercharge their divine powers with its significant essence. It stands just as the Irish poet Oscar Wilde (1854–1900) confirmed: Imitation is *the* sincerest compliment available on Earth.

The showrunner of life, just like the belief in God(s) or doctrines, such as karma and dharma, is often judged as a mere faith-based marvel or statement that can never be proved or disproved. No science, philosophy, or religion can claim to be able to "objectively" establish the non-existence of supernaturalism and God(s). Arguably, no mortal is able to make it known as a cold, hard fact that God(s) or any other invisible, abstract, unfathomable agencies ever [3] existed to influence the genesis of humanity. And so the cosmic premise remains imperceptible.

Destiny once was the preternatural [4] kickstarter of our major religions. They all wanted for themselves the meaning Destiny offered us humans.

Even the all-governing laws of cause and effect carry a connective notion of this mainstay of human sensemaking, right down to the claim of self-ordained fate among free-willing humanity. And ever since Destiny set the great stage, it circulates in the world's water supply. Everywhere. Little wonder that we find its ancient principles represented and incorporated in the divine personifications of our most enduring religions.

Prologue

Our independent melody of the universe has been with us since the dawn of civilizations, transcending any past or active tradition, faith, or creed. It is invoked worldwide, while its echoes sound more or less softly in almost every principal school of thought.

The very idea of the invisible order always made us ponder its promise of a beckoning future. What would be more critical in our transformative times than to pause, look back, take stock, think, and discuss the Destiny of humankind? That is even more vital now since we are walking the brink between a luminous tomorrow and an increasingly manifesting abyss.

Naturally, a good many past and modern thinkers, as well as some materialist and revolutionary-minded communism proponents, dismissed the idea of an elusive, invisible background "power," be it called God(s) or Destiny. Several of our best brains are still highly skeptical today. The world remains colorful; some of us even question the personal impact of specific determining laws of the universe and Nature. All too often, we tend to believe, or rather "will," what we perceive to represent our cherished self-image. Those of us that even postulate not to believe in anything at all, or rather claim to believe in *nothing*, are rendering themselves technically belief-less. This is a big fallacy because of one fact and trait we all have in common: We *do* believe in something subjectively, which is often driven by what we fear or desire. Human beings *feel* more than they think; many of us interpret our emotions as rational thoughts, taking each of these thoughts as "reality." Hence, no wonder so much cognitive dissonance[5] and so little tolerance abound, especially when contested with differing ideas.

Maybe we are just disappointed in our elders, their God(s), traditions, and omissions, or failures in our upbringing. So we drag our proverbial heels while telling ourselves and anyone who cares to listen that there's nothing to believe in or that we must not consider anything apart from our subjectively rational selves. Granted, some established religions caused terrible, inhumane acts, but we should not judge them just on their, albeit many, low moments and instead also try to see the good they do. Anyone should believe whatever they prefer since we are not who and what we believe to be, anyway. We are mostly highly subjective beings. That delivers even more reasons not to scoff at the *thought-feelings*, or rather *feeling-thoughts*, of others. We're all rowing the same boat, carrying forth our individual destinies. Whether we are aware of it or not or believe in anything, we all share in our collective human Destiny.

Anyway, most of our thoughts aren't as relevant as we think, so we better try to respect those of others. Let's not forget and forgive that producing sentiments about "not believing in anything" carries the added perk of garnering attention, just like those nihilistic notions often thrown about as gauntlets and challenges to a more traditional or religious status quo—and to raise the claimant's dopamine level.

It is often stated there is strength in numbers. The fact so many of us subscribe to specific concepts and faiths comes with legitimacy, proven or not. For there are beneficial elements in our ongoing, extensive acceptance of God(s), religions, and philosophies that deserve respect, tolerance, and understanding, even if we don't always agree on single entities, narratives, or details, and even if we are unable to share or reject the religious metaphors others hold dear.

The thing is, there *is* strength and safety in numbers.

Christianity, to date the world's largest and most successful organized religion, is swiftly losing followers in the so-called First World, even among white American evangelicals. Christianity's staggering ca. 2.38 billion upholders worldwide give evidence to the point that their faith carries incredible weight. The same goes for flourishing Islam, the next most extensive and rapidly expanding religion with ca. 1.9 billion global devotees and counting, followed by millions of Hindus, Buddhists, and then some.

Numbers *do* matter.

Worldwide, many, many millions believe in Destiny, also referring to it as fate. I'm terrible with numbers; nevertheless, let's look at some exemplary figures.

Nearly 50 percent of the British believe in Destiny[6] and state that important life events are foreordained. Even 46 percent of the United Kingdom's Christians say so.[7] As of early 2023, these sceptered isles counted 68,801,032 inhabitants. You do the math, please.

As many as 52 percent of Americans adhere to the notions of Destiny or fate.[8] The majority state to perceive a deeper pattern to life, with 52 percent saying they believe in fate, according to a 2015 report in The Washington Times.[9] Yes, you read that right: That would be the majority of the now estimated population of 334,233,854 inhabitants.[10] That's a lot, right?

In 2014, US researchers Konika Banerjee and Paul Bloom from the Yale Mind and Development Lab found that crediting a supernatural force like Destiny for determining what happens in life would not require religious beliefs. They are so correct. And it gets better. Even followers of organized faith confirmed there was no need to believe in God to accept the actions of an independent, preordainment agency.[11]

Participants were presented with questions to find out if they believed "life events happen for a reason." Partakers included the religious and non-religious. The study found the majority of both groups expressed belief in Destiny and fate.

Among subscribers to the existence of God, 84.8 percent expressed trust in fate, while just 2.2 percent said they did not believe in it. The rest were neutral. A total of 54.3 percent of atheists, agnostics, and freethinkers reported varying degrees of belief in fate. Those who did not believe in it accounted for 40 percent, and those who were neutral, 5.7 percent.

Participants were also asked to describe or characterize fate (a noun often used to express Destiny). Among the religious participants, 72.9 percent said fate was instructive. Others saw it as either fair (62.1 percent) or kind (54 percent). The group of non-believers described fate as "just a fact" in the cosmos.

Researchers also asked about the most significant event in the partakers' lives in the past five years. Twenty-four percent of non-believers and 53.1 percent of believers said fate had played a vital role in those events.

We haven't even looked at the large demographics in Latin America, India, China, or Russia, majorly invested in Destiny's guiding idea through local interpretations.

To me, all that data means the international interest and belief in the existence of Destiny results in such great numbers that this ancient principle should rank on par with all the other illustrious metaphysical and spiritual principles and faiths, in its own unique category and league, of course. Just saying. Not for no reason, Destiny hasn't joined the "Ozymandian [12] league" of slumbering giants of bygone beliefs.

Later in the book, we shall look beyond the anglophone world, discovering deeper connections with Destiny, fate, and karma in other cultures, religions, and philosophies. Ancient reasons await.

Humanity's relationships with Destiny's seminal concept and law are manifold and robust. Today, to some, it is a figure of speech or a meaningful metaphor. To others, Destiny is a notion from old books, an astrological almanac, or a romantic comedy: a force and state of being and experience far beyond our reach. And then some equate Destiny and especially fate—her darker epitome—with a kind of modern karma, interpreting the latter as a means of comeuppance out there to mop up baddies on auto settings. And, as seen above, to many of our fellow humans, Destiny is a valid concept, at least considered to have a hand in the flow of this world. We are looking at an undeniable cross-cultural and interspiritual omnipresence.

Our cosmic compass rose comes with many interpretations. It is often seen as a proverbial entity, a trope, a statement of character and standing, the red threat and clarion call of hero stories and movies, and the *raison d'être* of famous leaders and politicians like the "man of Destiny" Napoleon. Winston Churchill declared himself to have been "walking with Destiny" (also the title of a memoir on him) throughout his remarkable yet controversial life. Since time immemorial, this software of life has delivered massive momentum and magical mainstay to the spheres and many forms of special relationships, philosophy, religion, history, politics, literature, movies, and the music industry.

To this day, plenty of concern still exists that if the concepts of Destiny, and determinism for that matter, are indeed a proven fact or became "that popular thing" again, they could invalidate human moral responsibility exercised through our self- or God-granted self-determination, possibly leading to a plethora of excuses for bad choices, nether actions, and deeds. Why? Because anything could be interpreted as predetermined, i.e., outside our domain or control to decide against or not.

Such perilous limitations of human accountability and culpability are relevant topics and understandable moral worries. But what if we humans aren't the masters of the universe, no matter how much we'd like to run around with that label? And what if the whole strategic human self-ordination kit granted by God or ourselves is just a decoy or handy mirage? Imagine if the news outlets were plastered with flashes stating: SHOCKING EVIDENCE: DESTINY IS IN CONTROL, NOT HUMANITY.

Then what? Would we insist on clinging to the opposite? Probably. Would hell break loose? Likely not. Would our world religions crumble? Not so much since the majority adopted and developed their versions of holy divine providence from the original concept of Destiny anyway.

Isn't there perhaps far too much *angst* and too little trust in intuitive human awareness and innate moral thinking floating between our experts' learned brains and lips? Many of us are born with an inbuilt moral scope and are thus, for themselves, not necessarily in dire need of controlling sets of arbitrary rules. The intrinsic human tendency to try to live with goodness, based on cooperation and as much responsibility as possible, is a fact. Do we have a tendency to cheat, hoodwink, and even trick each other if the opportunity arises? Sure, but in most instances, that does not make us evil beings. We need to develop a lot more understanding of and for one another, our individual stories, circumstances, and the effects of the ravages of life that play on many of us.

Where would we be if a predetermining agency became the immutable fact of life (again)? Would we start to run amok? Declare war willy-nilly? Act selfishly and inhumanely for mere personal or corporate gain? Disregard and exploit the misbegotten and disenfranchised? Manipulate voters? Run corrupt rulerships?

Hold on a moment. All of the above points were and still are international issues.

Many political individuals or factions also abuse(d) the notion of *faux* Destiny to beautify unethical directions with eternity's invincible echo. Most of which, in time, led to ashes rather than laurels because their endeavors were never destined but wrongly claimed by misguided ideologies or toxic egos on steroids.

We know many kinds of Destiny: cosmic, natural, human, personal, divine, philosophical, national, political, religious, artistic, and lots more.

Our multifaceted topic is an impactful buzzword in movies or TV shows. It is a favorite moniker of shiver-inducing love-speak or an ennobling prerequisite of aggrandizing political egomaniacs or self-styled private or national exceptionalists.

Today, many, many millions, arguably a majority of people worldwide, accept various concepts of Destiny as a viable, underlying spiritual option far beyond its mythology. For millennia, this *original gangster* of time-honored phenomena has connected us with the unseen as the first fair and necessary guiding principle. And whatever happens, Destiny prevails as the primordial organizing force in the universe.

And it merrily stays as our great *continuum*, delivering thoughtfully spun threads running through the fabric of life, woven from the shimmering strands of universal laws, mysticism, imagination, and adventure.

Yet, Destiny is not a figment from a game. It may seem utterly philosophical and convincing, or shockingly limiting and even outmoded, utter tosh, for instance, to general skeptics and, especially, to devotees of scientism. Still, it is not just a holdover of ancient polytheism, nor a *Fata Morgana* or fictional chimera. It just is what it is. Always was. Always will be. And it may just be that unifying component we humans need to make it to the future.

Time to start pushing the big envelope.

Whether we accept it or not, the eternal thread is a part of our lives. It is even embedded in our material human build and our living force. The awareness of Destiny and fate are all around us. As said, we are talking about omnipresence here. We are saying, whispering, thinking, evoking, and dreaming of it every day.

We use idiomatic expressions like date or a deal with Destiny, all the things meant to be, the hand of fate, Destiny's wheel(s), a pull or twist of fate, and the call or irony of Destiny, whichever way the cookie crumbles, the dice may roll and whether the chips are going to be up or down.

My favorite Destiny metaphors are the mothership, the originator,, the supreme sense maker, Ananke's spindle, the software of life, the D Word, the cosmic choreography, the script of life, the grand design, the celestial blueprint, the cosmic compass, the universal symphony, the dance of Destiny, the tapestry of existence, the cosmic navigator, the celestial algorithm, the universe's plan, the game of serendipity, the river of everything, life's operating system, the mainstay, the foremost force, the melody of being, the compass rose, the real secret service, the Mona Lisa of principles, humanity's fairy Godmother, the cosmic law, the thread of everything, the lap of the Gods, and The All.

Our mothership performed the lead role in our quest for meaning, our imaginations, our hopes, and even our expectations in the agency of poetic justice. Neither the entertainment industry nor the worlds of music, literature, and art could do without it, thriving on the magic of a supra power.

It is important to note that Destiny does not translate to hard determinism, especially not to the bleak, responsibility-questioning variant of fatalism. Not all fatalism is created equal.

The Greco-Roman philosophical movement of *Stoicism* flourished on a liberating, ego-reduced acceptance and optimization of whatever life may bring. Modern scientific insights show that a moderate dose of accepting Destiny/fate improves our coping mechanisms, enabling us to overcome obstacles and move on less burdened and often faster. That's not limp fatalism. That's wisdom. Lemons, anyone?

A stoic attitude is a way to live well, to focus and deal with what is within our reach and make the best of what's there.

Life serves us a plethora of circumstances and situations we cannot change. Yet there is no ruse for inertia or bad excuses suggested for a life lived in harmony with a great principle. Destiny is multi-dimensional, dynamic, and symbiotic, the antithesis of defeatist notions or nihilistic doctrines. It empowers. It does not challenge or question a healthy dose of free will and self-fulfillment. Proactivity, drive, aspiration, and the readiness to seek self-transcending strength for a greater benefit are key ideals here.

So, whichever way we are persuaded and however we may judge or appreciate our topic, the fact is: We are here now; that's how the proverbial cookie indeed crumbled. Thus, it must be necessary.

The arch-principle of Destiny was and always will be a restorative *theriac* to an often iniquitous, unjust, and selfish world. Spindle and sphere, wheel and scales are still in full force. These concepts once introduced purpose, verity, identity, and the first shoots of meaning to an archaic world born from creative chaos. This supra entity preceded the religious systems that later borrowed many strands from the original fabric. Our contemporary world could do with a little, if not a lot, of that orderly principle of a good way to live in unity.

From the beginning, I had a sense of destiny, as though my life was assigned to me by fate and had to be fulfilled. This gave me an inner security, and, though I could never prove to myself, it proved itself to me. I did not have the certainty; it had me.

– CARL GUSTAV JUNG

CHAPTER 1

Origins of a Perennial Principle

Humanity loves to worship presumed supernatural and extraordinary beings: God(s), prophets, gurus, even celebrities, etc. Several religions and faith systems rule many of the invisible worlds of our spiritual needs throughout all cultures, geographies, and ethnicities. Inception myths and narratives generated impressive content and track records for those venerable beliefs and institutions that go back millennia. And the seminal concepts of Destiny—as legitimate as any of them—are no exception.

No one can escape Destiny.

— PLATO

But the grand blueprint should not be conflated with religion. Destiny hails from above and beyond any faith system. This is likely one reason my favorite force is more than alive and kicking today, despite no dedicated promotion, PR, or marketing efforts. No places of worship, no landmarks, priests, services, adorations, events, no rule books, no conditions, and no competition in the picture. Why? It is unnecessary. Its notion resides in so many of us—our reflections, hopes, and even trust in higher, if not poetic, justice. Confirmed by popular vote. Destiny is with us in many forms, not just in our everyday communications, books, art, movies, TV shows, and political and other ambitions. It shines internationally on the coveted, preordained, eternal bonds of our hearts and spirits, on time-and-space-spanning "meant-to-be" relationships. In many fields, Destiny and fate command unsurpassable quality through evocation and invocation, unbeatably unifying and democratic, due to the sheer absence of dogma, ulterior motives, control games, or financial interests. We don't *have* to call on the invisible unless we elect to do so. Are human self-determination and Destiny mutually exclusive?

It is not for no reason that the creators and story smiths of our organized faiths longingly adapted the metaphysical might of the great plan from polytheistic cultures. They went so far as to adopt the maxim of time and life itself to feature as a fundamental trait of their leading patriarchal overlords. The Abrahamic religions took off and grew swiftly and successfully because of their flexible attitude toward incorporating much older pagan components, symbols, pre-existing eternal personifications, and other narratives of myth and faith, pragmatically focused on filling voids in human sensitivity. So, no wonder Destiny was cleverly imported into religions to increase their importance with long-proven magnetic star quality and leadership. And why not? Faith knows neither plagiarism nor intellectual property infringement. It worked. Still does. Nothing is more successful than success.

But while we wonder whether knowing or believing in one or another element of Destiny is comparable with being religious, the answer is no. Our topic is an ancient, independent energy that emanates from the cosmic, human, metaphysical, and spiritual realms. It is a faith-independent force embedded in humanity's requirement for a higher source of attention, acceptance, balance, justice, and order. It is a legitimate spiritual alternative, and it can delight with a liberating perspective that continues to touch the lives of millions of people throughout the world.

This eternal and deeply human phenomenon always was and always will be a standalone, non-religious, meaningful power beyond comparison. Does being conscious of Destiny mean we are mere puppets remote-controlled by an unexplainable, incalculable force? Again, no. We are not expected to relinquish our wishes and actions. We're not told what to do unless called upon for a viable reason.

Our storied paradigm was and is a mentor, fairy Godmother, and inner voice, with us to help us seek self-development and venture into new frontiers on all levels. The actual "magic" always happened when humans and devised directions rose beyond all limitations as one. Yet sometimes it's just as well to close our eyes, listen and trust because we don't always know what's what, let alone what is right. Mostly we know little, anyway—very little. Still, we yearn for control while walking with one or the other big chip of illusion on our shoulder, but always in the company of natural necessity and inevitability.

Just like the flow of time, a concept of Destiny is innately present in most of us. It's all over the world as a virtue-inducing influence, deeply ingrained in our humanity, likely even genetic. No arbitrary, preconditioned guilt here. No masculine dominance. No ceremonies. No pomp. No cap-doffing deference. No elitist thinking. Non-doctrinal, clean slates for all. A principle that signifies Nature and open horizons. Our future. The eternal way forward.

N.B. This book does not aim to dissuade or evangelize readers revering established faiths. I won't argue against or diminish anyone's belief in any deity or thought school of choice, even if such a faith isn't freely chosen but the result of a particular and set cultural environment firmly internalized by family, peer group, and country. If a divine emanation is held in high esteem over a long time, it does *exist* through the histories, narratives, and unique places in its followers' hearts and hopes. That goes for all spiritual principles and entities; all of them are stewards of human Destiny.

First and foremost, we are all fellow humans. We are not our persuasions, which can enrich but also divide and burden us. Wherever the river flows, we are united in a shared, collective Destiny, even if we oppose each other or stand in competition. This ancient concept is free-flowing, all-encompassing, non-divisive, and unconditional. It costs nothing for the absence of hierarchical structures needing financing. There are no rituals to perform or laws of lifestyle to obey. We don't even have to believe in it. That quiet-yet-universal presence is underlined by enduring prevalence within our human dynamics and DNA.

Long away and far ago, our ancestors asked the very same questions we still raise today. What are we doing here? Do we matter? What is the meaning of all this? Where are we going? Who are we? How freely can we decide the purpose, shape, and direction of our life journey? What are our options, and what are the limits? How much are we guided without even wanting or realizing it? What is out there? And why?

In the past, humanity held strong beliefs in the laws of Destiny. It wasn't an alien concept to them to have their paths laid out and even be led by this mystical, ancient force of supreme balance that ruled serenely by their supreme might in the universe.

Our beautiful world *is* Planet Destiny, nurturing life and incredible evolution for millions of years. In the UK, the University of Southampton's Earth System Science professor Toby Tyrell stated recently in a study that our unique fertile habitat is an amazing exception in space. Other heavenly bodies did not fare so well. Professor Tyrell puts it down to fortuity. Fair enough. Or was our home planet singled out and protected by a cosmic force, even gifted with the favors of remarkable fortune?

For most of human history, cosmologies (world creation theorem) arose from the idea that everything that happened had to be incepted and sanctioned by non-human *uber*-beings. Many empires, kingdoms, and legendary narratives rose on the belief their leaders or prophets were destined for greatness and, sometimes, even ordained by God(s). Ancient civilizations believed that the foundations of their existence were based on the fact that Gods and demigods created and supported them and that these deities decided if earthly realms and leaderships would flourish or go under. Sometimes, the Gods bestowed particular, even luminous destinies on their often awe-inspiring favorites. However, even those perhaps less-entertaining yet deserving souls of conscience and character, those rare ones who stand tall for high principles and virtues, were promoted to elevation.

Over many years, increasingly, impressions emerged that not just the divine bunch but we mortal folk, too, could be capable of forging our futures. Philosophy and science enabled humankind to reflect on ourselves as rational creatures in charge, existing independently, reaching out toward our personal goals, and even influencing the course of Nature, if not the world. As ideologies, persuasions, and societies changed, the perceptions of Destiny and free will became more fluid and evolved.

In time, more concepts arose within and beyond official religions, while the ancient factuality of Destiny was, and is never, religious. Creeds and understanding of it inspired and vested world beliefs such as Judaism, Christianity, and Islam. The sacred books of all three Abrahamic religions feature Destiny in the form of God-driven foreknowledge and decree over anything and anyone, including respective ideas of an afterlife and the high and low fate of souls.

A splendid example from the Bible: Nifty-shifty *Jacob* is a perfect, although at first not evident, agent of Destiny chosen to fulfill a great mission for his God and his people. He even learns how and why to dodge conflict, strikes a covenant to hold peace, and walks away from vengeful battle and the typically unavoidable biblical fisticuffs to deliver on his Lord's design. Jacob wisened up, courtesy of a game-changing *Mizpah* moment. Genesis 31: [13] Why not look it up?

We now have differing ideas about both Destiny and religion, and quite a few of our modern notions challenge traditional worldviews that do not comply with our latest perceptions. Many of us like to think we have total control over our lives. At the same time, more and more of us believe the universe and its invisible forces play an important, if not prominent, role in caring about us and our wishes while conspiring to determine our often self-manifested path and future.

We all share an essential common aspect: humanity's penchant for a cosmic force. There exists an uncrushable need to believe in the presence of a higher rhyme and reason. That said, are we and our ways of living *indeed* the products of our actions entirely? Or is everything that's going on in our world a mere consequence of chance coincidence and random occurrences? Are we indeed willing and creating everything for ourselves while waiting for the goodies to come flying?

Is it all about us and what we desire? And, *is* there also a grand plan to support us, be it ancient, dormant, or quietly working in clandestine ways? Is there anyone, something out there, veiled within the wings of the stage of life and the realms of the unimaginable, waiting to return to the center of humankind's ever-changing arena to help us get back to who and what we are meant to be? Humanity has always looked for inspiration and a path of virtuous significance. We want to embody something special—deliberately chosen for a meaningful purpose.

It is far from surprising that Destiny and higher-calling-driven scripts and books such as *Star Trek*, the *Star Wars* franchise, *The Matrix*, and *The Lord of the Rings* trilogy have reached quasi-faith status with large followings that channel the universal significance supplied by these narratives into their own truths.

My take:

Just because something, anything, is ancient and mystical doesn't make it automatically right.

Just because something cannot (yet) be scientifically proven does not make it automatically wrong.

If something, anything, was and is anchored in our souls and traditions, even without hard evidence, it becomes our actuality. And even if we insist on *bivalence*—the idea that only two states of truth can be accepted as reality—any heartfelt entity or belief cannot be easily declared false if it subjectively works. Because if anything works, it is as valid as we wish, even true. Ask Neuroscience & Co.

How about a bit of time traveling? Let's get up close and personal with the backstory of Destiny.

What Exactly Is Destiny?

Varied concepts of Destiny anchored most, if not all, ancient civilizations. We already talked about how they were later adapted and adopted by the great world religions. To this day, a great many people worldwide believe in it, regardless of their persuasion or absence thereof.

Destiny is an ancient, international, universal, multicultural, seminal force, concept, and phenomenon represented by arcane cosmic forces, natural laws, multifaceted non-religious principles, and philosophical and theological personifications. And it is history's and spirituality's most constant, imperishable force, the original invisible hand.

Destiny is a teleological[14] notion of cosmological order shared with humanity and non-human beings. Its traditional cultural and philosophical axiom[15] consists of forever forward-looking, predetermined realities for single persons as well as groups, nations, systems, and even our planet. Another facet is the idea of certain no-matter-what style inevitabilities because of some great out-worldly purpose or rather mighty God's decree. Its legendary plan continues its impact on humanity from arguably before the bronze and iron ages straight through to our modern world as *the* debatable yet likely formative factor of the creation of religion. Time shall confirm.

We can define this phenomenon as a pre-envisaged or already decided course of opportunities and events during someone's or something's lifetime(s). Furthermore, Destiny is an ancient fact said to influence this world in a larger context and uniquely affect or even empower an individual. While it isn't static or absolutely unalterable but creative and flowing harmoniously with the agent's purpose and design, it also offers a reassuring notion of welcome permanence, certainty, and self-enforcement.

Let us examine the D-word's linguistic roots as per its usage in today's anglophone world. We have all heard, said, and read the term "Destiny" countless times. Since memory began, we have used this impactful noun (sadly, also often wrongly) in religion, philosophy, history, literature, politics, songs, movies, and more to address a pre-defined, specifically designed person, path, future, goal, or conclusion.

We may have thought, spoken, or written it ourselves when trying to describe an almost unexplainable, seemingly impossible, or even absurd scenario we've encountered. I bet it has been less than a few days since the expression popped up in a conversation or context near you that something happened due to fate, that Destiny *had her hand* in an outcome, that a couple's love was *written in the stars*, or that someone *followed their destined path*.

The concepts of Destiny are everywhere, fortifying our imagination and awareness with an invisible column–the pivot of being.

The Destiny of man is in his own soul.

– HERODOTUS

But what does this mystical word even mean? Let us look at the terminology.

Our noun, Destiny, developed from the Latin *"destinare,"* meaning "to establish, determine, or to affirm," and from the Latin "destino." [16]

The Latin term *destino* stems from way back to the pre-Latin Proto-Italic *de stanō*, which has its roots in the ancient Proto-Indo-European language, the latter having been spoken but not written from around 4500 BCE. [17]

Another definition of the Latin *"destino"* is "that which is woven or fixed with cords and threads." [18]

In Old French, *"destiner"* means "to determine," and *"destinée"* translates to the great D. Contrasting, we find it spelled *"destino"* in Italian, Spanish, and Portuguese.

Looking at its etymology, Destiny is commonly used to describe what is ordained or decided, designed to occur.

Take a look at another relative term: "destination." It refers to a specific, planned location where we wish to arrive.

As a dictionary term, we get a clear idea of Destiny as a concept dealing with getting from one determined life point to another. When we interpret this impression metaphysically and try to rationalize it, we understand how this specific "arrival" is supposed to take place. Like the facts of transportation and location in an exact time and space, we experience events on the way to arriving at that particular place.

A hint of the higher reason may also lead some of us to think our decisions were influenced by forces we do not completely understand, let alone control.

As a metaphysical concept, Destiny is an experience created by a series of forces we may or may not always have a say. For example, if we made a conscious decision to write a particular book, events in our lives influenced us to do exactly that, or someone strongly suggested to us to get going on that tome rather sooner than later—whichever way, we may simply have been "destined" to write this book all along. At the same time, if we seemingly accidentally started jotting down ideas without any prior intention or reason to ever write a proper book, but we did so anyway, it could still be predetermined. That book had to be written.

Simply relying on etymology and lexical meanings may be a bit too boring and barren. Synonyms for Destiny come to mind. When we look at different contexts and terms with the same or similar connotations and pay attention to cultural and historic overtones that come with such powerful words, we understand that it carries tremendous meaning for being synonymous with the big picture of Nature and the future. And that's also why Destiny is such a highly polarizing notion.

Not only individuals but all of humanity, peoples, states, societies, civilizations, and movements are still assigned their own destinies. For example, throughout history, the turn of phrase of a nation's Destiny is used abundantly to explain, elevate or even glorify all kinds of circumstances, not always for the best. Over time, sadly, too many characterless criminals borrowed its significance by wrongly claiming their appalling agenda decreed (or at least sanctioned) by Destiny. One example is Hitler, who brazenly construed the false vision of "*Lebensraum*" expansion he called "*German Destiny*" and instigated the catastrophic *Operation Barbarossa* (invasion of the Soviet Union) to lure his toxic mix of cadaverous-obedient and corrupt followers on the most horrid path of perverse national psychopathy.

Destiny or Fate?

In English, the other word we typically apply with or instead of Destiny is her slightly darker-clad sister, fate. Both terms often mean the same to many users but carry different connotations. Some prefer fate to describe a sense of resignation or inevitability, while others prefer Destiny since it evokes a feeling of hope or optimism.

At first glance, fate seems to be just a straight replacement for Destiny and vice versa. But fate is an entity that decides and manages the outcome of events in a person's life in an irrevocable fashion. Fate is both force and source of finality.

Destiny means something that's meant to be, while fate symbolizes a preconceived deal. Fate, in the more classical sense, is a pre-packaged affair, while pure Destiny navigates our journey in tandem with us. Both terms influence our human path, but fate has already carved each station in stone, while Destiny is the eternal voyage yet to be taken, forward-looking like a good travel companion.

An old translation of the Latin word *"fatum"* means "one's lot in life" and, more endearingly, "one's guiding spirit." Like Destiny, it commands an impressive etymology. Fate is derived from the Latin word *"fas, fari,"* which means "to speak," "to predict," or "to reveal a hidden fact through an oracle," an ambiguity of the Latin term *"fatum"* or *"fatum est,"* which means "that which has been spoken, that which is ordained." The three Roman Goddesses of Destiny were accordingly called *Fatae—the Fates*. A foregone conclusion. A fatality. A done deal. Finito.

> *Destiny is what you are supposed to do in life. Fate is what kicks you in the ass to make you do it.*
>
>   – HENRY MILLER

And yes, our modern word fate also stems from the Latin term *"fata,"* which means prediction. Our popular expressions "Fata Morgana" and "fairy" come to mind for all of the right reasons—etymological and meaningful connections include roots from the Latin *"fata,"* later translated to "fae, fay, and fairy." Remember the prescient *Lady of Avalon* and *Morgan le Fay* from the Arthurian legends? There you go.

Fate, both as expression and meaning, received rising attention and usage when the clever Romans, always keen to quickly adopt everything proven to work from Greece, (re)named the original Destiny trio of Goddesses the *Moirai—Clotho, Lachesis,* and especially *Atropos—*as their famous *Fatae*, the Fates—Nona, Decuma, and Morta—as per the etymology above. More on these amazing ladies a little later.

Since fate often expresses Destiny and vice versa, both are closely associated, yet somehow distinctly different, notions. Let's inspect.

Destiny applies when we are invited and given options to understand, adjust, and agree on our co-destined direction.

Fate applies when we are no longer asked what we think but, instead, get a kick up the behind.

You can control your Destiny, but not your fate.

– Paulo Coelho

Destiny gives the advantage of choosing which route to take, while fate is more a predetermined, unalterable course, sometimes seen as a one-way street. Fate is predominantly irrevocably woven to happen, no matter what.

Fate leads the willing and drags along the reluctant.

– Seneca

What the Stoic philosopher and statesman *Seneca* pointed out so succinctly is that Destiny guides those on board with the program, while fate pummels the stubborn and uninsightful.

Let us examine the two concepts of final fate and dazzling Destiny.

The Greeks began their relationship and mystic journey with the divine spinner Moira. Homer's *Iliad* and *Odyssey* initially hailed Moira (also called Aisa) as *the* Destiny, sometimes appearing as a cosmic, deterministic principle, another time via incarnation in a thread-bearing Goddess. The poet episodically mentions an intercepting Godfather, Zeus, grabbing the strands of Destiny or balancing a set of golden scales to determine the future of the Greek hero Achilles and the demise of the equally outstanding Trojan prince Hector. Yet, Destiny is usually represented by female personifications like the proto-Hellenic universe ruling principle Ananke and the three Moirai. Even the Gods had to answer to their personal Moira—Destiny—and accept a lower position in the hierarchy of destination designers.

In the early days of ancient Greek prose, Moira incorporated the meanings of desirable Destiny and deadly fate, both encapsulated in one formidable force to even tell the Gods what's what. There was no division. One power—one connection. One Destiny.

When the Romans conquered the Hellenic realms in 146 BCE, they assimilated most Greek deities and cheekily Latinized them. Thus, *fas, fari, fatum*—the oldest Latin term for Destiny—was applied to fit the new Roman incarnations of the Greco-classical three Moirai.

Consequently, the Moirai became the three Roman Fates.

Latin influenced many modern languages, including English. That's how, over many centuries, the widely used term fate entered literature and common expressions, while the English noun Destiny was adopted from the Latin *destinatio* for goal and *destino* and *destinare*, meaning perseverance and firm aim. Old French absorbed it for *"destiner"* and, later, for *"destin,"* meaning to destine—to predetermine a deliberate outcome.

The term fate—from the Latin *fatum est,* meaning decreed by Destiny or divine will—is traditionally interpreted as oppressive, immovable, and hostile. It is the opposite of dear Destiny and especially of Fortuna—luck or chance—the latter, though, only happens at the whim of the Goddess, a drawing of lots, or by blind luck, sometimes even as a coincidence. More on luck later. No wonder, thanks to our Roman predecessors, the kinship of linguistic etymology and meaning to terms such as fateful, fatal, and fatalism is lent enduringly. All this is mainly because of the Moira or, rather, the third Fata, the Greek Atropos (in tandem with her colleague *Moros*—the pathfinder of death) and the Roman Morta (the Latin word *mors* means death), who severs the thread of life with her shears. Consequently, lasting expressions such as fatality and mortality were created by the fearful interpretations of the Romans and through their language. Fate's meaning became a done deal.

The divine incarnations of the Greek Atropos and Moros represented non-negotiable fate, including the gloom of the scary connotation still with us in expressions like *mortal, moribund, mortified,* and *morose.*

This lifetime-limiting fate was seen as scary due to the human lack of control courtesy of Atropos's Roman sister Morta's overwhelming, snippy inevitability. These expressions created psychological tensions that also manifested in terror and bleak acceptance of what was perceived and interpreted to be fate. Regardless, the term fate is used a lot to express Destiny; consequently, we find the choice to call Destiny fate and vice versa in many ways throughout history. Fate's extension, doom—that particularly horrid fate, the entropy of hope—is another reason we have separate natures of an originally single entity in English.

Fate is sometimes also interpreted as an agency for retribution, dishing out consequences for assorted sins.

A note on fatalism. Many of us can be fatalistic without realizing it while feeling quite comfortable. Scientific findings relay that people with a fatalistic inclination may simply try to avoid feeling hurt overly much; therefore, they believe that whatever happened was unavoidable. So does a fatalistic stance help endure tough circumstances and deliver an explanation of what can be incomprehensible due to sheer enormity?

Apples and pears? Same root, different fruit? Dark side of the moon? The shadow behind the light?

Destiny defines, dedicates, designs, designates, and determines.

Fate fatigues and fatalizes and implies pessimism.

We are rewarded with a shining Destiny, whereas our feckless fate gets sealed.

Destiny is optimistic and flexibly modern, whereas fate can seem outdated due to its immutability. Destiny is *en vogue*; fate is not necessarily popular, despite its frequent synonymous usage.

According to the Roman poet Ovid (43 BCE–17 CE), the Goddess Venus tried in vain to prevent the assassination of her descendant, Julius Caesar. Despite the beauty's great powers, even she had to accept the will of fatum—decreed and delivered by the three Fates—as inevitably preordained and inscribed on eternal stone tables.

Destiny is meaningful. Fate leads to an inevitable conclusion, sometimes worthwhile yet not necessarily so. Destiny can resemble higher justice. In contrast, fate often signifies punishment. Destiny means boon. Fate means gloom. Fate is forced upon us by an invisible entity of ominous nature. Despite its classical branding as a decree by a mysterious agency, Destiny illuminates life with promise and opportunity, giving rise to hope and a higher calling. That's why no one gets too scared by the challenging-yet-shimmering path for the "chosen one." Fate often mirrors human fear of the Fatae-named divine personifications of Rome, perceived as unchangeable, whereas Destiny is more of a fluid projection.

Our Destiny is born with and works within us. Fate can loom to affect us from the outside. The idea of fate seems to lock us in, while Destiny opens up avenues.

The ancient Greeks had it right; they incorporated all departments of the original force into their first-ever avatar of Destiny—the principal Goddess Moira, including the light and darker aspects later named, interpreted, and translated to fate.

For the sake of differentiation, let's look at Destiny as the proverbial carrot, while fate is the stick. Destiny beckons; fate pulls or even pushes. Destiny offers; fate dictates. Destiny appears dynamic, while fate seems fixated. Destiny is potential; fate is the purveyor of limitation and entropy. Destiny is the great finished mosaic, where fate can inhabit its single pieces of different shapes and colors. Destiny gives us a chance, but fate may delay, deny, and even take it away.

Destiny is fluent and creative, yet fate can have an almost petrifying effect. We can end up befallen and struck by fate or, in contrast, be rewarded, if not blessed by, Destiny. It's the fate of a rose to blossom, bloom, and wither. But it's the rose's Destiny to be unforgettable and forever enrapture the beholder with her beauty, scent, and the promise of rebirth. For a long time, humanity has operated from fear of our final fate of demise and death. But that's not our Destiny; it's our Destiny to grow and evolve the shared spirit of this world.

It may seem as if it is our fate to perish as organic beings, but that's not the Destiny of our spirits. The spirit knows no fate, for it is destined.

By the way, chance may well be incorporated in any predetermined moment, like an element of good or bad luck, yet it is predominantly a random event that takes place without pre-decree. In comparison, we often perceive Destiny as floating on pure *panache*, whereas fate is a petrifying kick in the face. We are darlings of Destiny but the punching bags of fate. Fate is kitten-heeled Destiny's morbid sister in flat slippers. Destiny elevates us, but fate digs us a hole. Destiny is our fairy Godmother, and fate is a dominatrix. It is all down to human perception and interpretation. More often than not, it is tough and intense work to be in cahoots with the great design.

But how did fate get this image, that separate yet often similar identity?

The static and somehow gloomy concept of fate forms the foundation of much-debated thought schools such as fatalism, and, to some, it even reaches into the general perception of determinism. Both doctrines appear to withhold autonomy from humans entirely. These ideas go back to the ancient religious and theoretical times of Mesopotamia, Egypt, Greece, and Rome, and we find restrictive modes in other philosophies and religions all over the world. Fatalism is often criticized for fostering total dependence on a preordaining power, leading to inertia, since nothing significant a person thinks or wants would make sense under the cold eyes of a platinum fate that's already written in stone.

Even our thoughts and feelings would be pointless. A fatalistic life plan could involve denying any personal or moral responsibility, which, to the modern world, is an unacceptable construct. And it can mean not even a shred of a spark of hope is illuminating the way ahead. From an ethical point of view, that can easily look contemptible. Neuroscience and Co. developed new aspects on how much independence a human being may have—or, should we say, how little?

Determinism defines all events as results of previous events, causing other events from thereon according to natural laws. We'll talk about the evergreen cosmos of determinism versus free will later.

If we cannot get in harmony with the innate Destiny we are born with, we may feel the encounters and occurrences of our voyages acutely, whether they result from our actions or not. That can lead to perceived fate, an externally imposed burden weighing us down when it was, all along, in our power to accept the invitation to look over the fence. The lack of dialogue with our intrinsic nature and purposes and their source will lead to pinning negative experiences or unanswered expectations on an invisible agency.

How are determinism and fatalism entwined? Determinists are often judged to be fatalists as well, but that is not necessarily correct. Although the philosopher Aristotle advocated moral responsibility and did not believe in a mystical fate vis-à-vis human liberty, he accepted Logical Fatalism, meaning that the laws of the universe place worldly and human existence under the constraints of natural necessity. At the same time, the future can also rest on what humans feel to be true or not in the present moment. That is because not all occurrences happen due to necessity dictated by events of the past and the constraint of inevitability (Ananke).

Determinism marks the natural boundaries to our options, whereas philosophical fatalism, like Stoicism, is an inner way to deal with and accept any restraints in a refined manner that isn't always negative but pragmatic. Is there any sense in battling the unfightable outside our reach? It makes more sense to focus our strength and creativity on what we *can* successfully influence and shape.

If we brand fate to be oh so bad in the first place, we may get a taste of it from our prescription, pushing us to rethink our prejudice. Have we ever heard of tempting fate?

Furthermore, neither Destiny nor fate is here to punish us. The notion of Destiny supports human nature. It does not blame, and it does not condemn or convict. Destiny sends memos and books wake-up calls to educate. Yet not everything is destined or fated. Accidents happen, and so do coincidences. Chain events unravel, and so do reverse-engineered acts of self-fulfillment that don't stem from an inertia-driven perception of fatalism. Again, not all rests in the hands, the book, the scroll, the table, or whatever mortal-thought-transposed medium of any metaphysical or other force. As a consequence, there's no need to consider submission to any of them, let alone feel compelled to do so.

That is because we, the human family, are a real force to be reckoned with—as long as we do not hand over awareness of this fact and are not consumed by *hubris*, the arrogant attitude kicking even some of the cream of classical heroes from their high horses. But since we can learn a lot more about this misguided state of mind and action far too rife and growing in our modern age, let's take a quick look at Aristotle's interpretation:

Hubris consists in doing and saying things that cause shame to the victim, simply for the pleasure of it. Retaliation is not hubris, but revenge. Young men and the rich are hubristic because they think they are better than other people.

The cosmic agency is said to be allergic to hubris. Don't make it sneeze.

So, is Destiny just a purely human confabulation to help explain the scale of occurrences from fortunate and fateful?

Let's muse that there is no fate at all—just the original principle: Destiny. Unless fate is used as a synonym for Destiny, the often gloomy notion of fate arguably exists due to human (mis)interpretation. Could it be all in our heads, rendering religious and intellectual angst about all those many facts we cannot control or change? This book focuses predominantly on the effervescent realms of Destiny. The notion of Destiny was, is, and always will be at the forefront, even if we call it fate due to diverse interpretations and linguistics. It may come to us in the guise of retrospective confirmation, as a matter of personal or circumstantial interpretation of a particular outcome in the past. Perhaps our human need for a divided shining Destiny and an ominously bonding fate? [19]

Whatever endgame awaits, it will be performed by us mortals. That is all the more reason to turn the spotlight on mysterious individuals that hold it in their gift to see or predict the intricately spun patterns of the future—our Destiny. That takes us back to antiquity when the

Mothership ruled supreme, verbalized by oracles and diviners for glimpses of the future.

Snapshot of a Superforce

A few thousand years ago, Destiny was so "real" to our predecessors that they tried to decode the flow of its yarn. Divination was one of the central components of ancient understanding and everyday utilization.

Chrysippus (279–206 BCE), a one-off philosophical mastermind and second father of Stoicism, identified the law of causation—also called causal determinism—to be at the root of all that comes into being. He taught that the applied divine gift of foresight and its results were evidential of the perpetual, chain-like unraveling of all events producing human Destiny and causal determinism. To him, Destiny was identical to an all-encompassing entity of necessity and reason (Greek *logos*) that ruled the cosmos.

> *If it can be predicted, it must have been foreordained.*
> – CHRYSIPPUS, ON THE UNIVERSE

Back then, predictions felt rather compelling. Those in receipt of the gift of prophecy offered answers and encouraged reflective thinking, often challenging a person's fixed state of mind or beliefs. They were the sages, the Morgans, Merlins, and Obi-Wan Kenobis of their time. Often, they would speak in prose and riddles, rattling cages and upsetting the powers that be to shine a light on the path laid out by the overriding cosmic algorithm.

Enter the world-famous Oracle of Delphi in Greece, where the sight was articulated by its resident priestess: the Pythia. Or take the mighty Sibyls of Cumae, near today's Naples, Italy, and far beyond. Or the Roman drawing of Sortes (lot-casting), and not forgetting the wondrous Chaldean texts—enriching human imaginations, warning of perils, lifting hopes, and helping to make sense of the known world.

Such a notable predictor of events was called Mantis in the days of ancient Greece. A Mantis ranged a cut above most oracles since they were able to see the future, converse with the unseen, and tap into the will of Destiny granted rather inconspicuously to outstanding characters enlightened and directed by supreme dispensation. These chosen voices of cosmic advice often spoke in shrouded ways, metaphorically exploring whether tomorrow's chalice would taste sweet or bitter. Greek epics sing of tragic outcomes foretold and shattered hopes of changing the decree from on high. Fans of ancient history will know that many military exploits relied on the Sibyls and other seers and practitioners of prescience over time, just as we rely on special advisors today, especially concerning economic forecasts and the directions of our financial markets.

Upon closer examination of mythical Destiny and fate, it becomes clear why and how our foremothers assigned them to ease the uncertainty of auspicious or worrisome stages in life. The ability to preview what a person or group may meet in the future helped to feel prepared. Oracular answers were sought for the futures of families, whole nations, and even the then-known world. Not much has changed, as these are situations and factors many of us today will equally find extremely difficult to deal with since the largest part of human existence remains unsure and impossible to control. Our species continues to embrace any extra help to attain at least a few hints or whiffs of special foreknowledge to allow enhanced readiness for whatever awaits. After all, seeking certainty is a profoundly human trait that no arbitrary mindset, philosophy, or technological or other progress will easily reduce.

Artificial intelligence-driven quasi-oracles will likely become popular over the coming years because algorithms and datasets are getting so advanced that predictive expert systems may soon play integral parts in many fields. But will the dawn of dangerously-disruptive A.G.I. [20] (Artificial General Intelligence), ever be able to converse with our innate consciousness via "divinAItion" even in the case we'll awaken to the Singularity? [21] That said, imagine the enduring meaning and might of "Plan D" rooted in some uber-informed, non-biological, information-gathering agency reminiscent of Laplace's idea of a foreknowing Demon or mine of an ultra-computing entity courtesy of Ananke & Daughters— the only agency that does not require a cloud. An A.G.I. in the sky? Just a thought. After all, most human beings remain unable to learn from history how to avoid the same mistakes in the present and future, rendering mortal programmers and fact-feeders a little underwhelming, for that purpose.

Often, we want to know too much by trying to interpret random trivialities as messages from the mothership. In our modern age of social media and the need to be special, certain elements of conditioned reasoning and meaning, even unimportant scenarios, Freudian slips, or seeming coincidences, get fashionably detected as signage planted by the invisible force doling out cosmic nudges. While I admire Carl Gustav Jung's work, including his interesting Synchronicity and Meaningful Coincidence concepts, I do not recommend taking any such ideas too literally, expecting a winking universe at every given corner.

Adherence or overexposure to a perceived, uber-interpretative self-fulfilling Destiny can turn our lives into a labyrinth of expectations we may have difficulty navigating and streamlining with the lives we live. Conjuring up too many wishful manifestations of a desired outcome will neither lead to answers nor results.

Today, the concept of Destiny continues to highlight special life scenarios. Understanding the complexities of human existence may lead us to ponder whether a form of great choreography is out there that supports some, but not all, of us. Why do some of us thrive? Why do too many others suffer? Do both factions deserve to drink from a golden, silver, or tin cup of life? Are our life stories and experiences equivalent to rewards, punishments, or simply products of the proverbial luck of the draw, facilitated by fluke? Who decreed what and why? God(s)? Karma? Chance? Randomness? Determinism? Probability? Contingency? And, can we strive to earn, to deserve a good Destiny? Well, all that is the topic of my next book.

No doctrine or logic will ever fully explain what is at work in this world. And much less can anyone justify the reasoning and sense, or lack thereof, behind fortuitous and fateful events. Fairness and level playing fields can look like faraway ideas where good and evil, virtue and sin (but isn't sin a purely religious construct?) never play out as they should. And never mind all the moral narratives, fiction, or superhero blockbusters trying to keep us in a state of hopeful belief. Sadly, for the many, even applied meritocracy isn't as viable an idea in practice as in ideal theory.

We often gaze at skillfully crafted personae of human beacons that may deflect from what hides beneath an aura of merit. Being a wholesome person is a prize in itself to the innately virtuous who won't set their eyes on rewards in exchange for authentic excellence, anyway. But does it "pay," considering what is happening in this world at the expense of decent people?

We have no sustainable explanation for these discrepancies. So there remains the fact we don't have much control over most occurrences and third-party actions, and we are left to evaluate them in retrospect. Masters of the universe, we are not and never will be. We *can* become masters of well-delivered Human Destiny, though, but that, too, is for the next book.

Maybe the ancient theory still stands that if something has happened the way it did, good or bad, it may have always been meant to occur through a lack of alternatives or because it was necessary. The Stoic philosopher and Roman emperor Marcus Aurelius would agree. How can we even begin to expect an indifferent universe or dynamic higher force to unfold precisely to the tune of human morals and entitlement? What if the cosmos is indeed one enormous lot-casting entity that never apportions any meaning to humanity? That's exactly what our ancestors were concerned about: the bothersome fact that we don't matter and no one cares if we live. So they went to look for comforting and reassuring ideas, discovered time-ruling Destiny, and commissioned their best creatives to find a plethora of more or less interested but interesting Gods that reflected human beings and our traits like a precision mirror.

Who, or perhaps what, *is* in charge of our personal and collective cookies, cards, and dice? We have wondered about this for thousands of years, and here we are, still none the wiser, regardless of what or whom we believe in. We will soon address this age-old question no one has so far answered by going back in history to visit the most intriguing global Gods of Destiny.

In contrast, many events and consequences are open to interpretation. We find ourselves puzzled as to why something, in particular, happens to us. Yes, *us,* of all the people in the world? Instead of seeing the big picture around us, we tend to resign ourselves to the idea that everything we experience is a result of our own actions, our failings, or, preferably, our accomplishments. But that is not so. It is never only one or the other reason for whatever lifts or strikes us, but a cocktail named *"As Well As,"* on the Rocks, always mixed from at least two ingredients. We happen in tandem with the unseen. Sometimes more, sometimes less. Because of that, we never walk alone.

No wonder so many millions are so confident that spirits of the cosmos indeed mastermind us mortals, led by the agency no one ever fully fathomed or escaped.

Who Invented Destiny, and Why?

The concept of a grand cosmic scheme for the universe and all within, including our collective and individual journeys, arguably rose just around the time when civilizations generated large(r) settlements, class systems, and organized societies, like the Mesopotamian, Egyptian, and Minoan peoples when agriculture,[22] production, and trade became systemic. Yet, I am certain that Destiny's far earlier ideas, incarnations, and metaphysical actualities will become evident in the future, so watch this space.

But who or what started this continuing singularity that planted the seed for the development of high religions? Was it us, humanity, that created the pre-religious and pre-philosophical notion of Destiny, or was it the omni-spiritual principle's design to grow our need for it within us at the time of her arrival? Will we ever know who or what instigated this independent teleological cycle of meaning and forged the Mona Lisa of spiritual phenomena? Do we even have to?

One side of this mythic genesis suggests that Destiny either always existed or created itself (or, rather, herself) out of the purest chaos imaginable.

The other side supports the idea that humans simply invented it.

In fact, most polytheist and even animist religions recognized such a supreme power that stands behind all the different Gods, demons, and holy rocks. In classical Greek polytheism, Zeus, Hera, Apollo, and their colleagues were subject to an omnipotent and all-encompassing power – Fate (Moira, Ananke).

– Yuval Noah Harari, Sapiens

Again, instead of one or the other, both theories are valid in concert. We could have envisaged and thus invited the faceless supra force of orderly flow into our atavistic, undirected, uncertain conscious awareness that hasn't left us ever since, explaining our unquenchable gusto for its universal appeal. We may have followed up by giving this impersonal paradigm humanoid faces and attitudes to better match our anthropomorphic expectations. We humans like what we know; therefore, we know what we like. But why go for Destiny? Because it was the first and only power to whom we seriously counted, despite our fragility and insignificance. For the first time, we were taken into consideration by something, someone beyond our horizon obviously bothering enough to ponder and map out our existential paths. So we wished and welcomed the unbound and unconditional mother of our future spirituality with open arms.

Whichever is correct, one fact is clear: Destiny was neither created by God(s) nor by any of our engineered religions. Still, the first force inspired the cultivation of faith simply through its popularity and relevance. No religion worth its salt could compete with or do without Destiny. So, henceforth, they went on to copy and paste Destiny onto their

God(s). Unaware that they acted on the Mothership's design, guided by its threads while thinking it was their idea all along. All Gods work for Destiny for as long as humanity requires their presence and believes they help get through the night. However, our cosmic choreography is never a religion, despite the clever inclusion of its principles and meaning into codified faiths.

The times we live in now seem to run on reason and facts. In the Western hemisphere especially (or rather the Global North), many of us like to believe we are in charge of basically everything—the epitome of divine creation and a Eurocentric/USA-balanced system of longstanding cultural, global leadership. Nonetheless, the increasing perils and threats keep us waiting for an explanation, clarity, control, and hope. In that, we are no different from our pagan and polytheistic forebears. Our emotions and needs remain similar, if not the same. That's why ancient humans and savvy thinkers began to explain natural occurrences with supernatural activities and codified narratives many of us happily embrace today.

Humanity always tries to devise rational arguments for impactful events, especially those uncalled for. While sometimes, and a little too conveniently, the ability for pragmatic rationalization may be judged as a psychological flaw, it is basic human nature to do precisely that *vis-à-vis* unexplainable phenomena.

As homo sapiens do well not to rely on instinct and impulse too often, and since most of us lack command of special perception, we have to access mental facilities that allow us to plan for and make sense of our circumstances and environments. Human beings prefer to create attractive and logical narratives to explain better what our place in the universe might be. Or what it should be. Narratives are the key to how we tick ever since the word go! We can't help it; our brains are wired that way.

The reason why so many of us mortals are magnetically drawn to the seminal concept of Destiny lies in our primal urge to find significance in the world around us. And to this day, most of us refuse to accept that we could just be a mere product of random chance; therefore, we seek solace and significance in the idea of an intricate, mysterious design for the universe and our own lives. This all-encompassing primordial essence, soothing, frightening, and breathtaking, continues to enrapture us, weaving itself into our spirituality, values, and personal strategies. After all, we must be special to get assigned a direction, a path, and a unique destination.

In Hinduism, the impersonal *Rita* (or *rta*, the Sanskrit term for truth) reigns over the cosmos as the ancient moral principle of natural order operating everything, including universal, physical, and ethical realms, as well as those of human thought and agency. Out of Rita, the laws of karma and dharma pervaded almost all Asian philosophies with a sweeping sense of self-authored direction.

Rita also deserves our salute as an early influence on Western faith systems.

But the idea of a majestic essence alone is rarely enough for homo sapiens. We love to humanify and personify that which we struggle to grasp.

Ancient Egypt's female and male God(dess) *Shai* is one example of a Destiny-driving divine emanation, and so are the several Mesopotamian cultures' doctrines of the original force that spirited awe-inspiring divinities like *The Annunaki*. These great civilizations exported their philosophies throughout the then-known world and into the theological thought schools of Greece, Judah, and more.

Maybe the Greek poet Homer acutely sensed the uncertainty and trepidation around him, so he lent an extra layer of mystique to the defined Greek mythology, pantheon, and especially the role of Moira, i.e., Destiny, in his epic poems *Iliad* and *Odyssey*. And who knows if Homer's mental might did not inspire Hesiod to further develop the concept of divinity and Destiny in his *Theogony*?

We find raw force meeting a hostile environment in many tales of beginnings. Our human species suffered from many aspects of Nature's upper hand, craving a guiding principle, a power to define and underline our presence. Our ancestors were looking for a decreeing entity. Just as many small children believe their parents to be almost supernatural beings able to move mountains while keeping their precious babies safe forever, giving them continuous importance, attention, and responsible love, guiding them by good example and pointing a path in the right direction. And so humanity called: Is there anything, anyone out there? Mother?! All children long for their mothers when adversity looms.

Consequently, someone must have listened.

The primordial supra-forces of Destiny and necessity emerged from existential chaos in the early days of humanity, bearing order, structure, and pace.

Perhaps they served as ancient antidotes to the vast voids of an early version of nihilism, to keep from our door the wolf of realizing how superfluous the human race might be? Their presence enabled the first standards before faiths were conceived, morals and values pronounced and further developed by the great philosophers that refined and empowered humanity's views on ourselves and our role on this planet. The concepts of Destiny added a sense of past, present, and future by including us in the mythical and causal fabric that holds space in the universe. We are born with the desire to be singled out extraordinarily by a benevolent force while dreading to be earmarked for dire outcomes by a dark side of the same entity, yearning for paternal supervision with a bonus of free self-decree as pricey icing on the cake of destination.

Yet, even causation and logic cannot explain what is going down all around us.

Why was and is Destiny so attractive to humanity?

Many, if not most, ancient metaphysical concepts faded over time. Yet the grand mainstay mastered the fogs of forgetfulness and expanded its spiritual relevance throughout almost all cultures. Life's many bright and shaded moments are held together by the forethought of an incomprehensible yet stabilizing force that seems to whisper: *You are not alone, and your existence is neither pointless nor absurd.*

Even those who mock and reject Destiny and fate cannot help using and discussing both terms for their concise, irresistible, sometimes threatening meanings. The German philosopher Immanuel Kant, a compatibilist, imagined and debated fateful fallout from a belief in

Destiny while still featuring it prominently. He feared that we unreflective humans could just willy-nilly reject responsibility and sabotage proper moral codes. But although he dismissed ideas and laws of Destiny, Kant still minted them as mankind's ideal purpose.

Even this great thinker could not come up with a better word to rhyme with humanity. Bless him.

The ongoing emotional and cognitive relevance of the idea of Destiny is due to a very simple fact: It connects us with our most ancient human core awareness that there is a connective thread between and maybe even exceeding the validities of birth and death, beyond myth and dogma.

An Interspiritual Backstory

I've said it before, and I'll say it again: Destiny transcends all cosmogonies, mythologies, deities, and faith systems. Let us remember that it is a religiously neutral, independent spiritual phenomenon. As the antithesis of entropy, it inspired and influenced other principles and doctrines. Religions desired Destiny's tenets, powers, and options to decorate their divine personalities.

But what was it exactly that the concept of Destiny brought to the table hosting several evolving faiths?

The transformative agency gave humans certainty and stability, a mainstay. Through the great sense maker's predeterminations, our ancestors were able to explain and understand many of those mysterious and unfathomable things they encountered and swap diffuse dread with reasons and significance. Also, Destiny offered hope for guidance and even, on occasion, some intercepting moves of mythical might with regard to the application of higher and poetic justice, especially in cases of hubris. Everything feels a little better when we're not randomly bobbing on the waves of indifferent contingency alone, correct? Those were the days of the first steps toward the development of ethical codes, with Destiny as a consequential compass rose. Humanity desired that something even beyond Nature cared enough to include us in a grand design, be it on an individual or collective basis. Understandably, rulers and leadership aspirants waited in line to call themself Destiny's chosen ones, not always for the right reasons and with mixed outcomes. Destiny lent purpose, authority, and legitimacy to otherwise mere mortals with more or less virtuous characters. It granted ambitions to harvest alliance and loyalty with subjects and necessary associates. And Destiny resided above and beyond any cult, therefore offering spiritual flexibility, which was effectively included in various belief systems. Early religions saw the opportunity to become more convincing, and so they loved all of that. They still do.

When we reflect on the earliest thoughts about humanity's role and purpose, collective path, myths, and legends are still the best resources to understand our early attempts to get in tune with the workings of divine and human cooperation.

By inspecting artifacts and other cultural emblems, we can easily decipher that our forebears supplied a tangible humanoid image to those more or less invisible, unearthly forces that spun and ran the threads of being and time. Back then, and until today, such powers were still assigned to supernatural beings by their religious followers' veneration. In antiquity, almost anybody would swear their Gods walked among and conversed with mortals. Love and passion played an epic part in intricate control games.

Kind of nice, right? Personable deities. And even more charming, Ye Gods enjoyed mingling with us. All so essentially mortal, despite their deathlessness.

Legends and ballads sing of the lives of famous women and men whose paths were interwoven with the strands of Destiny, thus often demonstrating the futility of humanity trying to take total charge over their existence.

Humans often went one way; the Gods maneuvered otherwise, but practically, how, when, where, and why the dice rolled, or the threat got clipped was decreed almost exclusively by Destiny's edict. There was no getting away from it, neither for Gods nor mortals. And, since humans crave even slivers of certainty, oracles and sages were held in high esteem and were in even higher demand.

So it is no surprise that even, or especially, in our modern information age, clairvoyants and astrologers are as popular as ever. Courtesy of the internet, they have plenty more audiences to help and ways to profit from the variably mastered ancient art once reserved for those touched by Destiny. Anyroad, as it was then, it stands today: Only very few individuals were and are bestowed with *the sight*—the ability to presage and exercise foreknowledge. Rare characters may yet carry forward that complex gift of prediction clandestinely.

Mythologies of all civilizations present us with stories of ancient agents of Destiny crossing seas, Arcadian or perilous landscapes, quite aware that their lives, loves, hardships, conquests, and life battles flew along a challenging yet reliable thread the invisible spindle produced. It was deemed terribly plucky and even heroic to accept our preordained path no matter what.

> *For when the heart insists on its destiny, resisting the general blandishment, then the agony is great; so too the danger. Forces, however, will have been set in motion beyond the reckoning of the senses. Sequences of events from the corners of the world will draw gradually together, and miracles of coincidence bring the inevitable to pass.*
>
> – JOSEPH CAMPBELL, THE HERO WITH A THOUSAND FACES

Speaking of myths, consider the magic of *epos* and *mythos*. Myths are something our modern world can hardly be without; it seems we are mythologizing even more than our ancient predecessors. Mythos is Greek for *word*, referring to poetic stories and tales.

Mythology and philosophy are fantastic, different topics. Yet neither can be exclusively claimed by the Greeks or the West. Greece crowned poetic story glory with divine narratives and systematic theories of enduring Gods we will likely hold dear forever. But that kind of inspiration happened way before, in Mesopotamia, ancient Egypt, even earlier in the Indus Valley, and, highly likely, in other places. Great notions travel far, and so they did, stimulating and nurturing Mediterranean and Western mythology, philosophy, and theology. Myths and creeds are not necessarily divisive. New interpretations of foreign and own narratives paved the path to the inception of Greek philosophy.

Archaic Greek culture used the much older, slightly different term of *muthos* to authenticate and outline its creation chronicles. Muthos, interestingly, meant "truthful report" or "recital." For an easier read, I will continue to refer to myths and mythology—both absolute backbones of humanity, despite the fact Greek philosophers later sought to replace muthos with *logos*—reason and logic.

> *Myths are not lies. Nor are they detached stories. They are imaginative patterns, networks of powerful symbols that suggest particular ways of interpreting the world. They shape its meaning.*
> – MARY MIDGLEY, THE MYTHS WE LIVE BY

Before we start our brief journey across known and mainstream science-accepted cultures that venerated personified emblems of Destiny, I want to mention that these are by no means exhaustive or the last word on the history of Destiny and human achievement.

Long before the rise of Levantine, i.e., Mesopotamian, Egyptian, and Aegean civilizations, impressive cultural predecessors like Göbekli Tepe, ca. 9100–7300 BCE, and Catalhoyuk, ca. 7500–5700 BCE, were testimony that our history goes back much further than officially admitted. Both sites are situated in today's Türkiye, pointing to defined cultural success, spiritual beliefs, and activities beginning to steal a little thunder from certain claims laid by later societies.[23] Expect more discoveries, corrections, and fresh aspects of ancient sites predating today's generally agreed-upon interpretations of our past and the locations that hosted complex communities. Modern Türkiye's direct Mediterranean neighbors include the Indus Valley's Harappan culture (ca. 3300–1300 BCE), where cities like Mohenjo-Daro formed a distinguished array of civilizations going far back to times when, for example, the Ionian (Turkish) coast harbored pearls of human achievement long before other cultures rose. Albeit ranking well, neither Europe nor the Western world has sole rights to the crown of human advancement.

In the upcoming chapter, Gods of Destiny, we shall focus on divine emanations revered by great peoples that once thrived around the Mediterranean Sea and in and beyond Europe. Therefore, in this part of the book, we're not addressing seemingly similar principles of the very ancient belief system of Hinduism, going back to the time before 2000 BCE, or China's spiritual thought schools shining their light on its position as the oldest active civilization on this planet. We will, of course, visit their philosophies and views on Destiny later to explore some of the differences in definitions, perceptions, and narratives with respect to, for instance, karma and dharma. These two influential doctrines are not represented by a supernatural emanation, embodiment, or avatar but are entirely driven by human intentions and actions, inspired and masterminded by a universal concept. One that we could interpret as a self-issued "quasi-Destiny" but without a decreeing superpower or God(dess) involved.

The cultures and deities we will discuss soon brought immeasurable and enduring gifts to the world table while simultaneously casting long and sometimes dark shadows on what we now uphold as Western values of equality, freedom, and humanism. We need to view and understand them with the eyes and within the context of their time and circumstances.

Let's just mention that there appears to be growing speculation and scholarly and archeological evidence that Greek philosophy was indeed highly influenced by Vedic spirituality and philosophy, including the majestic cosmic order principle Rita. It is a space more than worthy of being watched.

Everything flows.

– HERACLITUS OF EPHESUS

CHAPTER 2

Destiny and Mythology

Gods of Destiny

Imagine a darkness so redolent with life that it requires no light to be radiant. Long ago and far away, Chaos draped its cloak of creation over the vast emptiness. The darkness formed anew, held high the torch, and smiled. And the nothingness bowed in awe and resigned.

– Helena Lind

Generally speaking, all spiritual concepts and God(s), retired and active, are trustees and stewards of human Destiny in varying capacities. But the ancient past had specialist teams running the options, threads, and flow of universal and human existence. Divine incarnations ruled the world throughout all bygone civilizations. Then, Destiny was spearheaded by sublime emanations guiding mere mortals and even their deathless peers throughout their eternal journeys. Destiny was never primarily theological but a pre-religious, order-balancing concept. And that hasn't changed, no matter how later "copycats" claimed their cover versions to stem from their God(s)' will.

In my book, all Goddesses and Gods, then and now, asleep or awake, carry equal validity; therefore, I apply the capital G to all of them.

And that's also why I write Destiny with a capital D.

Did, or do any God(s) of all sorts, including those Gods of Destiny, ever exist? Or were our foremothers just attributing powers and names to the principles of Nature, time, necessity, and inevitability, adding human behavioral traits and longings here and there?

In many ways, they did, and they do. To me, Gods of olde are as relevant as all those other time-honored divine reflections billions of theistic followers continue to worship worldwide today. Gods of Destiny were as, if not even more significant, than any established deities today. And somehow, they still are, as Destiny gets evoked continuously. Even atheists, agnostics, and Co, as per researchers' findings, are interested in it, despite many atheists' "normal" refusal to accept anything but a materialistic reality.

A total denial of relevancy of ancient principles and bygone deities would be pretty arrogant. Plus, it would mean questioning the legitimacy of such great codified faiths as those in the Jewish, the Christian, and the Muslim God(s), since their religions evolved from pre-existing, mostly polytheistic beliefs, divinities, and philosophy.

We humans, with our eternal spiritual leaning, are God-makers and, thus, just as productive as supernatural creators credited with bringing humanity into existence. We knew what we wanted and transferred our characteristics and requirements straight into the spheres of the cosmos and onto our divinities.

Men create Gods after their own image, not only with regard to their form but with regard to their mode of life.

— ARISTOTLE

Most Gods and members of notable pantheons display a bouquet of all-too-human traits. They appear egotistic, jealous, self-absorbed, dictatorial, and dogmatic, especially certain patriarchal specimens. We should not ignore that all Gods hold space as personified expressions of a deep human fear of uncertainty coupled with a yearning for order, justice, and a higher purpose. A lack of a designated future makes many, if not most of us, uncomfortable.

Ye Gods and we do not only seem to create each other—we equally need each other to keep going. Quite a few of the purveyors of personal paths we are to meet soon have drifted out of everyday awareness. Historians and writers keep them "alive" and remember them often fondly in their research and books.

The conundrum of whether humans command complete control over their lives continues to intrigue us. Take our prerogative to the neuro-biological as well as social construct of free will—what if it was but a partial illusion or the result of undetectable administration by forces of the cosmos, after all? Or those agreements upon seemingly material values such as diamonds, precious metals, money, stocks, and, to an extent, even real estate?

We can trace this riddle back to the rise of several Mediterranean and Asia Minor regions more than 6,000 years ago. Here, supernatural agency and human Destiny played a lead role and became the catalysts of magnificent myths, world-moving creations of art, architecture, and more. Awe-inspiring Mesopotamian kingdoms arose from and developed those fertile plains between the two great rivers, Euphrates and Tigris, spanning the location of today's Iraq, Iran, and parts of Syria, Türkiye, and Kuwait and as far as Egypt, founding legendary cities such as Assur, Nineveh, and Babylon with incredible resourcefulness, establishing high cultures, societal progress, and religious tolerance by employing fierce determination and ferocious armies.

O Mighty King, remember now that only Gods stay in eternal watch. Humans come, then go, that is the way fate decreed on the Tablets of Destiny. So someday you will depart, but 'til that distant day—sing, and dance. Eat your fill of warm cooked food and cool jugs of beer. Cherish the children your love gave life . Bathe away life's dirt in warm drawn waters. Pass the time in joy with your chosen wife. On the Tablets of Destiny, it is decreed for you to enjoy short pleasures for your short days. [24][25]

Masters of Mesopotamia

It was the Greeks that coined the term Mesopotamia—land between two streams—a then fruitful part of the world also believed to host the storied Garden of Eden. Between ca. 8000–2000 BCE, this region was the stage for formidable empires like the Sumerians, the Akkadians, the Amorites, the Babylonians, and the Assyrians.

Mesopotamia was the cradle of sheer ingenuity and at the heart of the fertile crescent. If ancient Greece later refined philosophy, ethics, and values and gifted us intricate art forms such as poetry, music, theater, and sculpture, right here, in the fields of abundance, they began to develop all those things already, possibly even earlier than 7000 BCE.

Let us take a quick look at a few of the many future-shaping inventions supplied from the banks of the two sacred rivers: mathematics, the *cuneiform script* (then considered to be of supernatural origin and the earliest writing system worldwide as per today's knowledge, dating back to at least ca. 3100 BCE), *ziggurats*: pyramidal temples crowned by a sanctum (the blueprint for the Biblical tale of the Tower of Babel), bookkeeping, the rotating axle with a spoked wheel, astronomy, irrigation systems, horticulture, architecture, the sailboat, the law, urban living, calendars, and the measuring of the flow of moments in sets of hours of sixty minutes and minutes of sixty seconds.

And they are credited with the creation of formal laws. The kings Ur-Nammu (2112–2095 BCE) and Hammurabi of Babylon and Mesopotamia (ca. 1792–1750 BCE) introduced the first proper codes of law to this world. Their legal approach encompassed most, if not all, aspects of life and human interaction. They are on show in Istanbul's Archaeology Museums and the Louvre Museum. The Laws of Hammurabi were carved into a 2.25-meter-high black basalt stone stele, appropriately reminiscent of a massive index finger. Its top relief shows Shamash, the ancient Akkadian justice deity and brother to the Ishtar/Inanna, Queen of Heaven, presenting the great law as measuring tape and rod to King Hammurabi.

One of the most spectacular offerings Mesopotamia gave us was its highly influential cosmogony *Enuma Elish—The Seven Tablets of Creation* and *The Epic of Gilgamesh*—both formative epics impacting several historic spiritual narratives, and even influencing the creations of the three main book religions: Judaism, Christianity, and Islam. The myth of the big flood in the *Gilgamesh* epos tells of the divine decision to reduce man's arrogance in tandem with, even then, the issue of overpopulation and hubris.

When in the height heaven was not named,
And the earth beneath did not yet bear a name,
And the primeval Apsu, who begat them,
And chaos, Tiamut, the mother of them both
Their waters were mingled together,
And no field was formed, no marsh was to be seen.
When of the Gods none had been called into being,
And none bore a name, and no destinies were ordained.
Then were created the Gods in the midst of heaven
Intro of the Eunuma Elish [26]

Let's meet the divine ordainers of Mesopotamian destinies:

The Annunaki—seven divine judges presiding over the Destiny of humankind:

An—top God and Lord of Heaven.

Enlil—executor of divine decrees and the Lord of the Winds.

Ninhursak—Lady of the Stony Ground (mountains), Goddess of Birth, and determiner of human Destiny.

Enki—Lord of the Sweet Waters/Rivers, ingenious creator, and Master of Destiny and Time.

Nanna—Lord of the Moon.

Inanna—Lady of Love, War, Queen of Heaven, the Morning, and the Evening Star (she remains famous under her other name: Ishtar).

Utu—Lord of Truth and Justice and twin brother to Inanna.

Mamitu—Mother of Creation and definitive Destiny. She's also one of the judges in the netherworld.

Manu—Chaldean Great Lord of Fate.

Nabu—Lord of Wisdom and Prophecy, keeper and scribe of the Tablet of the Destinies, and son of Marduk.

Namtar—dark fate and death personified.

The Tablets of Destiny or *Tablets of the Destinies*—initially believed to be under the control of Enki, Lord of Time and Destiny—granted world domination and knowledge of all futures ever to come to their owners. The *Enūma Eliš* epic describes how the fabled deity Marduk challenged and battled resident divine beings for ultimate power. These precious clay tablets were the record keepers of all information about the world's future as decreed and foretold by divine decree. They were guarded by the primordial Lady of Chaos, the salt sea Goddess Tiamat. Marduk overthrew and dispatched the glistening lady by hacking her to pieces and repurposing the body parts to create heaven, earth, and the Milky Way. While at it, he made the mighty rivers Euphrates and Tigris from the slain Tiamat's teary eyes, arguably also to mark a mythical triumph of patriarchy over the great yet manliness-threatening feminine principle. However, in doing so, the cosmos and world are therefore made of the legendary Goddess. Marduk swaggered on to seize the *Tablet of the Destinies* and became his pantheon's principal God and overlord.

About one fact, no doubt was present in the ancient lands of Sumer, Akkad, Assyria, Babylon, etc. Humans, by nature and in general, were dependent on *Simtu* or *šīmtu*, their decreed Destiny or fate, or *Isqu*, their lot in life.

The design of Destiny as a principle was called *Nam;* it also meant that what is. [27]

Most Mesopotamians found little capacity to shape their lives themselves. They existed solely to serve totalitarian Gods in every possible way while relying heavily on divination and omens as pointers to the likely direction Destiny may prescribe. [28]

A rare and different example of an early self-determining human is the extraordinary Sumerian hero-king Gilgamesh, who dared to explore the secret of eternal life only to accept his mortality.

All Mesopotamian deities had to content themselves with the unquestionable authority of the parallel force of Destiny, residing above and beside Nature, Gods, and humanity alike, reaching far beyond Mesopotamian astronomy and celestial divination.

Personal Destiny and fate seem to have relied on the blessings of omens, either promising good luck or warning of impending misfortune. We find more individual methodologies encapsulated in the leading concept of The Four Guardian Spirits or Creators of Destiny.

Meet Ilu and Istaru, and Lamassu and Sedu—winged special, i.e., supportive demons that looked after their mortal protégés and gifted them with very special Simtu/Destiny:

> Spirituality—Ilu, personal spirit (male), offering luck, happiness, and good fortune.
>
> Personal fate—Istaru, companion deity (female), giving protection, fate, or Destiny.
>
> Individual characteristics—Lamassu, a spirit (female), granting protection.
>
> Life force—the God Sedu, endowing mortals with the energy to live.

And then there was/were the cosmic force(s) called *Me(s)*, [29] Sumerian ideal forms standing behind the motions and workings of the universe, distributed by the orderly design(s) of *gis-hur(s)*, both entities closely connected with the distribution of specific divine decrees of Destiny and the art forms synonymous with civilization in the lands of the two great streams. Many *Mes* get mentioned in the myth of Inanna and Enki, in which the Goddess steals a great many *Mes* from their keeper, Enki. These objectified powers of *Me* were involved in all crucial mindsets and concepts like happiness and essential gifts or actions like music. *Me(s)* could even take physical forms or act as connectors between Gods and humans.

The Four Guardian Spirits of Mesopotamia and the Persian/ Zoroastrian *Faravahar* were among a group of exceptional winged beings that later inspired the world's expanding penchant for angels, a theme that is still going strong. They were the originals, though. Humanity always craved caring bearers of hope and celestial entities that stood as intermediaries between the worlds and, winged or not, even acted as intercepting agents of Destiny.

This world could do with a few such guardian spirits that are not the product of Hollywood but ready to guide humanity properly, right?

Egypt—Jewel of Destiny

Let us now venture to the shores of the Nile to meet its determiners.

The land of the pharaohs was a shimmering gem in the crown of great cultures that hugged the Mediterranean Sea, and it lasted for nearly 3,000 years (ca. 3100–332 BCE).

Ancient Egyptians entertained a profound connection with their destinies and deities. They idealized carriage of the divine within their innermost sanctum—their own enlivened heart. The reigning pharaoh shone as brightly as the sun, an earthly personification of divinity ruling the kingdom(s), leading their people through peace and war, abundance, and famine. Ideally, the pharaoh did this as steadily and reliably as the great river Nile, in constant communication with the Gods of the lands of Egypt, which they called *Kemet* or *Kmt* (their script mainly represented consonants)—this ancient name of Egypt translating to "black earth." The realm's Destiny was synonymous with the individual citizen, especially during the early centuries. Kemet's mythology is rich and inspiring; its worldviews are unique, and they continue to fascinate and captivate modern imagination thousands of years after ancient Egypt's heyday. All Egyptians felt like living parts of the motherland's Destiny.

Egyptian achievements are in practice to this day: medicine, surgery, astronomy, sacred hieroglyph script, papyrus paper, ink, accounting, geometry, grain mills, make-up, mummification, advanced agriculture, and irrigation systems.

And the calendar—Egypt invented the 365-day year of twelve months and thirty days, later slightly corrected through a leap year by King Ptolemy III (280–222 BCE), adding one day every four years. Egyptian and Greek cultures merged in the 275 years of the Ptolemaic dynasty's rulership over Egypt. They reigned in Alexandria as pharaonic crown bearers with classical Hellenic looks, education, and genes. The infamous Cleopatra was the last queen of Egypt; it fell into the collection of Roman provinces after her suicide.

Ancient Egyptians rightly revered cats, albeit not always in a fashion that modern feline aficionados would condone. Egypt loved life, beauty, and poetry. Tremendous stories were told throughout the two kingdoms, and unique, important spiritual works were authored in the most aesthetic script ever—sacred hieroglyphs. Narratives were inscribed on the walls of temples and tombs, and legendary tomes were inked using a prototype of our paper—papyrus—for the famous scrolls. To name just a few eternal ancient Egyptian books: the *Berlin Papyrus*, a philosophical, ego-dissolving dialogue between a human and his soul (ca. 2000 BCE); *The Tale of Sinuhe*, carrying Destiny and free human will as a central theme (around ca. 1875 BCE); *the* blueprint journey of the soul through an epic afterlife—*The Book of the Dead* (ca. 1500 BCE)—an igniting inspiration for later world religions' own versions of what to expect of the worlds hereafter. But the idea of a rebirth after physical death was uniquely created and documented on the storied shores of the river Nile. We read it there first.

Egypt's pantheon hosted some of the most unforgettable deities in the world. Isis, Horus, Osiris, and Amun are names that continue to sing both the myth and history of this outstanding realm. We are here, though, to focus on their Gods of Destiny.

Neith—ancient creatrix of the cosmos and High Lady of the thread of life.

The Seven Hathors—lovely incarnations of the Great Goddess (see below).

Renenet or Renenutet—cobra Deity providing abundance in the way of fortune, pure luck, and material serendipity, able to soften a person's too-harsh Destiny while also bringing forth dark fate where required. An Egyptian version for the later luck Goddesses Tyche and Fortuna?

Meskhenet—Goddess of birth and determiner of fate, providing the decree in purpose, status, career, and rank. She was said to write a newborn child's path on the birthstone.

Hemsut—transcendent Goddess of fate and protection, represented the spirit of life—the *Ka*, the Egyptian blueprint of an immortal soul.

Shai/Shait—both names mean "that which is ordained"— the incarnation of Egyptian Destiny. When donning his male form, Shai was romantically linked with Renenet or Renenutet, a Goddess of Destiny.

The belief in Shai—the Egyptian word for personified Destiny—interwove the lives of all inhabitants of this magnificent culture. From early on, Egyptians of their time saw themselves as collective participants in the realm's written story.

Individual Destiny was the other big theme that took center stage with the rise of Upper and Lower Egypt—the red and the black countries. Egyptians took pride in living and dying as predetermined beings under divine guidance. Because of great devotion, they believed their roadmap could be altered either through merit or with the aid of the Gods. Exceptionally gifted souls were able to co-steer the courses of Destiny through their excellence and special status. Here, virtue begot special attention.

Divine Shai even took the top of the monotheistically inclined heretic King Akhenaten's religious revolution agenda, which explicitly declared Shai a fundamental part of his mono-sun-God, Aten, while abolishing the complete Egyptian pantheon in style, at least for a while. Nonetheless, Pharaoh Akenaten insisted:

The Aten is the Shai who gives life.

While the civilizations of Greece and Rome ostensibly relied on the three Moirai and three Parcae/Fates, the kingdoms of Egypt, since early days, also featured seven female deities of Destiny.

Those seven entities signified the great cosmic Goddess Hathor—Great Lady of many names. They acted as her seven-pronged magnificent extensions called the Seven Hathors—mighty spirits of life, death, and everything in between and beyond.

Representations of the Goddess Hathor manifesting as seven beautiful women and/or seven adorable cows, symbolizing the determinations of life and death—were known as Ladies of the Universe, Sky Storm, Beings from the Land of Silence, and more magical titles.
    – GEORGE HART, A DICTIONARY OF EGYPTIAN GODS AND GODDESSES

Some historical sources also link the Seven Hathors to the cosmic system of Pleiades.

The highly diverse Hathor was one of the most beloved and powerful divine ladies. She represented love, sexuality, and fertility. Hathor also welcomed souls to the afterlife and guided them on their journey through the netherworld like an affectionate mother. Yet, she was also the destructive Eye of Ra, acting guardian of the sun God.

The Shai was the source of all being, courtesy of the eternal presence of the blue-golden thread. This worldview reached the lofty heights of several famous doctrines and avatars of an original mover in ancient Greece.

Transcontinental and Proto-Arabian Destinies

The Hittite Empire dominated large parts of Asia Minor, today's Türkiye (capital Hattusa, Anatolia), Syria, and beyond (ca. 1650–1200 BCE).

The Hittites looked up to the weaving Goddesses Papaya and Istustaya—both entwining the strands of life.

They also venerated the Mesopotamian top Goddess Inanna, more widely known as the famous Ishtar.

The ancient Middle East and the proto-Arabian peninsula relied on the wise spiritual rulership of three mighty Goddesses who were principally worshiped at Mecca and also at Palmyra.

Manāt—the Semitic prime Goddess of Destiny, luck, time, and death, assisted by her sisters.

Allāt—Goddess of prosperity, war, and peace.

Al-Uzzā—Goddess of power, love, and protection.

Helming Greek Destiny

For thousands of years, ancient cultures revered and relied on the mythical powers of the prime force, and splendid representatives of ancient Greek Destiny remain prominent to this day. Ancient Greece (ca. 1180–323 BCE), in eclectic concert with the earlier Sumerian, Akkadian, Indo-European, Egyptian, and later the Roman civilization, laid the foundations for Western culture. These realms fired and inspired philosophy, spirituality, and religion. The much older Mesopotamian and Egyptian cultures influenced Greek cosmogonies and conceptions of their pantheon and spirit worlds.

Greek creation and inception narratives, myths, and poetry describing Destiny's might are highly inspirational and also the most enduring, impressive, and valid ideas. For me, the Greco-Roman concepts of Destiny are the gold standard of Western destinies. *The* Destiny.

Some of the magnificent gifts Greece gave the world include the Olympics, geometry, democracy, science, lighthouses, medicine, engineering, sculpture of the divine and human physique, logic, rhetoric, theater (tragedy, drama, narrative art), aqueducts (Athens' free water supply), elections, higher education, the Greek alphabet, optics and perspective, naval military fleets (men-o-wars), and identity-creating philosophy.

Inspired by their rich mythology and Egyptian, Western Asian, and Indic thought schools, the Greeks founded unique philosophies, one of the most remarkable contributions to the betterment of humanity. They did not invent wisdom *per se* since that was to be had aplenty from other civilizations too. Yet they became masters of reason, logical thinking, and defining complexities. Their philosophers dared to examine the validity of purely theologian concepts. The upper echelons of ancient Greece revered beauty, yet in contrast, the Greeks were obsessed with, wait for it: death! Beauty was all good to them, whereas death, well, was best to be avoided wherever, if possible. They abhorred the thought of finality, so it is not surprising Classical Greece produced some of the most fascinating concepts of the grand design.

They called their first documented Destiny Moira—the lot or portion in life. Moira *was* Destiny, and the poet Homer describes her authority impressively in his epics, the *Iliad* and the *Odyssey* (ca. 700–800 BCE). Even the Gods could not stand in the way of Moira. The *Iliad* is more than a seemingly obvious saga singing the praises of bunches of remote-controlled heroes just out to campaign and kill for an elusive kick to brutish kings' fragile senses of selfhood and doubtable concepts of *macho* honor. King Priam's pretty son, Paris, charmed Queen Helen of Sparta into eloping with him, thus serving the cuckolded husband and his peers a perfect reason to start a war for the sake of wounded pride (and to get their paws on Troy's unique location and riches, but that didn't sound cool). Albeit a brutal epos, to me, the *Iliad* almost has the quality of an anti-war narrative since it painfully observes the futility of war and violence. Some protagonists even portray early forms of remorse, conscientiousness, compassion, mindfulness, and even individual choices in the human spectrum of traits that would become so important to the later Greek philosophy superstars.

No man or woman born, coward or brave, can shun their destiny.

– HOMER, ILIAD

Despite Destiny directing the *Iliad*'s protagonists, we see glimpses and tendencies, if not clear signs, of rising ideas about human freedom.

In his second epic, the *Odyssey*, Homer tells of one man's archetypal battle against the will and whims of certain Olympians. Odysseus (Ulysses) is a many-faceted hero whose long, winding journey home gets pushed and pulled between dangerous divine designs and his intentions. The *Odyssey* gives us the effect of human choices and, yes, evident freedom of choice and responsibility, but we best listen to Zeus himself, who laments:

> *Ah, how shameless—the way these mortals blame the Gods. From us alone, they say, come all their miseries, yes, but they themselves, with their own reckless ways compound their pains beyond their proper share.* [30]

So man's wishes and actions are far worse than whatever Destiny could decree? Interesting point.

And later in the story, the cute messenger God Hermes tells a bewitching nymph Calypso to let Odysseus go to fulfill the benevolent yet adamant bidding of Moira.

Now Zeus commands you to send him off with all good speed, it is not his fate to die here, far from his own people. Destiny still ordains that he shall see his loved ones, reach his high-roofed house, his native land at last. [31]

Even the famous Gods of the Greek pantheon had, like mere mortals, their preordained destinies, courtesy of their own Moira—the femininely inspired, embodied, and pantheon-independent principle of higher order and wisdom, set to gift her creative spark to major strands of Greek philosophy. [32]

The first inception of archaic Greek Destiny occurred in primordial times, in the days of *muthos,* narrated in early descriptions of the universe's origins. And so the genesis of these foreordaining forces kicked off.

Ancient Greek Destiny seems to have been initiated with the appearance of Moira, from *meros* [33]—lot—referring to the share in life she assigned to humans. She *was* Destiny incarnate, and the mythical Homer first mentions her as the mistress of the thread of life in his *Iliad*—the great poem about the Trojan War, and the *Odyssey*—outlining how the hero Odysseus or Ulysses fares on his long, complicated journey home. Both masterpieces are today assumed to have been written around 725 and 675 BCE, even likely by more than one "Homer." It makes sense that Moira must have been *the* Destiny Goddess before she is mentioned in the era of Homerian narratives. It should be noted that at that time, she already represents a kind of open option, not just an immutable fate, but a Destiny that allows humans to make their own decisions without too much constraint from the apportioned decree, apart from meaningful stepping stones and the unfortunate facts of mortality. Moira offered a good deal of flexibility unless it was time to die. She also acted in concert with Godfather Zeus, who was sometimes assigned as her dad, with her mother, Themis, the Goddess of Justice. Moira spun Destiny's threads with full knowledge of everyone's path in life, its stages and milestones right down to the end. Spinning and weaving were essential and exclusive feminine domains. Without those artisan skills of the women of antiquity, all those tough yet vain guys would have had little to wear apart from animal skins. Consequently, our predecessors saw the fabric of the world and each life in it as intricately spun and woven by divine ladies' fair and able hands. We know more than one version of Moira's origins, as she was also revered as the daughter of Nyx— the reigning lady of the starlit night. Moira looked after everybody's existence, not just the mundane life journeys of mere mortals but also titans, demigods, demons, and even the major deities.

Her mythical concept of order appeared just and even moral—an absolute first in the rough-and-tough world of Gods and mortals.

Character is destiny. Mortals are immortals, and immortals are mortals. The one living the other's death and dying the other's life.
                                            – HERACLITUS, GREEK PHILOSOPHER

Heraclitus' observation embodies supreme wisdom. Our important word character, referring to a person's innate, upright moral qualities, comes from the ancient Greek *charactĩr*, meaning a unique inscription, a brand stamped on a surface or etched in it. [34]

We are our Destiny; it is inscribed in our being. Hesiod (ca. 750–650 BCE), in his *Theogony*, tells not of one Moira but three *Moirai*, [35] also daughters of Zeus and Themis. Hesiod's Zeus preordains Destiny with his justice-spinning offspring. In another description, the Moirai are the daughters of the dark Goddess Nyx.

Plato, the philosopher and creator of Natural Theology (an experience-based theory of an immortal soul and the existence of a creative divine agent), revealed the three Moirai as daughters of the faceless principle and primordial Goddess Ananke (universal world necessity). Her three amazing girls—Clotho, Lachesis, and Atropos—represented a human's past, present, and future. The Greeks idolized even more divine female personifications of Destiny, namely Aisa, a sister in meaning to the one Moira, and the philosophically rationalized but divinized principles Pepromene and Heimarmene. [36]

The powers of Destiny—the foremost principle—ruled independently, albeit connected to and in cooperation with the Gods of the Greek pantheon.

There dwelled much spiritedness within those representatives of humanity that populated the shores embracing the Aegean Sea. They feared and cherished their divine role models and added a portion of extra respect for the world's future-spinning "over-ladies."

Who were these predominantly female, divine embodiments always speaking the first and last words?

> Ananke [37] (*Ἀνάγκη*)—primeval Goddess and the faceless principle of Necessity—Protogenos, i.e., first Goddess and the force of Destiny, representing love, healing, and wisdom in the Orphic Cosmogony. She self-formed from chaos as the resolute, supreme ruler over everything, offering cosmic balance, carrying a torch of enlightenment and purpose above and beyond any system or religion.

Chronos/Khronos—The Principle of Time, also born from divine chaos—husband to Ananke. Together, they crushed the egg of creation and made the world. The flowing concept of time plays a vital part in the idea of Destiny. Time, the invisible, transient force, witnessed the past, represents the here and now, and can see into the future. The measuring of time is more than an ancient necessity—it is an ongoing human obsession, for it mainly works against us. To rule time would mean overcoming the mortal domain. Ananke and Chronos produced the incarnation of life, kindness, and light.

Phanes[38]—a golden-winged Prime Guardian of the Cosmos and Creation, female and male.

Adrasteia—the Inexorable—erstwhile Nymph turned Goddess of Inescapability and Vengeance, also an incarnation of Nemesis.

Tekmor—the Purpose—Inevitable Ordainer of Boundaries—the embodiment of the order of life.

Poros—the Path—a deity of plenty, repentance, and the road of life.

Aisa—the Determiner—Provider of a person's lot, a personification of ordained fate.

Moira—the even-handed Might of Destiny and allotted individual portions in life (described in Homer's *Iliad*).

Tyche—Goddess of Chance, human and political, even national Luck, or the lack thereof. Her divine actions sometimes represent destined forms of chance, good or (even deserved) bad fortune, while her unpredictable moodiness often drove these situations. She was also the personification of abundance and depicted holding a horn of plenty (cornucopia) filled with pleasant gifts for mankind.

Moros, Ker, and Thanatos—the Deadly Brothers—Moros guides toward life's expiration; Ker deals with ferocious dying circumstances until Thanatos delivers a tranquil passing with his light hand. These guys were one of the reasons fate received such a negative rap, because our scary Desti-Bros acted at the behest of Atropos—the third Moira and terminator of a person's earthly existence.

The Keres—three dispatchers of savage deaths—demonically divine variations of Ker.

The Erynies—Alekto, Megaera, and Tisiphon—female demons of unending wrath sent to deal with perpetrators that violated the natural code of necessity by committing and getting away with horrible acts left unpunished. These ladies, also known in Rome as The Furies, cleverly dubbed The Eumenides, which euphemistically translates to The Benign Ones, were a perfect girl squad—fatality guaranteed.

Pepromene—philosophical principle and Goddess of the fulfillment of an individual and vocational journey.

Heimarmene—Inescapable Law of the Universe and our world, philosophical principle, and determiner of the inevitable Destiny of physical realms. She masterminded cause and effect and was revered by the Milesian Nature Philosophers of Ionia—the motherland of Greek philosophy (today's west coast of Anatolia/Türkiye).

Pepromene and especially Heimarmene were refined, conceptualized re-personifications of the great Ananke, embodying two departments—the personal and the universal.

Nemesis—Goddess of Retribution and Hand of Destiny—the beautiful bane of the arrogant, the corrupt, and those that succumb to hubris or hybris (Greek for excessive pride or the human delusion to be divine). This principled interceptor not only incorporated but nurtured the ideal of higher justice and divine retribution that humanity has craved ever since. She could give and take both bliss and destruction.

Dike—Goddess of Order, Fair Judgment, and gifted abundance, daughter of Themis—Goddess of Justice. She was one of the three Horei sisters (natural time deities, Dike, Eirene, and Eunomia).

These philosophically refined incarnations of principles and deities represent the change in ancient Greek awareness and perception, looking for a more individual and increasingly ethical representation.

Last but not least—the famous triple threat, the anti-linear forces of the spheres:

The Moirai—Clotho—the Spinner

Lachesis—the Unbending

Atropos—the Inexorable

Goddesses of spinning, measuring, and ending an individual's thread of light and life. Moira/Moirai also stems from the Greek *meros*—lot, portion. [39]

The Moirai represent the concepts of yesterday, today, and tomorrow—nothing scary if we all have our wits and a touch of realism about us and accept that beginning, middle part, and a definitive end are the prerequisite of any story, be it a drama, an epos or a comedy. The Moirai actually sang these three-pronged Destinies of anyone with a soul. Yes, you read right: They sang life.

Come, gentle powers, well-born, benign, famed, Atrops, Lachesis, and Clotho named, unchanged, aerial, wandering in the night, untamed, invisible to mortal sight; Moirai, all-producing, all-destroying, hear, regard the incense and the holy prayer; propitious listen to these rites inclined and far avert distress, with placid mind.

– Orphic Hymn 59 To the Moirai, translated by Taylor

Clotho spun the thread of human life. Lachesis took it over to measure a person's lifetime and decreed when it was time for Atropos to use her shears and cut the yarn, issuing expiry.

Carl Gustav Jung, Swiss psychiatrist and creator of analytical psychology, thought when the number three appears in our dreams it represents the Moirai or Fates, pointing to a significant juncture.

The ancient Greeks had Destiny writ large all over their mythology and everyday lives. We are indeed talking about Destiny with a capital D. But in contrast to the later adopters of their Destiny, the Greeks saw only important things of some scale masterminded by their fabulous feminine force, whereas the Romans subscribed for the platinum package including everything in life and beyond being spun by their ladies of fate. [40]

In his *Theogony* (poetic creation theory), the writer Hesiod outlines how the high principle of divine decree came into this world, personified by the three Moirai.

The philosopher Plato (ca. 427–347 BCE), in his *Republic*, also referred to Ananke as the astounding primordial Goddess of necessity, cosmic stability, purpose, circumstance, and even of constraint and compulsion (needs must, as the saying goes)—an outstanding supernatural being who, when she saw fit, created herself straight out of chaos. Furthermore, she represented all-embracing celestial love and healing, superior to any Olympians.

> *The spindle turns on the knees of Necessity; and on the upper surface of each circle is a siren, who goes round with them, hymning a single tone or note. The eight together form one harmony; and roundabout, at equal intervals, there is another band, three in number, each sitting upon her throne: these are the Fates, daughters of Necessity, who are clothed in white robes and have chaplets upon their heads. Lachesis, Clotho, and Atropos, who accompany with their voices the harmony of the sirens— Lachesis singing of the past, Clotho of the present, Atropos of the future; Clotho from time to time assisting with a touch of*

her right hand the revolution of the outer circle of the whorl or
spindle, and Atropos with her left-hand touching and guiding the
inner ones, and Lachesis laying hold of either in turn, first with
one hand and then with the other.

– Plato, The Republic, The Myth of Er

Essentially, everything sprang from Ananke's will, lap, spindle, and hand. Faceless Ananke meant more than a mighty archaic Goddess; no one could ever avoid this cosmic principle.

Even the Gods don't fight against Ananke.

– Simonides

And they knew why.

Necessity is not just a mythological and metaphysical term. It is also used concerning determinism since its philosophical interpretation refers to a world where all that occurs is driven by necessity—yesterday, now, and tomorrow. We have physical and logical necessity. [41] Necessity, determinism, and free will are weighty topics at the heart of many different theories and opinions from the desks of Chrysippus to Aristotle, to Kant, and beyond. [42]

Ananke remained an elusive outsider, often perceived as cruel. But
it is important that at an early stage, religious and philosophical
speculation closely linked Ananke to the elements of the world's
existence (among which Goethe included her too).

– Otto Brendel, Symbolism of the Sphere

Over time, the original fountainhead, Ananke, was lent a stern public image. No wonder—her qualities rivaled, if not obliterated, all other deities, including the masculine varieties. And Ananke and the Moirai, The Destinies, were not the type of power humans could haggle with or impress with sacrifices or by praying and paying lip service. Ananke's carefully reinterpreted, severe public persona was not always justified, though. Where would we as homo sapiens be, and where would the world be without the laws of necessity? Absent the clear insight that something, even everything, is what it is. Enigmatic Ananke, i.e., necessity and purpose, inspired Victor Hugo to his novel, *The Hunchback of Notre Dame*. Later, Hugo even acknowledged Ananke as the first principle of love. We are talking about necessity in a higher form, not always worldly, not driven by base intentions, and especially not selfish or politically motivated. It is a natural, spiritual necessity to bring about what has to happen for the progression of this world, including the pursuit of ethical goals and good choices, to further decent expansion and well-intended, exercised advancement of humanity. This necessity is the ancient voice of purpose within our souls, telling us what is right, hopefully louder than the enticing noise produced by those who want us to believe whatever serves their objectives.

Our inner Ananke is crucial.

Ananke must above all be regarded as cosmic force, that is, as the ruling law in the Universe; thus ... the super-personal, cosmic significance of "the All" ruled by Ananke as well, can be accepted as certain. It represents in the Universe the inviolability of cause and effect and does so as dual essence, as a mythical personage belonging to the oldest theogony or as the earliest philosophical concept of the mechanics of natural events.

– Otto Brendel, Symbolism of the Sphere

Back to Ananke's three daughters—the Moirai, mistresses of universal, divine, and human time and their different departments.

Clotho produces the string of life, often depicted as a maiden bearing a spindle. Lachesis takes care of the precious thread and decides how long a person shall live. Atropos is tasked to cut the thread and bring finality to a being when their defined time has come. Just like in most great movies, plays, or stories, our three Moirai represent the three acts of life: setup, build, and resolution.

Clotho delivers Emergence, Lachesis sorts Vitality, and Atropos fulfills Denouement.

These ladies were not necessarily always mentioned in the Super League of deities residing atop Mount Olympus. No one knows the See of Destiny's location; even the mighty Greek pantheon lacked dominion over the lots that Ananke, the Moirai, and Co. assigned. They, too, had to play ball.

To the Moirai (or Fates), the might of Zeus must bow, and by the Immortals' purpose, all these things had come to pass, or by the Moirai's ordinance.

— QUINTUS SMYRNAEUS, THE FALL OF TROY

Two Greek luminaries, the philosopher Heraclitus (ca. 540–480 BCE) and the historian Herodotus (ca. 484–425 BCE), saw Destiny as an innate trait, if not quality, of a person's unique character and soul. They considered it a supernatural gift, granted by a female personification of the highest order, lovingly bestowed by the Supra-Mother, the one that created order out of chaos. This gift resembled an invisible crown, often at the cost of personal sacrifice. The preordained direction of our path, teamed with superhuman aspirations, can lead to outstanding achievements. And to this day, Destiny and heroism forever go together like cream and apple pie. Just as Destiny and virtuousness are a dream team as well because the spinning Goddesses also represented justice and fairness. Human character, in combination with the threaded journey, was seen as a combination of the finest kind, often leading to the desired and destined outcome.

Let us briefly give a special salute to the philosopher Plato (427–347 BCE). He was the creator's creator. Noble-born Plato, who penned tragedies before he became a student of Socrates (469–399 BCE), suggested the visible world was crafted by a divine principle, a supreme yet not-embodied entity, while the laws of cosmic Destiny ruled the universe. This provident artisan he called Demiurge, Greek for producer. Mighty, yet not all-mighty. Who says that a God(dess) has to be all-powerful anyway? Plato had traveled to important parts of his world. He founded the first "university"—the Academy—and next to his doctrines, theories, dialogues, and famous myths like *Atlantis*, the *Myth of Er,* and the *Allegory of the Cave*, he created the core of Western philosophy and metaphysics. His idea—that a meaningful spiritual world exists beyond the visible realm—influenced Judaism, Christianity, Islam, and beyond with a visionary perspective on a benevolent, creative principle performing in concert with Destiny. Plato gave us unparalleled impressions of the immortality of our souls, an afterlife, reincarnation (or rather transmigration), goodness, and high love. To him, life and death weren't dead-end streets but revolving doors of renewed purpose and self-development. Plato encouraged ideally ethical humanity to co-author their destinies and seek harmony with it instead of feeling wholly bound by seemingly stringent laws.

But was Plato a forerunner of a monotheistic, all-powerful God as later construed by Christian scholars? Naturally, such a "handy" concept proved quite irresistible since claiming that the most eminent philosopher's idea of a prime artisan niftily supported Christianity with added gravitas and backstory to the otherwise primarily Judaic evolution of our book-based faiths. We can get quite far by misinterpretations. Yet neither Socrates nor Plato nor any other of the seven Greek sages believed in a sole omnipotent deity, as that's just not how they rolled.

Plato's student, Aristotle, who wrote the splendid *Nicomachean Ethics*, clearly learned a lot from his mentor. Like everybody else, then and today, Plato was a man of his time and personal circumstances. Therefore, he deserves to be humored for some of his views on, for example, the societal position of women (seen as inferior to men in his day), Attic democracy, censorship, the military, and justice. When we look at many of our political leaders, we could all use a bit of that idealistic, perfect society guided by philosopher kings that Plato envisaged instead of the tragic clownery abounding these days.

The divinely provident Demiurge—I feel that a far earlier concept may have inspired far-traveled and well-read Plato regarding supernatural creatorship: that of the Egyptian sun God Aten in concert with Destiny God(dess) Shai/it (ca. 1350–1335 BCE). No wonder Plato's artisan, despite being later described by the Neoplatonic philosopher Proclus

(412–485 CE) to be in a creative partnership with Ananke, i.e., cosmic Destiny herself, was developed into a co-role model for respective Godly attributions that assimilated many qualities of their surrounding territories' polytheistic inspirators. All female elements were, of course, later redacted and edited out of these respective traditions. Long before the children of Palestine finally embraced and enforced monotheism around 600 BCE, the Israelite God Yahweh was consort to the Canaanite mother Goddess Ashera, the chief lady of divination, foreknowledge, and sagacity. The Christian God openly chose Mary as the mother of his USP—their human-born son Jeshua. And Allah, the former moon God, had three daughters—Allāt, Manāt, and Al-Uzzā—already worshiped at Mecca. But I digress.

It is time to bid farewell to the overwhelming culture and philosophy of ancient Greece, their mythology and pantheon, which impressed the rapidly rising Lords of Italy tremendously. They liked it so much that they simply adopted most Hellenic Gods and repurposed and renamed them. If they worked for the Greeks, they would work for the Romans.

Savvy, labor- and time-saving. After all, these guys were busy building the mega-empire of its time and conquering the world they did, including noble Hellas. Meet the Romans.

The Roman Agency of Fatum

Rome, the first modern world power (ca. 625 BCE–476 CE), rose from surrounding lands when a small settlement on a group of Italian hills grabbed the staff to become the leading force in the ancient world. These masters of splendid organization were known for their pragmatism, resourcefulness, strict hierarchy, class system, discipline, and ruthlessness.

In contrast, their fluid religion was rather non-dogmatic; hence, Romans always showed curiosity and tolerance toward other faiths and their deities, especially if they came with added benefits. They were not as romantic and spiritual as the Greeks but far more practical and goal-focused.

As a result, little Rome began to ascend as a factual mega-power. A solid attachment to Destiny held their growing world together with the shiny threads of success. Ancient Rome remains an identity-building element of Western culture and civilization. The world owes a massive debt of gratitude to these she-wolf-raised, toga-donning creators. They gave us enduring architecture, cement, paved roads, sophisticated high-rise aqueducts, the Latin alphabet, the Julian calendar, philosophy, rhetoric, law, literature, the art of government and administration, and a highly influential language.

Over time, Rome forced many countries into subjugation thanks to her highly functional military system and expansive stratagem. Rome entertained the proven practice of brain-draining her occupied territories, especially Greece, by exporting a large part of its fine intelligentsia to serve in Roman education and as consultants.

Captive Greece took captive her fierce conqueror and instilled her arts in rustic Latium.

– HORACE, ROMAN POET

Other nations' deities infiltrated the traditional Roman system. Their state religion centered on the major Greek Goddesses and Gods that were energetically rebranded à la Roma.

Rome's literary gems include *The Aeneid* by Virgil (70–19 BCE), *Metamorphoses* by Ovid (43 BCE–17 CE), *Naturalis Historia* by Pliny (23–79 CE), a blueprint for encyclopedias, *De Natura Deorum* and *De Divinatione* by Cicero (106–43 BCE), *On the Nature of the Universe* by Lucretius (99–55 BCE) and *The Meditations* of Marcus Aurelius (121–180 CE).

Roman culture was open to any supernatural force that "worked" for others, and other beliefs were tolerated. So, after initial disturbances, the later foothold and spread of Christianity happened quite swiftly. But back to the earlier heyday, during which the Roman Empire and her citizens strongly believed in the powers of Destiny and cherished their own destinizing pantheon, with Jupiter as managing director, the Latin version of the imported Godfather Zeus, possibly co-inspiring later adoption of predetermination by the Christian God.

Necessitas—Necessity—a Roman equivalent to the Greek Ananke.

Fatae—The Fates—The Sparing Ones—spinners and bringers of Destiny, Roman versions of the three Greek Moirai, also called the Parcae (birth Goddesses), often pictured using distaff and spindle, scales, and shears:

Nona—The Ninth • Decima—The Tenth • Morta—The End or Death.

Fortuna—Good Luck and Chance, Mistress of the Rota Fortunae—The Wheel of Fortune, and the Cornucopia (horn of plenty), bringer of prosperity to humans and cities—Rome's answer to the Greek Goddess Tyche. Often depicted with covered eyes to represent blind luck.

The Camenae—nymphs and prophetesses, singers of Destiny to children:

Carmenta—The Oracle • Antevorta—The Future • Postelevisionerta—The Past • Egeria—The Wise Counsellor.

Janus—The Arched Passage/Doorway, two-faced primordial God of time, beginnings, transitions, and endings.

Anna Perenna—Eternal Stream—bestower of the infinite year—Goddess of time and the circle of the year.

Invidia—Goddess of Divine Retribution, Rome's answer to Greece's Nemesis.

Justitia—Mother of Divine Justice and the Law of Custom.

The Furies—Alecto, Megaera, and Tisiphone—the three Roman counterparts of the Greek Erinyes, three female demons of vengeance and special agents to assist Invidia and Justitia in punishing selected evil deeds and mindsets (like hubris) as per the decree of Destiny.

Nortia—the Etruscan Goddess of Destiny—an eminent deity in the Etruscan culture (ca. 800–300 BCE) that ruled over large parts of Italy way before Rome rose to absolute power. Rome conquered Etruria and absorbed its art, trade, and the Goddess Nortia. In the same style as when taking a shine to the magnificent Greek pantheon, they morphed and Latinized when turning Greece into a Roman province. Nortia was equalized with the Roman Necessitas and Fortuna. The Romans knew not only how to fight and occupy; they cultivated the art of adaptation, always learning from the best: the Etruscans, Greeks, and far beyond.

Providentia—an important divine principle embodying the wisdom of foreknowing the future and providing solutions for all eventualities. Feminine-stylized Providentia looked ahead with prudent foresight and precaution. She was revered as one of the Roman state virtues and served as inspiration for Christianity's divine providence, many works of art, and lending noble gravitas to insurance companies and anything in need of utmost integrity. Providentia *provided* insight and direction for what tomorrow holds in store and how to make the best of that.

In Latin mythology, the Greek Destiny emanations Ananke and the three Moirai re-emerged as the nail-bearing Necessitas. The three Fates Romans also called the Parcae (after the Latin *pars*—part or lot). The Fates, also respectfully called Mothers of Destiny, were pronounced daughters of Jupiter, Rome's equivalent to Zeus, and Justitia, the Goddess of Justice.

Let us take a quick look at the tasks of the Roman Fates. Their name stems from the Latin *fatum*—that which has been spoken, that which is ordained and *fas, fari*—to speak and to presage. They spun and spoke Roman Destiny.

Nona, the Ninth, was invoked to spin the thread of life for the soon-to-be-born children of, ideally, nine-month-pregnant mothers-to-be. Decima, or Decuma, the Tenth, measured or weighed a newborn's time and future in the first month of their life and decided on his or their worldly existence and set of fortunes. And, finally, Morta, the Bringer of Death, cuts the thread of life.

Nona enables Conception • Decuma empowers Vitality • Morta directs Transition via Death.

The Fates became synonymous with a brand of inescapable finality that flew from their decisions and actions, a crystallization of human fear of what is outside our reach. Quite undeservedly so because Nona and Decuma, just like the Greek Clotho and Lachesis, were companions, givers, and keepers of life, while Morta and Atropos just expedited the human spirit into full circle and progressed their clients to the in-between and otherworld(s).

The influential early Christian writer Tertullian of Carthage (ca. 160– 240 CE) even describes a *Fata Scribunda*—the Fate who writes—who superintended the Book of Life. [43]

The Goddess Necessitas nailed the decrees spoken by the Fates, supernaturally rubber-stamping the supreme authority's mandate. In both mythologies, these female deities represent the spirits of necessity and fulfillment of life and death. To this day, we use the expression "to nail something," meaning to make something finite or to seal the deal.

NECESSITAS (Gr. Ἀνάγκη/Ananke), in Orphic theology, the personification of absolute necessity. She appears as the mother of the Moerae (Fates), as the wife of Demiurges (Fashioner of the World) and mother of Heimarmenē (destiny). Her power is irresistible, even greater than that of the Gods; to her was due the strife (battles with Titans, Giants) that raged amongst them of old, before the rule of love began; the world revolves round the spindle, which she holds in her lap. According to the Egyptian theory, she is one of the four deities present at the birth of every human being, her companions being the Daemon (guardian spirit), Tyche (Fortune) and Eros. On the citadel of Corinth, there was a temple sacred to her and Bia (Violence), which none were permitted to enter.

– PLATO, REP. 616 C, SYMP. 195C

The Roman Necessitas is represented in the well-known ode of Horace (i. 35) as the forerunner and companion of Fortuna, holding in her brazen hand huge nails, a clamp, and molten lead, symbolical of fixedness and tenacity.

– MACROBIUS, SATURNALIA, I. 19; PAUSANIAS II. 4. 6., FROM THE 1911 ENCYCLOPÆDIA BRITANNICA

Fortuna, the whimsical Lady Luck, was, and is, a regular sunbeam to most folks, notwithstanding that she does much more than grant surprise jackpots. For she also bears a certain darkness and endgame since she is prone to impulsive decisions, often depicted blindfolded, like Justice. She was easily distracted by a moment's flavor or a bemused mood, resulting in the decree of bad luck or good luck as obvious options. This mistress of preordained caprice was revered in several contexts and under a good two dozen different names. The Goddess Fortuna remained a firm favorite with poets and gamblers for more than two millennia and is beloved and evoked all around the modern world. Small lucky charms bearing smiling Lady Fortuna's pretty head encircled by a gloriole symbolizing her wheel continue to be popular tokens.

Human necessity triggers our need for reason, for purpose, accepting what makes sense or what cannot be changed, and it seems so much more trustworthy than fortune. Luck comes as a gift or a challenge that may bless or befall us wholly undeserved. As a result, humanity ostensibly fancies Fortuna while reserving respect for the necessities that come with the cosmic principle. Still, we must not forget that Destiny often incorporates this amiable Goddess's business as well. To this day, serious wealth is called a fortune, while the Fortune 500 ranks the biggest and most significant companies in the US, not to mention the influential business magazine Fortune.

Destiny will find a way.

– VIRGIL

European Gods of Destiny

The Celtic civilizations that shaped Europe and further afield for thousands of years and were hailed as a leading culture of the British Isles (ca. 700 BCE–ongoing) looked to a Destiny deity emanating in the forms of three divining sisters. Macha, Babd, and Anu represent one mighty incarnation as Morrigan—the Great Queen of Life, war, and Death.

Destiny plays an integral part in Celtic mythological narratives. The Celts lived in tribal yet refined societies that excelled at music, poetry, the ornamental arts of their time, metalwork, and fine pottery while being fierce warriors who did not seem to fear to die, thanks to their transcendent philosophy represented by learned and gifted priestesses, diviners, healers, bards, and Druids. Women were on an equal footing with men and, at times, even had several husbands. Private life was less restricted than in other cultures, offering emotional and erotic liberties and flexibility.

The Anglo-Saxon (ca. 400–1066 CE) view on individual Destiny focused on Urd—both the name of the Nordic Norn that weaves "what is to come to pass" and the Well of Destiny beneath Yggdrasil, the Sacred Ash Tree, and on the term Wurd/Wyrd, the fabric of life.

The old Anglo-Saxon knotted symbol for Wyrd expresses this very well. Germanic tribes also revered this flexible and adjustable concept encompassing the past, present, and future of mankind and any worldly occurrences. Anglo-Saxon philosophy was highly influenced by Norse mythology. The waters of the Well of Wyrd provide the roots of Yggdrasil with an unending supply of Destiny that returns to the well as drops from the World Tree's boughs.

Destiny/Wyrd goes always as she must.

– BEOWULF

Mokosh/Mokoš—the ancient Slavic Goddess of Destiny, fertility, spinning, and weaving provides the water of life and focuses on the protection of women. Motherly Mokosh was even Christianized and is continuously highly esteemed throughout Eastern Europe.

Our little trip back in time to meet the deities that ran the realms of Destiny in antiquity concludes here.

Norse Destiny—The Norms of the Norns

Over time, the lords and ladies of the North (ca. 790–1066 CE) took a giant leaf out of classic Greek and Roman cosmogonies by featuring an interesting, unusually impermanent take on how their versions of the three Moirai or Fates ran their lives and even those of the Gods.

Meet the Norse Ladies of Destiny:

Urd or Urðr—The Past, Verdandi or Verðandi—The Present, and Skuld—The Future.

They are the triple guardians of Urd or Urðarbrunnr—the well of Destiny, reigning over life and death from within the shades of Yggdrasil—the great ash tree that connects the cosmos with the nine worlds.

The Nordic epithet for Destiny and fate is *Wyrd.*

According to Norse mythology, the Norns are the three supernatural ladies who spin and weave the lace of Wyrd and carve the Destinies of Gods and men, anyone born into the world of the living, on pieces of wood. These three spinners can only shape the early versions of human destinies, while their carvings aren't meant to be absolute and final. As opposed to the Moirai or Fates, the Norns suggest and predict how a person may lead their life, while that individual can still change the course of their life depending on the flow of water within the Well of Urd (Destiny) over in the Norse otherworld. The flow of water symbolizes the passage of time and Destiny. But let us not forget the web and images the Norns weave and carve are valid and influential over what happens in the future. Norse civilizations used the casting of runes to divine their destinies and relied on seers and sages to advise on their endeavors.

It is time for Ragnarök—the Destiny of the Gods. The Poetic Edda describes how principal Norse Aesir deities like Odin, Freyr, Thor, and Loki of Asgard will eventually perish in the twilight of many natural disasters, followed by a renaissance of life and a renewed, reinvigorated pantheon. Humanity will be reinstated through two surviving human beings—a fascinating concept. Everything is fluent. Already, before the Aesir deities reigned the Vanir Gods of Vanaheim. They were in charge before the Asgardians, but due to a war between the two divine teams, the Vanirs were absorbed into the famous league of Norse Gods.

Imagine Goddesses of serendipity and fortune unconditionally on our sides, singing at our cradles, weaving lightful paths, and handing out gifts of fortitude and endurance. Genetics come to mind—our biological makeup will always have a bearing on what we can and will or will not do, no matter how powerful our desires are and how meticulously we plan our moves.

In times of olde as today, both human Destiny, genetics, and epigenetics are directly interwoven. If we were gifted with a sharp and shrewd thinker's brain, a healthy physique, and an upbeat, self-possessed personality, we easily appeared to be or perhaps even *were* competent and able. And we would have been seen as naturally destined for great exploits and achievements, as leadership-, spouse-, and hero/ine- material. That is how human beacons are still idealized today.

Between Antiquity and Modernity

At this point, we may well pause to ponder how our ancestors felt about the meaning of life. Because in their worldview, everything awaiting them on the road ahead was previously written by invisible hands.

How humanity perceived their lives and futures was guided by two sources of knowledge and belief—philosophy and theology. If we compare the challenges our foremothers had to master to explain how life and the universe function, we may realize it came at the cost of a lot of anxiety and time spent with introspection trying to understand the occurrences around and beyond them.

Let us return to the age of polytheism to put out our feelers to perceive how the ancients worked their worlds back then. Polytheism offered us a way to understand and accept their aspirations and desires, explaining all kinds of phenomena while expecting limited power over the environment they lived in.

While antiquity generated a lot of wisdom, aesthetics, poetry, and art, life was hard and short. A common cold, a small wound, or a broken limb could lead to death. The majority of women were kept under the rule of male relatives, often uneducated, suffering under increasingly patriarchal structures, and treated as second-class beings. Childbirth was dangerous, with child and maternal mortality being incredibly high—usually more than 50 percent. Sons were "worth" a lot more than daughters. Tutelage only existed for the affluent and influential. Natural disasters caused even more bewilderment than today. Men could be commanded to sacrifice themselves in wars at any given moment, and lives, villages, towns, and even cities were upended, if not destroyed, at the whim of an overlord. Gods were humanly vested with the authorship and creation of almost everything that took place, which made it far easier to get away with despotism. Societies and leaderships were predominantly built upon cruel hierarchies, absolute inequality, and the consequent disregard for human or animal pain and life; thereby, serfdom and slavery were rife. Most of our times and civilizations so far worshiped good looks, physical strength, and selfish ferociousness while rejecting anyone and anything that did not fit the clichés of efficiency and absence of weakness. Sounds familiar, somehow?

Mother Nature, like love, wasn't romanticized then, and her deified representatives were experienced as far more challenging, albeit generous as well, so our forebears felt obliged to pray for and give thanks for each cycle, each harvest, and any non-eventful time that went by without too great hardships. Humans, then, knew they were not in charge. We are likely going full circle soon in the experience of acts of Nature that may drive us to question our pet idea that humanity simply has to be the measure and master of all things.

Nights were pitch-dark, and the firmament shimmering with stars appeared like a comforting vision of a world of wonders. To eat fresh, well-baked bread with honey or olives was a joy—something to look forward to. A small piece of polished amber was a breathtaking treasure. And a finely pleated linen wrap was worn with elegant pleasure. Woolen fabrics of the time were cherished protectors from the elements, and a few sips of coolish wine made us wish to party with our respective pantheon and get into trouble with a shapely nymph. Peace, if so to be had, was a daily blessing, a gift from Destiny, instead of being taken for granted.

There was no easy way to understand natural phenomena, such as lightning, storms, and rain, and survive the many other challenges of Nature. Our human experience before the invention of proper agriculture, mining, and architecture alone explains why our ancestors believed they were ruled by powers far beyond their reach. The belief in Destiny ensured we did not feel meaningless but somehow counted and were significant for an unseen principle to predesign our adventures. Destiny offered hope, explanations, and an invisible thread to follow.

Mythologies gave our foremothers plenty of reasons to assume there were forces at work deciding how and where the world had to go, which persons should be admired, followed, and placed on a pedestal, and which ones should continue to serve as their enablers. It is clear how our need for parental guidance and attention ushered in the rise of early religions reflective of mankind's self-sabotaging F.U.D. syndrome (fear, uncertainty, and doubt).

With the progress of societal development, more profound views on the role of life in society and the universe broke free. If our predecessors could remain undefeated in battle or had the charm and diplomacy to prevent an invasion, they were individuals of a much higher ascribed worth than others not as lucky to be able to employ chutzpah, skills, traits, and winsome personalities to best effect. And accordingly, it became a tantalizing trend to think of those more capable and fortunate of us as Destiny's darlings or pets—divinely decreed to be unique, well-designed for greatness, riches, and whatever was out there worth having.

While most of us preferred to subscribe to codified and authoritarian top-down models of belief when determining human direction, some stood tall, investing higher conviction in particular abilities of humanity instead of believing in remote God(s) alone.

That's when Greek and Roman philosophy checked in that chatroom, focusing on new ways of understanding the universe's workings and how humans should evaluate and actualize themselves. Philosophy also enhanced fresh thinking on how to encounter life best and how to treat our fellow beings.

Classic philosophy asked those niggling questions about our role in the great play and began to debate the existence of God(s) and their degree of involvement with humanity. No wonder philosophy emerged as the primary avenue for understanding human behaviors, ethics, morality, freedom, and the meaning of life. As Greek and Roman philosophy became more mainstream, it inspired and intermingled with traditional beliefs, especially when coining a standard for seeking certitude. While philosophy never debunked the existence of mythology and religion, it helped to clarify the initial, often slightly blinded, relationship with their statements.

Destiny's Diviners

While consciously flowing with the presence of any given day is a wise way to conduct the dance of existence, we humans are wedged between the compartments of yesterday's effects on today's results and, especially, tomorrow's consequences or surprises. Always wanting to know our future is one of our pet intentions. What's going to happen, when, and how? And what can we do to ensure a good outcome? Today, we rely on weather forecasts, stock market and trend analysts, lifestyle coaches and mentors, and many consult clairvoyants and astrologers to find out what tomorrow has in store or whether we'll find what we're looking for. A long time ago, seeing into the future or even accessing the great design's agenda was called divination, and those gifted with the above were diviners.

The term divination stems from the Latin word *divinare*, from *divus* for God and *divinus* for the ability to predict something and be divinely inspired. *Divinare* means to explore the will and pleasure of the Gods. Cicero, an appointed Roman augur, called divination the Greek practice of finding the future. [44]

Destiny and divination were a winning combination. The eternal human wish to learn about the next chapter crystallized this relationship. The Stoic philosopher Chrysippus coined the notion that if something could be divined, it would be destined. He had a point because if something is successfully prognosticated, an echo of predetermination seems a natural conclusion. In ancient times, diviners and oracles were greatly trusted to predict the future. Many claimed mysterious connections to the planning desk of Destiny. Ancient civilizations believed that every individual, and even whole nations, had their uniquely designated path. If details of those paths could be unshrouded, it was akin to foreseeing the future.

Some later religions that relied exclusively on revelations or visions of prophets weren't exactly fond of the practice of prediction since they preferred devotees to stick to an ideally unshakable faith that did not ask for pointers, let alone evidence of what their good God may be up to. Those same organizations insist human beings have free will to choose whether they act on their innermost intentions or simply on prescribed guidance. That also led to religious followers seeking alternative knowledge of what lay ahead under strict camouflage.

Many rulers tried to avoid predictions about their royal fortunes by declaring high treason on anyone for even just having a king's horoscope read, let alone commissioning the prognostic art of a well-connected seeress.

An ethical diviner or predictor can be called a prophet, too, albeit one without a purely dogmatic agenda and, hopefully, with much less ego.

And whichever way we swing it, the custom of divination and seeking of oracles predate any established religion. We need not be surprised that ancient prescience left a lasting impression on today's world. After all, many of us are still fascinated by the possibility of catching glimpses of our future and going for it in great numbers.

It is difficult, if not impossible, to squash a living being's interest in even the most minor details of tomorrow, personal or global. We will always be curious about what's around the corner, which is fine, no matter what anyone says.

Since it is in our nature to feel uncertain about the road ahead rather quickly, we are prone to question it swiftly. No wonder we need to *know* as much as possible to meet whatever awaits in as prepared a state as necessary. Thereby, the deliberations of the ancient art of the zodiac have produced horoscopes for considerable millennia. A veritable army of cousins named tarot, numerology, palm reading, fortune telling, crystal ball gazing, etc., populate one of the biggest and most enduring world arenas offering advice, encouragement, and solace to millions since the days before antiquity, across all cultures and belief systems.

The powers that be always liked to keep us on a loyalty-centered, need-to-know basis, so no wonder they were and are still critical, if not condemning, of any kind of prediction unless it works in a specific interest and for their benefit. Some Gods, or rather their interpreters, just don't seem to like us to be too inquisitive, and nor do they like competition.

But human curiosity to know, influence, and, where possible, renegotiate the terms and conditions of our journey cannot be subdued. And why should only God(s) know what may lie ahead, especially if they are not in the habit of sharing their classified information with us? Well, actually, the Gods of the past were far more generous in that regard, as they humored mortals to seek and find answers through divination, prophetic dreams, and the interpretation of omens. Any of these methods can be both illuminating or deceptive since the outcomes don't just depend on a seer's connection with the invisible but also on their very integrity, their motivation, and their associations. It is pretty easy to tap into someone's trepidation and their F.U.D[45]., or to even cold read and tell them what they obviously want and need to hear, only to lead them astray for ulterior objectives.

It was, and will always remain, a tough job to convey the whispers of Destiny fairly and responsibly while withstanding the many temptations to abuse the gift of being in tune and sync with the threads of light for egotistic and corrupt reasons or the greed for misguiding influence and unnecessary riches.

We know that the great civilizations of Mesopotamia, Egypt, China, India, Greece, and Rome, and even the ancient Mesoamerican and Mexican cultures,[46] were connected with their respective powers of Destiny by employing mystical options to be let in on the directions of the mesh of life and time.

Star-gazing was a science that remained as such until a few hundred years ago. Astronomy and astrology were held in similar esteem. Despite the fact that this status changed, we still like to partake in the current art of it, big time. In 2017, researchers found that nearly 30 percent of Americans believed in astrology across all persuasions or the absence thereof.[47]

We should respect their choice with grace and tolerance before unjustly judging them for going woo-woo. Nobody knows what may be called "real" fifty years from now. Or ever.

Divination also served as a process of exploring what has happened in the past and why. It could be dubbed an early form of psychotherapy since it engaged the advice-seeking party to explore intentions and circumstances intensely. Seers were the go-to solution for all events hidden in the past, the present, and the mysteries of what the future may bring, employing their special knowledge, rituals, and ability to decipher ominous signs and use various tools to receive answers from transcendent agencies.

Conversing with spiritual forces or consulting deities to gain insight into individual and national destinies was nothing unusual in times gone by. From rulers to rustics—everybody wanted to find out what kind of a future lay ahead to get an advantage over those that didn't know, as in wars and political feuds. Any awareness of impending dangers or strikes by Lady Luck was of great comfort. As a result, the many means of divination never fell out of favor or fashion. Even today, these ancient traditions remain popular and influential throughout almost all cultures.

No matter what we believe or belittle today, genuine divination can provide a relevant perspective on the intricate patterns spun or woven for those who like to add another dimension to navigating our journeys. The needful exploration of the hidden resides comfortably in the company of the open-minded across all ages.

In Mesopotamia, diviners were revered for their ability to interact with divine entities and understand signs and messages conveyed in animal livers. Gods were implored to share their knowledge via soothsayers, who would answer questions of those who could not hear celestial voices or read in the Tablets of Destinies. [48]

Egyptian sages would ask the Gods for advice on everyday and even legal decisions. They employed readings of animal entrails, omens, and dreams to find the most auspicious constellations and moments for their seekers. [49]

In Greece, at first, the Earth Mother's Oracle of Dodona and, later, the Oracle of Delphi, were ports of call for comers of high and low status wanting to consult the priestesses about the upcoming context and future, ranging from personal affairs to public policies. At Delphi, Themis, the Goddess of Justice, and Apollon, the God of verity and the arts, spoke through an entranced Pythia, who relayed answers and messages in often poetic and mysterious words.

The Greeks believed Delphi to be the center, the omphalos, or navel of the world. One of the resident Pythia's most legendary divinations was her prophecy of the rocky path that awaited one Oedipus, who went on to unknowingly kill his father and marry his mother. Sophocles, the fifth-century BCE master of tragedy, describes Oedipus, the textbook tragic hero, as an outstandingly brave, intelligent, and gifted man. He went beyond his youth's spiritual and physical wounds and solved the notorious Theban Sphinx's riddle while trying to find clues to his life's questions. Sadly, he had to shoulder a heavy burden. Through a dense and painful process of self-discovery, Oedipus undergoes multiple transformations, from an abandoned bastard son to a wise, respected, and beloved king. Oracular Destiny, voiced by the Pythia, was inescapable. He suffered a bitter fate triggered as a consequence of the cursed misdemeanors of his useless father, King Laius, whom, as per the prophecy of the Delphi's priestess, Oedipus unknowingly dispatched from the face of the earth only to go on to marry his own mother and become a great sovereign. Destiny cannot be outwitted. Golden years were uprooted by fateful facts that led Oedipus to accept full responsibility. He blinded himself and left Thebes for good, wandering around the wilderness guided by his loyal daughter, Antigone. One version of the parable has it that when it was time to leave the world of the living, as foretold, Oedipus descended into the sacred earth of Colonus outside Athens.

Interestingly, Colonus was dedicated to the previously mentioned Erynnies or Eumenides—three awe-inspiring personifications of immutable Destiny, now kindly extending eternal peace to Oedipus' injured spirit.

Rome's leaders and luminaries banked on clairvoyant statements of their institutional augurs who monitored and interpreted the flight of birds to optimize Roman endeavors and strategies to win or maintain their gods' goodwill. Furthermore, Romans relied on the records from the Sibylline oracle named *libri fatales*—The Books of Fate (Fatum). Nobility and lesser-born Roman citizens alike employed the services of privately operating diviners that also offered a drawing of the lots to determine the invisible design.

Divination remains an international phenomenon.

Whether we turn to the Confucian *I Ching*—the *Book of Changes*, pervading global culture and even science with its philosophical clarity—or the study of Destiny, luck, feng shui, and the four pillars of Destiny called Bazi, consult the traditional Nadi palm leaf astrology of India, which inspires with enriching wisdom: Envisaging the future sharpens our focus to make the best and most of the time we have. The wish to divine our future is an element of our natural existence.

Let us name two well-known diviners from Western history. England's Queen Elizabeth I (1533–1603) had good reasons to trust her philosopher, seer, and strategist, the polymath John Dee (1527–1608), who, against many odds, predicted that England would prevail against the invasion of the Spanish Armada (1588). A storm, foreseen by the multiply gifted Dee, devastated the Spanish fleet, keeping England safe. Over across the Channel, French physician Michel de Nostredame (1503–1566), world-famous under his Latinized name Nostradamus, not only advised royalty but envisaged the future in 942 four-line stanzas.

Sitting alone at night in secret study that is placed on the brass tripod. A slight flame comes out of the emptiness and makes successful that which should never be believed in vain.

– NOSTRADAMUS, THE PROPHECIES

Many of his creatively written crypto-visions can be interpreted to be pretty accurate; some are still waiting in the wings of time to come to pass finally. Today, we like our horoscopes, mystical magazines, and Tarot reading as much as our predecessors, with the benefit of multimedia and the internet. And we are still trying to look ahead at our paths, just as we did thousands of years ago.

Considering the ongoing adherence to the sight and the knowledge gained by our foremothers from vocational oracles, is there still the need for such expert predictors today? The answer is that we do not have enough ethical diviners about now. Our own counsel is only rarely a satisfactory or reliable source when it comes to evaluating, to "divining" our individual, let alone global, Destiny.

Far-seeing, principled guides who visualize the future from a responsible and authentic setting can pull us out of inertia and show us a direction.

CHAPTER 3

Faithful Destiny

What decrees our Destiny? In the pure theologian world, the answer would be that Destiny is decided by God(s), eventually performed by more or less devout homo sapiens but still pre-orchestrated and delivered by God(s) entirely.

Let's briefly examine the much-discussed etymology of the term *religion*. Some authors derived it to stem from the Latin *(re)ligare,* which means to bind. Other sources claim that religion goes back to the translation of *religio,* for organized respect for the Gods, casually put.

Destiny's seminal cosmic order is the primary reason civilizations developed organized religions in the first place.

Taking the necessity of a common ethical ground to uphold as much peace as possible during the rise and demise of civilizations in the past, we understand that without an agreed cultural and religious code, many societies may have never risen or just wreaked havoc. The religions still leading much of humanity's spirituality had positive and even harmonizing effects on the brutal and ego-haunted aspects of homo sapiens. From antiquity to modernity, a lot of goodness and kindness was brought into being by well-meaning individuals who, in the name of their respective denominations, invested and even sacrificed much to help their communities try to ease the often heavy burden of being mortal.

Religion as a primary provider for a connection with and achieving Destiny is a long-term concept—starting from the era of ancient beliefs about the universe, right up to the present, with many of us continuously viewing religion as the main, if not the sole, source of their spirituality. Indeed, religion still offers a steady source of ideas for understanding the unknown, prompting generations into embracing the world of faith to generate echoes of life's values.

While science often seems to frown upon the idea of salvation or the existence of supernatural entities, statistics show that impressive majorities still believe in (a) supreme being(s) guiding them, the cosmos, and Nature. This may be down to the fact that so many children born into their parents' social and religious environments are rarely given a chance without the persuasion or even pressure to adopt the belief systems of their elders. Guilty as charged, I advocate giving children the freedom to grow up open-minded and without influencing their spirituality. Instead, we should encourage them to seek their paths, answers, and leanings, especially since knowledge and perspectives are at our fingertips these days. Kids should not be lured in by showers of gifts, lavish ceremonies, and overboard attention to make attractive a faith they are expected to adopt by their biotope.

In my book, children aren't possessions; they don't belong to their parents or families but are entitled to form their own views and decide their own steps. Just because something is part of an accepted tradition does not make it automatically ideal, especially not in our modern world.

Many nations utilized religion to bolster state-building and the creation of laws and dominion, and this is an ongoing strategy. Established religion is still one of the most important influencers and movers of humankind, with the three book devotions promoting the idea of free will under the eye of an all-powerful governor—God.

Self-determination became a vital element of the core branding in the three world religions, pointing out that the wise, gracious, and caring God bestowed humankind with free will to decide whether or not to follow his prefabricated moral path. Ostensibly, self-determination, embedded in the prominent religions, including manifold rules and laws, allows humans to freely manage personal choices while providing multi-pronged value to the ruling system. The faith-full citizen is automatically baked into the resident regime's code and any resulting demands while bearing full responsibility plus the burden of authority-imposed consequences. It is almost a kind of societal Destiny by command.

Isn't this a Fata Morgana of personal empowerment that can result in systematic bondage? It may be one of the prices we have to pay for the concept of controlled worldly order, or rather indoctrination on many levels, all for our benefit and best interest, of course. Whose best-vested interests would that be?

Render therefore unto Caesar the things which are Caesar's; and unto God the things that are God's.
— MATT. 22:2, KING JAMES BIBLE

For good reason, religions are in cahoots with earthly leadership and governance so that they can rely on mutual, system-bolstering back-scratching:

Give, and it shall be given unto you; good measure, pressed down, and shaken together, and running over, shall men give into your bosom.
— LUKE 6:38, KING JAMES BIBLE

The monotheistic take on human Destiny lies in the proposal of a universal God who will reward everyone following him and his set of rules, but not just yet. Being and acting philosophically virtuous, i.e., for its own sake, no longer was a primary philosophical objective to seek. Instead, God's authored morality is the benchmark all subscribers to his paradigm must adopt and obey.

In contrast, Hinduism presents an intriguing mix of human freedom and divine mentorship when it comes to determining our steps. For Hindus, karma shapes the current path of life, which means that the gifts or challenges faced, such as the circumstances of birth or the type of family, are consequences of our decisions in our previous existence. This concept could be interpreted as a form of self-determined Destiny or a fair chance to improve an individual's "fate" through better choices in their current life under the divine influence to regulate dharma to provide balance.

Before we take a clear-eyed look at the handling of Destiny by the religions that follow just one deity, let us visit early monotheism. Remember Aten, the sun God of King Akhenaten, mentioned earlier? Recap: Akhenaten (ca. 1353–1335 BCE) canceled all other ancient Gods of Egypt but one—Shai/Shait—leading to a unique "merger" of Destiny and the sacred principle of his only God, Aten.

Heretic King Akhenaten declared all other Gods null and void, bar his favorite lodestars, the Aten, and Shai, the hermaphrodite personification of Destiny, which melded into one supreme being. This revolutionary pharaoh established the first monotheistic cult and a new capital of Egypt: Amarna. They said he was crazy, but what a trailblazer and forerunner this guy was in retrospect. Later monotheistic religions took a massive leaf out of his book and poetry. They should pay royalties to him and Zoroaster.

If you are interested, look up *The Great Hymn to the Aten* and Psalm 104 in the Old Testament, as well as Plato's *Timaeus* (ca. 360 BCE), especially the idea of a cosmic producer, a Demiurge, in cooperation with The Ananke (necessity, purpose). From Egypt with love?

The unusual notion of just one God who would promise incentives to everyone following his ideology was initially an unknown quantity for the spoilt, multi-deity folks of the past. Due to the uptick in paternalistic cultures, God had to be masculine-ish, surely. Instead of inspiring and even challenging us to naturally want to be good, to do better by others, and to have higher standards of human conduct, the demand to simply fall into line slightly differed from the old approach. Virtue was no longer a personal ideal or freely chosen path of a shared philosophy, let alone innate inclination, but a written code of conduct.

The philosophical necessity for any person to harmonize, if not improve their being by freely trying to make better decisions, acting less selfishly and more humanely as part of a decent character, was no longer the first aim. There was a God channeling Destiny while insisting on regulating every human step.

The world's three most-established monotheistic religions have in common the existence of an all-knowing, all-powerful, all-seeing God who shapes the universe with his personality traits. This God is not a spectator who watches over people's activities—this entity also has a direct handle on everything.

In our revelation-based religions, God declares absolute intent to punish those who venture or stay outside of his code. In contrast, he is prepared to signal salvation to all those who obey and perform as expected. He even grants them the right to subdue the earth to gain dominion over all in exchange. Sadly, the often inhumane and self-absorbed results are visible everywhere and will be felt even more acutely in the nearer future. Granted, it's not just us that caused what's coming, but our hubris possibly led us to forget the world moves without asking our permission. It always has and always will.

Mankind owns its destiny, and its destiny is the earth. We are destroying it until we have no destiny.

– Frida Kahlo

The loudest argument in support of religion as a driver of mankind's existence was the introduction of theistic causality, which is the idea that everything the cosmos would enfold is caused by that sole entity, the one behind all events.

And most codified faiths and philosophies also claim to be fountains and keepers of ultimate truth.

Thus, one of the challenges religions display is that their all-knowing God adopted the realm of Destiny, claiming that he has already predetermined actions or occurrences. But isn't he, or rather his authors, perhaps weakening their decree of human beings autonomously living in this world? If he is indeed omnipotent and a lord of human Destiny, our existence is predeterministic. But how is there any place or use for free will under such a God?

So while a divine ruler decides and knows all that'll go down in the future, humans are still fully responsible for our predesigned actions. Essentially, it's up to us to follow the path set forth by God or stray from it altogether. Since an omnipotent God was willing and able to concoct plans for every single human on earth, including the option of salvation, the trajectory of humankind is crafted in line with his self-fulfilling prophecy. The good people who lean towards monotheism walk a path solely painted with colors from God's all-encompassing power palette. These great faiths champion human autonomy, meaning we can also undertake actions beyond the prescribed code and potentially defy the preordained future that God may envision. With a staunch belief in God, we remain responsible and bound by an unwavering commitment to a predetermined divine fatum.

Our great book religions absorbed and modified pre-existing polytheistic faiths and philosophies, likely one reason for their swift and continued success.

We're not here to talk about the monotheistic Abrahamic religions alone but also to find out how the other active and no-less-splendid religious philosophies operate in this world and their positions about Destiny.

Destiny's Realization in Active World Views [50]

Judaism

Following blueprints of spiritual influences from surrounding realms, Judaism—the first "book religion" to alight from Canaan (Palestine) between 1800–1000 BCE, still holds the copyright, trademark, and patent to a single-God-led organized religion. Official monotheism seems not to have been in full swing until around 600 BCE. The Jewish belief system grew from several local movements resting on the sacred texts of *The Tanakh*, which include *The Torah* (also called the Hebrew Bible), the first five books of the Old Testament, the books of the prophets, and further scriptures. As per the narrative of Judaism, a covenant was agreed upon between Yahweh and the patriarch Abraham. The prophet Moses received direct divine instructions on two tablets made of stone directly from his God while atop Mount Sinai—the ten commandments. *The Talmud* outlines a theological history and a multitude of rules and laws for Jews to follow. Judaism reveres and celebrates life, holding several views on possible options in the hereafter, culminating in the expectation of resurrection. Today, Judaism comprises three main branches: the Reform, Orthodox and Conservative movements.

In the Kingdom of Freedom, one's destiny is realised.
— ALBERT H. FRIEDLÄNDER [51]

The original organized monotheistic religion confidently entrusts free choice and responsibility in the hands of its followers while all happens per Hashem's will. And anyway, all Jews, as a people, are connected through a preordained and shared eternal Destiny, *Goral,* [52] and a collective high purpose. The Destiny of the community, *Ye'ood,* [53] ranks above the personal journey. Being Jewish transcends far beyond the religious realm as an influential and unique spiritual, emotional, and cultural awareness, inspiring admiration and inspiration. The Jewish identity collectively represents an extraordinary, incomparable Destiny spanning time and ages with spirited tenacity and inimitability. The concept of *Bashert*—the Yiddish word for Destiny—has great significance for many devotees of the Jewish faith. Bashert/Beshert [54] refers to the divinely chosen ideal partners in love, life, and the realms of the soul. This notion of providence expands the idea of the most favorable relationship through a deep inner and even outward connection, the vision of a perfect match—*Mazal* [55]—good fortune.

Everything is foreseen—yet free will is given. The world is judged with goodness and all is according to the majority of deeds.
— RABBI AKIVA BEN YOSEF

Christianity

In the first century CE, the second Abrahamic religion, namely Christianity, followed in the footsteps of Judaism by anchoring their newly created faith mainly on the life and death of Yeshua, or Jesus— the son of God and his disciple-written gospels. This Christian concept offers that upon physical expiration, all true followers are incentivized to dwell in heaven while the bad ones will be booked into hell. From Jerusalem, the once small Judaic sect later branded Christianity advanced throughout the known world on the foundation of the Bible, consisting of the Old Hebrew Testament and their self-developed New Testament. So far, Christianity remains the most successful religious movement ever, having made it from an obscure cult in the Roman province of Judea to Rome herself, growing rapidly and expanding throughout almost all parts of the world. Rome's Emperor Constantine (280–237CE), a ruthless yet savvy lip-serving champion of Christianity, declared Christendom the official religion of his traditionally polytheistic realm. It was a deliberate decision that went on to serve him well. [56]

Just like many of our modern world's politicians and public personalities, he was by no means the first nor the last ambitious power player to utilize religious symbolism and lingo for his or his goals. Christianity remains the largest religion on this planet. Beyond the original Roman Catholic, the Eastern-Orthodox, and the Protestant denominations exist several thousands of other churches.

For over 2,000 years, Christianity's omniscient God has granted humanity free volition under the premise of moral accountability for their actions while claiming charge over Christian Destiny.

> *For I know the thoughts that I think toward you, saith the LORD,*
> *thoughts of peace, and not of evil, to give you an expected end.*
> *– JEREMIAH 29:11, KING JAMES BIBLE*

In the Book of Genesis, despite being forbidden by God, Adam and Eve execute self-determination by deciding to sample some fruit from the tree of revelation. Since then, God, disappointed by Adam and Eve's betrayal of his perfect divine plan, has rejected responsibility for anything evil or harmful, including natural events. Because God is always only good, and he is praised for letting his devotees decide which way they want to seek and pursue their Destiny.

The mind of a man plans his way, but the Lord directs his steps.
– PROVERBS 16:9

A therapeutic notion of universal wisdom is the American Christian theologian Reinhold Niebuhr's famous *Serenity Prayer*, written in 1933:

God, grant me the serenity to accept the things I cannot change, the courage to change the things I can, and the wisdom to know the difference.

Its peaceful acceptance of "what is" seems reminiscent of Stoic and Eastern world views. Reinhold Niebuhr is the author of *The Nature and Destiny of Man*, an important book and mainstay of modern Christian ethics.

Islam

Islamic religion rose around the early seventh century CE from the Arabian capitals of Mecca and Medina. The term *Islam* translates to surrender. As per its tradition, it was started by the prophet Muhammad through revelations bestowed by the archangel Gabriel. Islam, today, is the number two world religion and the fastest-growing global faith. *The Quran* is Islam's holy book. As to Islam's notion of a life beyond life, Allah decrees the moment when a Muslim has to die. After death, Muslims expect their souls to remain in an in-between state awaiting resurrection. The world owes a great deal of gratitude to advanced Islamic thinkers who, assisted by Mediterranean scholars during the not-always-so-dark Middle Ages, rediscovered many nearly forgotten works of classic philosophy. Muslim achievements include the further development of astronomy, architecture, mathematics, medicine, and ornamental art. Islam knows two principal communities: Shia and Sunni.

> *The Lord has created and balanced all things and has fixed their destinies and guided them.*
>
> – The Quran 87:2

Quadar or *Al-Quadr* is Arabic for divine Destiny predetermined and known by Allah and written in *The Preserved Tablet* (*Al-Lawhu 'l-Mahfuz/Mahfooz*), an Islamic book of Destiny. The whole spectrum of time and what is good and bad in the world, including all living beings' actions, was decided and handwritten by Allah long before the creation of the universe.

The concept of *Taqdir* or *Taqdeer* (preordaining a person's lot or measure) was originally related to pre-Islamic fatalistic predestination, adapted as Allah's absolute claim to detailed foreknowledge of everything. He wrote each believer's life path from birth to the afterlife. Muslims enjoy the ability of independent will, so they are challenged to behave virtuously, carrying full responsibility for their actions throughout the trials and tribulations of life seen as tests of their subservience to Allah. The annual festival of Laylat al-Qadr (Night of Destiny) commemorates Muhammad's first vision of the Quran. It also signifies Allah's decree of next year's Destiny, which is set in motion by his angelic agents.

> *Allah has created and balanced all things and has fixed their destinies and guided them.*
>
> – The Quran 87:2-3

Zoroastrianism

Despite the fact this legendary concept is upheld by a minority these days, we need to acknowledge the inspirational Persian faith. All dualistic, mono-God religions took more than a page of the concepts of good and evil from the book of the greatest empire the world has ever seen. This spiritual tradition was Persian state religion from ca. 600 BCE to 650 CE, sadly ended by the Muslim *conquista*. Zoroastrianism also spread to Central Asia. It rests on the life story of the role-model inspirator Zarathustra, or Zoroaster.

He is thought to have lived around 1200–1500 BCE, but no one knows for sure. Under the guidance of six luminous beings, Zoroaster's prophetic visions revealed the existence of the good God Ahura Mazda (wise lord), who created the universe while fighting his evil counterpart Angra Mainu or Ahriman (the destructive spirit) for millennia, until one day Ahura Mazda would, it was hoped, win this war of good against evil. His followers were expected to lead responsible and virtuous lives, thus empowering their kind God through human fortitude. Failure to do so would strengthen Angra Mainu's evil agenda. Zoroaster taught truthfulness, compassion, justice, and everything supporting a long life crowned by immortality. He introduced a set of convincing tenets, including good thoughts, good words, and good deeds. Zoroastrians esteem holy scriptures—the *Avesta*—and the concepts of heaven and hell. Meet dualism on all levels—an advanced formula for monotheism.

Sound familiar? Opposing ideas of light and darkness were already woven into much older Mesopotamian and Egyptian faiths, like the formative narrative of Osiris versus Seth leading to Isis's triumph over evil and death. Or Ma'at versus Isfet—justice vis-à-vis injustice. But Zoroastrianism developed the concept into a fine art. Little wonder their original version of good versus evil intensely influenced the core branding and USP of all three Abrahamic religions. Zoroastrian principles shone when Judaism declared official monotheism and adopted certain elements that became the moral and ethical backbone of the three book faiths. Estimates suggest that today, there remain 100,000 to 200,000 active Zoroastrians or Parsis worldwide. [57]

In this belief system, the Destiny of the universe, our world, and all inhabitants lies in the caring hands of Ahura Mazda. Humans have free choice, though, to decide between the wise and misguided spirit world. Virtuous humans can attain an enlightened state through positive thoughts and deeds, with no fatalism but proactive cooperation with the divine. [58]

On a historical note, Zurvan—the God of infinite time—existed long before he inspired Zurvanism (ca. 300–700 BCE), a fatalistic, some say heretic, religious movement associated with Zoroastrianism.

His followers believed Zurvan to be the one and almighty balanced and originally non-dualistic divinity that controls everything in this world, including humans' thoughts, feelings, and actions. All-knowing Zurvan created (or rather birthed) the personified (Zoroastrian) twin principles or spirits of the good Ahura Mazda (Zoroastrian creator and ruler of the universe) and the evil Ahriman (Angra Mainyu), lord of the constraints of time and a perfect baddie (a blueprint for Lucifer or rather the devil?).

Let us turn to Eastern philosophies and religious concepts now and run our Destiny check on some of the polytheistic, non-dualistic, and non-theistic views and philosophies gracing our sphere.

Asian realms developed beliefs in support of the idea that people could better understand their destinies based on actions or choices they may have made in the past with reflection on the here and now. Take the Hindu and Buddhist concept of karma, wherein we have a handle on what our life will be like in our next reincarnation based on the choices and actions delivered during our dharma this time.

Hinduism

This faith goes back to a spiritual aggregation of ancient Sanskrit narratives and epics such as the *Vedas*, the *Ramayana*, the *Upanishads*, the *Mahabharata,* and the *Bhagavad Gita*. Hinduism is over 5,000, if not 6,000, years old, making it the most ancient of active world religions. It is based on life goals such as dharma (cosmic order), karma (human deeds), samsara (cycle of rebirth), moksha (liberation from karma and samsara), and maya (the illusion of the world). Hindus believe in reincarnation and millions of deities. We can only name a few of their impressive Devis: Parvati/Shakti—Goddess of the Enduring Power of Life—Saraswati—Goddess of Wisdom and the Arts—and Lakshmi— Goddess of Good Fortune and Material Abundance. And for Devas: Vishnu—Creator of the Universe—Shiva—Caretaker of the Universe— and, of course, Brahma—God of Absolute Truth. All Hindu deities are legitimate parts of a single Godly oneness. Hinduism is based on the two columns of *Vedānta* and *Tantra*, incorporating both dualistic and non-dualistic notions.

Hinduism upholds an intricate and divisive caste system that can be hard to understand for Western onlookers, especially with respect for women's rights and social equality. Hindus don't feel pushed to be seen worshiping at any temple or feeding an organizational religious apparatus. Their infinite Godly principle is found within humanity as well as in supernatural entities.

Fate and free will both play an equal role in our destinies.

– INDIAN PROVERB

India's, or rather Bhārat's,[59] to name it properly, assertive alighting from the shadows of British colonialism remains a realm of philosophers and seekers. We should not interpret Vedic and Hindu philosophy as meek fatalism. Hindus venerate both a great design and freedom of choice. Destiny acts through the laws of karma and dharma; the Hindu existence is shaped based on previous lives, efforts, and deeds. Karma would not be actionable without human volition and moral and ethical responsibility. Hinduism gives absolute credence to samsara— reincarnation. An actual life's allotted path can be altered through divine grace and virtuous actions. A Western pet prejudice labeling Hindus as fatalists is without realistic grounds as they strive to be proactive co-authors of their destinies. Worth mentioning is the Indian conviction that each newborn human gets their unalterable Destiny written upon the forehead by God Brahma. Many Indian marriage matches come about through the guidance of Destiny and the skillful deciphering of horoscopes to establish if the stars and the predetermined paths of a potential couple may align.

> *As the young calf is able to recognize its mother from among a thousand cows, so does karma find the person destined to experience it.*
>
> – MAHABHARATA BOOK 13

Buddhism

Siddhartha Gautama, an Indic prince—later renamed the Buddha (the enlightened one)—founded this spiritual movement 2,500 years ago, which is consistently growing to this day. Buddhists embrace amiable virtues such as kindness, patience, and compassion.

Life is lived by the laws of intentional karma and belief in the soul's rebirth. Instead of adhering to any form of deity, Buddhists seek enlightenment and the divine within themselves, living by the Four Noble Truths, addressing suffering, its inevitability, its cause, its end, and a proactive way to avoid it. Following the Eightfold Path—respecting life, accepting truthful existence, avoiding hurting others, exercising thought control, meditation, rejecting evil, doing good deeds for others, and liberating the self from evil—enables Buddhists to reach their highest goal: the state of Nirvana, i.e., perfect harmony.

Buddhism is a non-dualistic belief built on the experience of the two-fold doctrine of absolute and relative truth. No reward or punishment system for good or bad actions in this philosophy, just the consequences of the ancient principles of cause and effect that influence a person's Destiny. It is of particular interest that Buddhists are China's largest singular belief group today. [60]

Buddhists don't believe in unalterable and immutable Destiny set in stone; however, they reckon with the cosmic principle of cause and effect, which governs the unfolding of their self-caused destinies under the wheel of life and suffering, or samsara, that they've previously molded themselves. Their paths aren't bound by a rigid precondition but instead include manageable personal factors, such as virtuousness, spiritual devotion, constructive aspirations, and, above all, mindful, karmic actions. Buddhists have some freedom of agency, but since they reject any notion of selfhood, they don't see free will as an inherent human prerogative. Buddhist Destiny means to achieve enlightenment through dharma.

> *I do not believe in a fate that falls on men however they act; but I do believe in a fate that falls on them unless they act. Just as one can make a lot of garlands from a heap of flowers, so man, subject to birth and death as he is, should make himself a lot of good karma.*
>
> — THE BUDDHA

Sikh(ism)

This relatively young faith (ca. 500 years old) originates from India (Punjab). It was founded by the sage Guru Nanak. Sikhs (learners) combine the idea of "the one God," expanding on and encompassing other monotheistic religions with the revered teachings of their holy scripture, *Sri Guru Granth Sahib*. Sikhs believe in Waheguru—their Wonderful God—and the concept of reincarnation while celebrating absolute equality on all human levels, including that women and men enjoy the same rights and significance. Sikhs ideally focus on God instead of mundane self-centeredness. They aspire to a life of service, responsibility, and deep contemplation. Sikhs expect the human soul to join the great sphere of Nature after wrapping up material existence. The center of worship is Durbar Sahib—the Golden Temple in Amritsar.

Destiny plays a substantial part in this unique religion that teaches unity and equality. Sikhs also believe that everything in life happens because of God's will—Hukam—a divine order that governs the universe. But this doesn't mean that Sikhs don't have free will.

Hukam is all-pervasive; it exists in everything. To Sikhs, even the most minor action impacts the whole world. Sikhs believe in a divinely preordained and selfless form of Destiny, which is influenced by karma but adaptable through veritable human efforts.

> *By one's own actions, nothing can be done; destiny was pre-determined from the very beginning. By great good fortune, I meet my God, and then all pain of separation departs.*
>
> – Guru Arjan Dev Ji

Jainism

The Jains' more than 2,600-year-old Indic faith is trans-theistic, i.e., situated between a belief in deities and atheism. They promote non-violence and believe in the immutable Niyati—Destiny—interacting with other elements such as karma, dharma, human nature, personal initiatives, causality, and time in a self-managed universe. Jains avoid evil and prefer a compassionate vegan or vegetarian lifestyle to prevent or at least limit harm to animals and plants.

Jains believe in the human soul's constant refinement, if not perfection, of the human soul through reincarnation in four material forms known as The Four Destinies (gatis). Depending on the individual's merit or lack thereof, the cycle of rebirth awaits as either a human, an animal or plant, a supernatural being, or a hellish entity (echoes in Plato's *Myth of Er*). The individual always chooses the next Destiny due to full responsibility for the ethical and moral qualities of all deeds. Only well-performed human destinies will lead to deliverance from bondage to the cycle, though. Jainism is thought to be eternal and claims that it may even be the oldest known faith on this planet.

> *Do not injure, abuse, oppress, enslave, insult, torment, torture, or kill any creature or living being.*
>
> – Lord Mahavira

Daoism

This uncategorizable ca. 2,500-year-old Chinese cosmic and religious philosophy is based on constant transformation and deep connection with primordial Nature. It rests on the *Daoteching*, said to be created by the divine thinker Lao Tzu, or Laozi (571 BCE–unknown). The term Dao translates to The Way or The Path to achieve balance with the laws and motions of Nature and the universe. Daoists do not revere or follow the arbitrary rules of any deity. This belief is non-dualistic; good and evil are seen as relative. Still, since the Dao celebrates internal and external harmony to attain oneness and contentment, it incorporates the opposing yet complementing principles of yin and yang. Safe landing in a cozy or nasty hereafter is not at the forefront of this life-embracing thought world. Instead, the human spirit becomes a part of the cosmos. The Dao arts of "letting go," "stillness," and "going with the flow" conquered modern spirituality and linguistics for a reason. Daoism is still a venerated influence in today's predominantly atheist China.

This philosophy finds fulfillment in fully embracing their Destiny in life. The Dao is the source of Destiny in tandem with human agency. Daoists venerate Ming—a flexible order of Destiny that can even be turned from negative to positive. Ming also translates to Life and Command.

The way of the Creative works through change and transformation, so that each thing receives its true nature and destiny and comes into permanent accord with the Great Harmony: this is what furthers and what perseveres.

– THE I CHING

Another related concept called Yuan or Yuanfeng—fateful coincidence—determines the Destiny of relationships based on conditions by the past and a person's predetermined preferences or dislikes. It works like destinal magnetism, creating connections of many kinds: familiar, casual, romantic, and even professional. The principle of

Mingfen relates to the decree of fate. Furthermore, Daoists know sixty divine emanations in charge of Destiny during measured time spans.

And then Tianming—celestial Destiny—the highest form of a person's heavenly guided conduct is predominantly achieved from self-education, or, as Lao Tzu called it, through "self-cultivation"—leading to an ultimate wholeness.

Confucianism

This ancient Chinese thought school was founded by Kong Qiu or Confucius (551–479 BCE). This worldview is deeply humanistic, promoting harmonic values that rest on personified or theistic Heaven—Tiān and The Deity—Shàngdi. Goodness, unity, and discipline are relevant in this divinely oriented philosophy seeking a meaningful middle path. Heaven consists of a plethora of celestial beings strongly connected to the world of mankind in a universal wholeness. Pursuit and existence of an afterlife is not a priority in Ruism. The dualistic concepts of yin and yang bear deep significance for many if not most, areas of life and human nature. Yin represents feminine and yang masculine aspects, darkness and light, different yet complemental. Ruism remains a strong source of general wisdom, and we are currently seeing a renaissance of this philosophy's impact in China.

This Chinese philosophy accepts the natural force of all that is unavoidable and uncontrollable, such as old age or death. Simultaneously, it is a heavenly mandate of personal ethics and virtues. Hence, the principle of Tianming or Ming—celestial Destiny—is highly revered. It signifies aspects of heavenly preordination that lie beyond human control, ordered to manifest as a destined role and path during and beyond the human journey through the universe. Confucianism teaches that anyone may alter their Destiny with courage and purpose.

Don't let your past determine your destiny.
– KONG QIU, THE ANALECTS AND THE I CHING [61]

Both Daoism and Confucianism were influenced by Buddhism; these three faith movements share in the predominance of moral and ethical tenets to improve humanity without the leadership of a top God.

While Confucianism includes reverence of Destiny, the altruistic philosopher Mozi (ca. 470–391 BCE) insisted on human freedom and equality under the guidance of heaven. He challenged Confucianism and Daoism for fostering a limp acceptance of an immutable fate. Mozi favored a proactive attitude to author a worthy Destiny. He thought that human beings could be improved by teaching them to be compassionate and just.

Shinto

Japan's native faith likely harks back to about 1000 BCE. It unites several strands of ancient tribal cults without featuring a specific major deity or a prophet. We find neither a formal holy scripture nor firmly prescribed rules or tenets. Shinto means Way of the Divine (Kami). It esteems a variety of deities, such as the male and female cosmic creator couple Izanagi (heaven) and Izanamithe (earth), that gave life to the sun Goddess Amaterasu and other supernatural beings. Followers of Shinto revere their ancestors, sacred animals, natural beauty and harmony, and other manifestations and acts of Nature. Worship takes place at Kami shrines.

The sanguine Shinto belief system is rooted in historic Japanese cultural and community values. Destiny is vital to the Japanese, albeit in a less religious but traditional and folkloristic fashion. Dividing concepts like good and evil play no fundamental role here. The endearing ancient Asian myth of *The Red String of Destiny* remains as popular as ever, as is the drawing of fortune slips (o-mikuji) upon leaving a shrine after a ceremony or prayer to reveal future perks of Destiny.

Even the stone you trip over is part of your destiny.

– JAPANESE PROVERB

And while we're here, we should also visit other schools of thought that play a growing global role today.

Let's look at two open-minded thought worlds that transcend faiths and limitations for completeness.

Omnism

This non-organized belief embraces all religions, faiths, and philosophies there were and are in a unifying and tolerant way. To omnists, verity and wisdom are present in all spiritualities, while no religion can claim the fountainhead of absolute truth. The term stems from the Latin *omnis* for all and every. Omnism was started and named by the British poet and lawyer Philip James Bailey (1816–1902). It is a fair and modern way to explore and cherish all directions—bygone and actual, polytheistic and otherwise—for enlightening and beneficial gems are set into all faiths despite the darker aspects found in most religions.

Religion is all true in part but none in totality.

– PHILIP JAMES BAILEY, FESTUS

Omnists handle the cosmic and human concepts of Destiny in individual and open-hearted ways due to the multi-pronged spiritual approach of this non-aligned worldview.

Humanism

Anything but a religion, Humanism is an essential common sense-based philosophy that puts the advancement of the dignified human experience at the heart of its moral thought world. There are no Gods, no scriptures, and no dogma. The views of Humanism go back to the Northern Italian Renaissance (fourteenth to the seventeenth century), inspired by the rediscovery of Greco-Roman philosophy. Its foundation is credited to the poet Francesco Petrarca (1304–1374), also called the father of the Renaissance.

And so on earth, our destiny is with us from our birth.
        – Francesco Petrarca, Poems from the Canzoniere

Modern Humanism emphasizes complete responsibility for our destinies in a natural universe without a need for dogmatic divine overlording. Supernatural powers have no place in current humanistic thinking, but there exists Theistic Humanism purporting a contrasting spiritual and transcendent position. The respectful, ethically shared benefit of a dignified, humane society is at the heart of this empathetic, adaptive, freedom, and positive life-focused perspective to build a better future for all stakeholders. [62]

Since the ongoing decline of institutional religions, especially Christianity, in the Western world is relatively swift, let's acknowledge these fast-growing, no-God(s)-no-religion notions since they are as valid as any other philosophy.

The United States is booking a continuous fall of the Christian faith while the so-called "Nones"—non-affiliated people, agnostics, atheists, self-determined or practitioners of alternative transcendence, etc.—are on a robust up-and-up. [63]

The same effect is felt in the United Kingdom, where "no religion" is a rapidly growing trend. This turning away from Christianity constitutes a "slow, unplanned and almost unnoticed revolution," says Professor Linda Woodhead, author of *The Rise Of 'No Religion' In Britain: The Emergence of a New Cultural Majority.* [64]

Atheism, Agnosticism, and Co.

Atheism is the disbelief in or lack of belief in the existence of God(s). Atheists tend to love science. This assumed and declared objective reality and logic-based perspective hold no space for supernaturality or God(s). Many atheists opine that religious beliefs are based on warped mindsets, persuasion, manipulation, or even fraud.

Agnosticism is the belief that it is impossible to experience or know whether or not God(s) exist(s). But agnostics don't necessarily deny the existence of God(s). To them, any knowledge we have about supernaturals comes from second-hand sources, such as religious or mythological texts, and thus, can't be confirmed.

Quite a few atheists and agnostics consider Destiny or fate because they are religion and system-independent ancient and natural principles non-involved in organized faiths. Some even subscribe to the idea of a great plan. Similarly, free will and determinism are chosen notions.

Some atheists seem to almost worship reality and reason, while agnostics keep their options open regarding any supernatural phenomenon.

It is no surprise to find atheists, especially agnostics, considering the non-dogmatic concept of a non-theistic cosmic power. [65]

Increasingly, rising numbers of us are looking toward our own emotional and even mystical experiences instead of internalizing the often anguish-reducing pre-pack revelations established faiths have to offer. The same goes for seeking options in atheism or scientism, the latter sadly often reminiscent of just another zealous religiosity under the diktat of deterministic, atavistic processes in our brain and its metabolism. The overwhelming majority of us humans need to believe in something, albeit mostly not fanatically or in the guise of magical thinking. Scared of chaos, risks, emptiness, and cold, hard facts, we're still yearning for a space to feel calm and recognized in meaningful order and routine, something to hold on to when fear and uncertainty rise. Please look it up. However, human spirituality does not necessarily require any theological authority, lead system, or "whateverism."

New Age and Esoteric Spirituality

Our final international thought realm is touching those with little interest in affiliation to codified religions. The New Age movement began as early as the eighteenth century with the teachings of the Swedish theologian and mystic Emanuel Swedenborg (1688–1772). Its modern rise of steady growth to a worldwide phenomenon began in the 1970s.

New Age is based on esoteric traditions that attempt to foster peace and harmony through alternative and ancient approaches. Practitioners often believe that divinity is prevalent throughout the universe and within humanity.

Communicating with non-human entities, such as angels or masters, is quite popular. New Age followers seek to experience untapped wisdom considered lost because of humanity's spiritual degeneration. The ancient knowledge of conversing with the Gods outside a fixed system was swept into semi-oblivion over time, only to change through the advent of the liberating Age of Aquarius, an endearing mix of different traditions.

We find strong, often omnism-based heart notes of Kabbalah, Christianity, Paganism, Buddhism, Hinduism, and many other directions.

The New Thought Alliance—based on a nineteenth-century movement focused on divinity and life mastery within the mind of homo sapiens—is widely celebrated, as is the connected Law of Attraction.

The New Age asserts an alternative way to live, one that yields a higher purpose in a spiritual sense. Healing plays a strong tune, achieved via methodologies such as meditation, yoga, qigong, reiki, mandala drawing, crystal therapy, etc. Through kindness and holistic approaches like veganism, meditation, hypnosis, shamanism, and transcendental experiences, New Agers encounter and fill essential parts of their universe with meaning.

The adoration and identification with the Great Mother Goddess is one of the foremost trends of esoteric thinking, as are seeking and reaching full potential, solace, and a feeling of belonging, while materialism and selfishness are not predominant currents. No wonder Modern Paganism and even ancient polytheisms are on the up-and-up in all Western countries, not just statistically.

Many followers of New Age spirituality accept Destiny as a main factor in human life, presaged eons ago by a loving, nurturing cosmic principle. The process of finding themselves by reconnecting with the universe as the mother of human Destiny is at the heart of many followers. Instead of clinging to a single line of belief, New Age advocates are spoilt with many paths to experience their unique destinies, developing inroads to an abundant future.

Instead of merely looking to the unseen forces of the universe to gather clues of what the future may bring, the New Age invites everyone to look inside through introspection, awareness development, and the achievement of self-actualization.

Alternative spirituality's reconciliation of human liberty with the different views on how the universe or an omnipotent being may manifest is neither mainstream nor traditional. Many believe these practices are, at best, hocus-pocus, woo-woo, or even just another mass delusion. Established religions, as well as scientific and some contemporary schools of philosophy, believe the New Age movement to mislead or even abuse human gullibility.

Excuse the whataboutism: Considering all the practical good that organized denominations can offer, the New Age won't be any worse in treating followers as easy marks than the greed, brutality, corruption, and wool-pulling performed by established denominations and their offshoots over the last two millennia. Surely, Wicca and paganism may not be everyone's logical cup of tea, but neither can certain practices and ideas within normative faiths produce validity versus analytical and critical evaluation. All human beliefs can unite in the identical human longing for sparks of light to illuminate the darkness with a few moments of hope.

Spiritual towns like Glastonbury (a possible location of the ancient Isle of Avalon of the Arthurian legends) and Totnes in the UK, Asheville, Boulder, and Sedona in the United States, and many popular Ashrams and Yoga resorts in India are buzzing hubs for the international spiritual community. The rise of such alternative beliefs invites insight into how we feel about our realities and destinies and, perhaps, the lack of being at home in their Western lives and traditional values, especially during this sizzling age. Maybe humankind is still far too unaware of its nature and spiritual potential. Esoteric and alternative beliefs may provide confidence in the fact that we are more than mere supplicants, sheep, and subjects—but proud individual beings amid the extraordinary context of our shared spiritual experience.

Humans follow the ancient tendency to long for something to hold on to, something that gives us a higher sense of being, ideally inducing the will and ability to transcend ourselves, or, understandably, something that offers a warm and fuzzy feeling of surety and belonging. Religions come and go; Gods rise and fade, casting shadows and shining light.

One day, the now-dominant faith systems established over the last two millennia will slowly begin their own slipping into the twilight and join the distant memory zone already populated by olden Gods and cults. What's been done well will stick and be carried forward, with the rest to serve as an instructive, even cautionary tale to the spiritual movements of the future.

Everything flows, said Heraclitus. It may seem unimaginable now, but there it is, tomorrow's trademark: the heightened absence of impossibility. Regardless, will there ever be a world without faith or hope? Likely not, despite the growing movement of Americans, for example, who identify as unaffiliated to any system or describe their existing spirituality as "nothing in particular." They don't seem to be in any rush to find a belief system to fit their needs and expectations. Many feel connected with a higher power, or Nature and earth, yet preferably without churches, temples, financial interests, or institutional places and bodies. One way or another, humanity's inner voids and vacuums will always demand supernatural attention.

There are many options to believe or not believe these days and plenty of ways to experience or judge our choices from different perspectives.

African Civilizations

The notion of Destiny appears widespread among the nations of Africa, forming an essential element within the different philosophical contexts. In the historical view and depending on their geological location, a number of African civilizations believe in universal and human Destiny decreed by their supreme being(s). In contrast, others adhere to the idea that their ancestors control the life paths of their descendants by connecting with the living and preventing them from doing evil.

Several tribes adhere(d) to varying concepts of their existence, all related to the involvement of supernatural powers. [66] Death was seen as the final stage of a man in the physical form but not spiritually. The dead went to a peaceful place while still existing among their families as guiding spirits. In essence, they were destined for a life after death. Fate and Destiny in African tribes are experienced as a human state that exists between the spiritual realm and Nature. For instance, the *Akans* venerate a concept of Destiny (Nkrabea) that enables them to exercise free will due to the general character of divinely decreed Destiny. The *Esan* people of West Nigeria hold strong beliefs in a flexible form that does not include notions of fatalism. [67] The *Yoruba* believe that Destiny rules humans as positive or negative Ori—which the Supreme Deity Olodumare decides. Furthermore, the Yoruba can elect their future Destiny upon birth. Certain aspects of their journey can be altered by the external influences of guardian spirits, sorcerers, and character. [68]

Although many African communities abandoned these beliefs in favor of Christianity and Islam, some still adhere to their ancient traditions. [69]

The hand that rocks the cradle rules the nation and its destiny.
– SOUTH AFRICAN PROVERB

You have little power over what's not yours.
– ZIMBABWEAN APHORISM

If you pick up one end of the stick you also pick up the other.
– ETHIOPIAN PROVERB

He who is unable to dance says that the yard is stony.
– MASAI SAYING

If the moon loves you—why worry about the stars.
– AFRICAN PROVERB

For sources and further reading, see notes. [70]

The Aboriginal Civilization in Australia

Destiny and fate are elements in the beliefs of Australia's aboriginal culture, going by the poetic oral tradition that the beloved lands thousands of generations of their peoples occupied once were a gift from Destiny. [71] The concepts of predestination could be seen as evident in the ancient Australians' main deity—Baiame, or Sky Father—prominent in their more than 65,000-year-old mythological universalism called *The Dreaming* or *The Dreamtime*. Ancestral spirits that took the forms of trees or rocks may also represent a notion of fate. However, some researchers question whether Destiny or fate existed in Australia's aboriginal culture due to the absence of meaningful terms in their diverse languages. [72]

The land owns us.

– AUSTRALIAN ABORIGINAL PROVERB

For excellent sources and further reading, see notes. [73 74 75]

Native American Nations

Every tribe in the Native American spirituality had its narratives, rituals, and legends that spell out its Destiny. There is evidence of beliefs in the existence of spirits that control their life paths. As per Native American traditions in the Pacific Northwest, all living beings are watched over by the great Guardian Spirit. [76] The most widespread and influential indigenous religious movement practiced by Native Americans in the north was the Peyote religion. [77] These civilizations made it through and beyond the genocide that possibly cost the lives of 95 percent of Native Americans, caused by brutal European conquests and the consequences of self-styled imperialistic American Exceptionalism branded *Manifest Destiny*—a perverse misnomer wrongly abusing the ancient principle to lend mythological gravitas to the corrupt intention to prioritize the interests of white settlers and new Americans. Let us hope their incredible resilience and spirited survival will offer modern Indigenous Americans a comforting sense of prevailing cultural and spiritual Destiny. [78]

> *Sometimes I go about in pity for myself, and all the while, a great wind carries me across the sky.*
>
> – OJIBWE APHORISM

> *All dreams spin out from the same web.*
>
> – HOPI SAYING

Eastern European Destinies

Destiny is a relevant factor of life in almost all regions of Eastern Europe. A Pew Research conducted in 2017 examined how many religious people believed in fate. Let's take a look at a few examples: Armenia (83%), Bosnia (80%), Georgia (73%), Ukraine (71%), Estonia (62%), Russia (60%), Greece (59%) and Poland (56%). Non-religious and other unaffiliated respondents also confirmed a heightened interest in a destinal life. [79]

Slavic nations know the Rozaniče, originally ancestral dispensers of pre-decreed life that kept relevance as birth spirits, as well as Rodjenice and Sudice, emanations responsible for the prearrangement of a child's life journey. [80]

The philosophical concept of Avoš (pure fortune) offers a hopeful spin on life and prescribes a remedy to prevent adverse events: relying on sheer and jolly old luck. Avoš and Sudba—fate—are influential factors of life in Russia.

> *Always count on a miracle.*
>
> – AVOŠ

The Dólya is a mythical Russian being that either offers lifelong friendly assistance or a tendency to ruin her protege's existence. A good

Dólyushka supports a cheerful, protected Destiny, whereas a bad Dólya delivers elements of dark personal fate. And since this female spirit is with us for as long as we live, Russians accept that no one can escape her. [81]

> *Not even your horse will get you away from your Dólya.*
> — RUSSIAN PROVERB

Whether Destiny is externally immutable and written in stone or subject to our influence has been an ongoing debate ever since we raised our eyes to gaze at the firmament, wondering what lies beyond the visible world and what stimulates our spirit and aspiration for the future, ordained by a principle respectful of the complementary power of humanity.

Takeaway: Destiny is a religion-independent principle. Over the last 2,000-plus years, great religions vested versions of Destiny into their personified divinity narratives to address the long-standing human propensity for the first force to enhance their capacity. And why not? That's how life works: Everything is based on fluent perception valid until another page turns and the caravan moves on.

Divine Providence

This affiliate concept's name stems from the Greek term *Theia Pronoia* for divine foreknowledge and the Latin *providentia* for looking ahead, initially rooted in the Greco-Roman Goddess principle of the same name. But as per the book-religious divine providence, everything in the cosmos and here on earth is created and decided by the loving, immutable wisdom of God. He knows all truths (for there indeed are many) and benevolently holds eternity, mankind, and their future under His caring predetermination while humanity is granted self-determination to decide between good and evil. All three Mosaic religions subscribe to this concept individually.

Plato and later philosophers already exemplified free choice in concert with original providence to address an artisan-creator shared leadership of Destiny.

The Christian twentieth-century existentialist philosopher and theologian Paul Tillich (1886–1965) saw Destiny not just as something that happens to us but as a consciousness that is formed in our *Kairos*— Greek for opportune moment—as well as time and individual history, personal nature, vocation, and actions.

Man is asked to make of himself what he is supposed to become to fulfill his destiny.

Destiny is not a strange power which determines what shall happen to me. It is myself as given, formed by Nature, history, and myself. My destiny is the basis of my freedom; my freedom participates in shaping my destiny.

Providence is not interference; it is creation. It uses all factors, both those given by freedom and those given by destiny, in creatively directing everything toward its fulfillment. Providence is "the divine condition" which is present in every group of finite conditions and in the totality of finite conditions. It is not an additional factor, a miraculous physical or mental interference in terms of supra-naturalism. It is the quality of inner directedness present in every situation. The man who believes in providence does not believe that a special divine activity will alter the conditions of finitude and estrangement. He believes and asserts with the courage of faith that no situation whatsoever can frustrate the fulfillment of his ultimate destiny.

– Paul Tillich, Systematic Theology I

Since we have now covered a bit of general information about several of the great civilizations, their polytheistic cultures, and quick introductions of a few philosophies that give Destiny center stage, it is time to explore the literal *take* of their monotheistic follow-ups on the first force in the universe.

Theodicy

This paradigm vindicates how an all-knowing God can allow evil to happen without intervening or trying to free the world from evil and sorrow.

Theodicy (from the Greek *Theos,* meaning God, and *Dike* for the justice Goddess/principle) was promoted by Augustine of Hippo (354 – 430 CE) and the German philosopher and mathematician Gottfried Leibniz (1646–1716). The latter basically trademarked the term in his book of the same title. Furthermore, Leibniz explained the motley state of almighty God's imperfect world creation, plus the necessity of suffering as a deliberate result of limited human mentality and too little capability for appropriate agency. It looks as if some divine producers require their goods delivered with a spin-doctored caveat emptor or disclaimer, including the human experience.

So we are looking at a construct of theological philosophy concerned with justifying God's goodness in the face of evil. For Christianity, it was introduced as a defense, or whitewash, since God just had to be seen to have created the world out of nothing but love, so evil was not a necessary consequence of his immaculate creation but an entirely human disposition or "willed action" beyond God's responsibility. Anything wrong, harmful, or evil is on humanity. And because God didn't create evil in the first place, it is not his job to abolish it. But then God created humankind in his own image, right?

This nifty doctrine is also elaborated in Islam. All Abrahamic religions promote that God granted reason to us and thus the ability to make the right choices. If something goes pear-shaped, it's not God's problem, with the slight exception of Judaism, where the consequences can be interpreted as corrective measures, here or beyond.

And all that includes natural disasters, which, realistically, are deterministic and neither good nor bad, apart from their effect on living beings. Therefore, the three Abrahamic Gods won't intervene to stop earthquakes, remedy famines, or stop climate change. But perhaps it's just because their almightiness does not stretch far enough.

So it's all down to us, with the big difference of the introduction of Jesus, humankind's advocate, who not only spoke up for us but even took over and carried our sins. This metaphorical superhero with a heavy, painful Destiny understood what it is like to be human.

Theodicy tries to reconcile the idea of a kindly God who created this perfect world by adding a human experience rife with suffering and injustice. The remedy to this dualistic knot is always postponed to a rewarding afterlife, rendering all pains and inequities part and parcel of the rocky road to paradise. It is like a moral parachute saving the omniscient one from being identified as the architect of a beautiful yet hostile, brutal, and anything-but-perfect world when the human race has to bleed and compete for salvation.

Protestant Christians promoted God's total control plus the option of salvation via predestination. The Calvinists even introduced single predestination for the good eggs—also to keep God out of the firing line and then the notion of double predestination for the reprobate, the latter being a ticket to hell for those unfavorable to a benevolent God and those he condemned to go down there in the first place. It feels as if humanity was generously granted free volition and the resulting responsibility for their individual choices not to niggle an (in)disputably all-powerful God with a few meaningful questions.

So, in case of climate catastrophes or personal tragedies, especially involving children, it's not the celestial penthouse's doing but all down to human mis-whatever. But if it's bright and beautiful, it's thanks to God. It reminds me of "your son just broke the neighbor's glass vase" versus "my son just won a medal in sports."

Just how can we have free will if a specific God or dominion knows and has already determined our future as individuals and as humankind?

In contrast, Destiny does not require any arbitrary reasoning since no religious ifs or buts and, especially, no conditional promises are involved.

To Believe or Not to Believe

In 2011, researchers at the University of Oxford found plenty of us across many nations naturally drawn to expect some form of hereafter. Even though atheism, agnosticism, and deism are on the rise across the globe, we experience a strong tendency to believe in the existence of supernatural entities. [82]

In 2014, two separate Yale studies established that non-religious people, too, believe in fate (i.e., Destiny), which offers supportive order, meaning, and the surety that life isn't just random but filled with reason and sense. And managing often painful questions like *"why did this happen?"* And especially, *"why on Earth did this happen to me?"* [83]

Whether we like it or not, and whatever arguments anyone may harbor against an invisible agency directing our lives, it is clear that we decide with our hearts *and* minds for that which supports a better deal with life's challenges.

Even though I am thoroughly non-religious, I wholeheartedly support the importance of tolerant, evolving faiths, particularly the significance of spirituality per se. An uplifting belief can indeed play a vital part in a person's self-actualization, as long as it is adopted absent of any dogma and notwithstanding healthy skepticism.

If so elected, our spirituality can be a personal standpoint when pursuing heightened awareness in unity with a particular concept or might.

Spirituality comprises multiple metaphysical ideas; it also promotes actions that can propel individuals and even nations to rise and move forward. Because of the benefits faith can provide to a human being, it can also become a salient factor in discussing how humankind may best approach our future.

Apart from humanism, pantheism [84] offers another favorable option. It is an all-encompassing belief system rooted in several world religions and philosophies, embracing the idea that the universe, Nature, and humanity are on par with a non-personified divine.

And we must not forget omnism—the inclusive notion that connects us with any chosen aspect of higher consciousness outside of any selected religion. Omnism embraces all persuasions while also being independent of them.

Considering a supreme being in the mix and the promise of an afterlife, we become more vigilant with our actions and inner calling due to the fear of judgment and consequences and for reasons of inner emptiness. Without divine guidance, many of us may lose hope and fall prey to existential angst about our destinies.

Life is short, the art long, opportunity fleeting, experience treacherous, judgment difficult.

– HIPPOCRATES

Another thinker who cannot be accused of wearing rose-tinted glasses was the English philosopher and determinist Thomas Hobbes, who described human existence as:

Solitary, poor, nasty, brutish, and short.

With religion as a prime pilot of our lives, the concept of an omnipotent God's promise of salvation, forgiveness, and paradise allows human beings to find comfort and look forward to the future, knowing their fulfillment of moral obligations and endurance of challenges may lead to a rewarding afterlife and even resurrection.

My pretty old-fashioned idea is that the entire process of dealing with the experiences of our realities is part of our Destiny, making life a moving and ever-changing destination—an aspiration and goal, without any guarantees, though. And it's fine just like that.

A life purpose can remedy that dreadful "*Hobbes feeling*," especially when all seems mundane and pointless. Yet purpose is not a universal antidote because our lives can be meaningful and absurd for everyone. And a significant life purpose does not automatically consist of education, career, wealth, and fame. It is often innate and not necessarily external. A balanced existence without dependence on anything, not even third-party evaluation, and without climbing the social and societal ladder can still be pretty pleasant, even fun, and thus meaningful. As is living with a sense of faith that a higher principle offers guidance and harmonization of shared ethical values. It can even be purposeful to be a Hedonist and decide on existing happily without much ambition and just try to enjoy being here, in the moment, as much as possible or run after success and lots of money and, most importantly, make good stuff happen for others as part of modern eudaimonia.

Instead of instilling fear that we are alone in dealing with the nitty-gritty of each waking day, a connection with a greater force turns our focus on a co-determined Destiny.

With the idea that our destinies extend far beyond our lives, we can excel in our motivation to be and do as good as possible, with lasting effects that transcend us, affecting generations to come with our caring legacy.

Destiny's spiritual identity as an all-embracing phenomenon depends mainly on our perception and interpretation.

But we should always resist and prevent the arbitrary construction of undeserved privilege on the one hand and false entitlement on the other. We should always seek to enhance the ability to create resilience in communities devastated by injustice, discrimination, calamities, wars, and other events that may crush individual and collective spirit. A sense of Destiny may empower a personality with permanence. It allows us to see that obstacles, no matter how bad they seem, do not necessarily derail our mission of overcoming challenges and finding some of that coveted purpose in our lives.

Only open-minded faiths and philosophies deliver values we can utilize in the ways we live our lives, letting us add personal meaning to daily struggles and calls to action. We have it in us to become who we're meant to be, going forward with the guidance of our innate ethical compass rose we originally all called our own.

Our Relationship with Gods and Destiny

Humanity eagerly cultivated the idea that we are fashioned by and even after supernatural beings in charge of the universe. In many religions and mythologies, Gods and their spokespersons were often described as having human-like forms and characteristics. They even knew all our languages. So humans elected to believe that we rank high above all other living creatures. Indeed, our specialness and perhaps even our rationality looked a lot like handy confirmation of our superiority over animals, for example. A massive misconception, in my book.

We've always kept a close relationship with supreme beings for many reasons. No wonder, as mentioned before, that we like nothing better than to exalt ourselves and create many emanations after our fair likeness, matching our actual needs of the moment in time, culture, and history. Many tales exist of how mortals could directly converse with deities and their agents. Such "interactions" with higher beings are hard to comprehend for a critical mind unless experienced personally and more regularly. Lore about how the Gods engaged with and directly aided humans are testament to humanity always aspiring to be the most favored species in the universe, deserving of divine attention, acceptance, and even intervention, notwithstanding miracles in exchange for mortal commodities of sacrifices (in the beginning), ostensive worship, and through intense subservience and prayer, later on.

According to the Bible, Adam and Eve enjoyed direct, privileged engagement with God before their temptation. In Christianity and other related religions, the concept of perceived and interpreted sin almost automatically distances humans from God. The expulsion of the first woman and man from paradise was promptly and unforgivingly extended to all the generations afoot. Our book religions promoted that, through continued repentance and the renewal of the child-like relationship with their God, humans could apply and even qualify for redemption through ritualized communication with the supreme father figure through measured supplication, praise, and prayer.

Why did interaction with God or his vested representatives become such a desired concept? By getting close to an entity that postulates to control human Destiny, our forefathers may have calculated they would likely secure pole position to receive enhanced clues on how to get what they wanted or, at best, achieve some certainty about their destinies to keep their fears at bay. Not so different from what the Destiny-whispering oracles and seers sought in the past—to get a glimpse of the original plan.

Without such acquired surety, life can appear stressful and dangerous. With a controller of cosmic approval firmly in place, it may pay to barter the best possible outcomes through obedience and rapport, i.e., thus trying to renegotiate options.

Several schools of thought disputed and even denied the existence of "real" Gods, and demigods still claimed these beings were necessities when it came to explaining the world to humanity and making life more livable. And more controllable, too.

God(s), supernatural entities, and other omnipotent forces were declared necessary to make sense of quandaries like the beginning of the world and the relevance of human existence. Specific God(s) even dictate(d) completely conforming mortal conduct while demonstrating streaks of envy, vindictiveness, and egomania with more or less subtle hints of narcissism, just like authoritarian dads.

We like to view ourselves as essential characters in stories that feature divine entities, placing sense in Nature's expressions. For example, when volcanoes erupt or lightning strikes, our forebears believed the Gods were displeased and needed appeasing with a ritual, like a blood-sprinkled sacrifice or a big roast. In any case, a lot of that was carnivorous and dead-meat oriented.

By grasping the Gods' sentiments, the ancients hoped to escape the wrath of their bosses and, through satisfactory actions, earn their favor. The Gods' moods helped our ancestors to come to terms with their often almost dystopian environment and bring meaning to their harsh existence.

Ancient mythologies sing of numerous mortals or lesser deities defying the will of higher beings. That usually resulted in personal tragedy, albeit with the spark of triumphant spiritedness challenging blind, cadaver obedience.

With these narratives rose the realization that, no matter how intelligent and logical humans try to be, it would remain a great feat for mere mortals to outwit our God(s) and manipulate their desired outcomes.

God-Like Beingness?

(Wo)man, as per the world book religions, such as Judaism, Christianity, and Islam, was created after the image of God. In contrast, Hinduism promotes natural divinity in everything, including human beings. Greek and Roman mythology gave us whimsical yet often amiable and entertaining Gods—attractive but unsurpassable supernatural beings that would, now and again, visit and sometimes elevate and reward a human, occasionally getting up to no good or even falling in love with us.

Antiquity's mortals cherished walking with supreme beings. Accordingly, we created and re-adopted their specialness, traits, looks, and style, reflecting our wishes and tastes.

Since the beginning, humans placed themselves—confirmed by some of the holy scriptures—in the position to outrank all other entities on earth, claiming deity-designed exceptional qualities.

As a result, animals, albeit sentient, were treated as inferior; hence, many of us still take the ill-advised liberty to exploit, torture, and devour them in obscene quantities. This misconception still posits us to corrupt our environment as we want. For now. The jury is out.

We dominate an animal, cultivate a plant and develop technology for our benefit, but how would we like it if it went the other way around to get the upper hand on us?

And we also love to celebrate fellow mortals that seem to resemble our image of God(s). We love fawning over celebrities, billionaires, and modern fictional characters. In classic Greek mythology, heroes like Hercules, Odysseus, Perseus, Theseus, and the enlightened artist Orpheus were connected with the Gods. They went on perilous journeys to master tasks only those with extraordinary abilities could accomplish. The divine ones even chose some mortals to dwell with them in the halls of eternity or find new life in a celestial constellation instead of dying.

While these narratives may just be myths, they carry a significance that evolves with time. Also, it is possible that myths and legends were created according to actual events, refining wishful thinking that human beings with above-average aptitude could be as superhuman as a demigod(dess).

Although the ancients held on to beliefs that Gods manage Nature and that we were essentially under their mercy, many discoveries enabled us to see beyond our mortal station and advance. Since humanity's ability to be creative, rise to many challenges, and overcome obstacles knows few bounds, we intentionally shaped the world. With the progress of technology, we have begun to adjust how we view the world. Improvements in medicine allowed us to update our understanding of human biology and anatomy, even to delay mortality for a bit.

By adopting skills and knowledge to do the once seemingly impossible, humankind began to produce schools of thought that rejected the idea of higher beings and, instead, found divine traces, if not evidence, in ourselves.

It is neither valid nor necessary to pin everything on a supernatural entity as the prime cause of all events. It does not matter if a God, any God, isn't almighty but playing their part in concert with the great principle in the universe. No one can be all-everything.

Destiny offers options we can choose to act upon. Moral responsibility may become a natural human desire to practice innate, intrinsic ethics and values instead of being pressed upon us through governing expectations and rules. Going easy on dogma and orthodoxy would neither stop the world from turning nor render millennia of belief null and void nor end in an infinite abyss of living without direction or purpose.

This captivating notion raises a question about our relationship with the divine. Despite the philosophical, cultural, and technological strides we've made as a species, many of us still crave authoritative systems. Faith can serve as a moral compass, keeping us on a path of, sadly, otherwise often self-declared exceptionality and exclusive self-rightness. Society was always wary of independent thinkers who stray from the beaten path, explore alternative thought realms, or, even worse, create their own worldviews or reject organized religion altogether. The mere notion of leading an independent spiritual existence is enough to give proper dogmatists nasty chills. Thus, religions have always emphasized the doctrine of God(s)-made predetermined fate, to keep people in check under common beliefs. Whether we like it or not, that still offers a way of introducing a kind of order to chaos and infusing life with a sense of purpose, even if it means submitting to a particular systemized faith.

Ethical values and responsibility are possible via the ability to act in liberty, ideally in concert with a non-dogmatic principle. I recommend you look up Plato's concept of the Demiurge (*Timaeus,* ca. 360 BCE). More on that in the next book.

What about a universe without figurative or abstract Gods and religions?

In the humanist approach, we have control over the meaning of our life and, subsequently, our Destiny, resting on the assumption that no omnipotent being causes or influences events in our lives. Here, we exist without any need to rely on a divine plan and are free to provide meaning to our existence by being both directors of and actors in our movies. In the absence of any deity or parental emanation to lead us on the "proper" path, no toolbox of fixed morals we must adhere to, just our own decency is available. No reward awaits us in an afterworld. Humanity alone is in charge of creating import for our existence.

The Danish thinker Soren Kierkegaard (1813–1855) advocated personal access to faith, philosophy, and human Destiny instead of exclusively using organized religion. He was also one of the fathers of existentialism, a philosophical notion later solidified by Jean-Paul Sartre (1905–1980) with a single statement:

Existence precedes essence.

To Sartre, we are *"condemned to be free."* To discover any meaning in life, we need to live with the anguish of knowing we exist in a world that is wholly unconcerned with us. Not a single damn given because, existentialists claim, life is meaningless.

As Jean-Paul Sartre would put it, we'd need to *encounter* ourselves first to define our existence and create purpose. Our consciousness would fashion our way of life and help us sort and select our thoughts and actions, determining the person we shall become to define ourselves, our freedom, and our Destiny.

So, as we encounter the world, we piece together portions of perceptions of our experience. And consequently, we will understand the ancient wisdom that nothing is ever the same.

> No man ever steps into the same river twice, for it is not the same river and he is not the same man.
>
> – HERACLITUS

Without a constant in the presence of continuous randomness, we interpret our environment as meaningless until we create our own significance.

Without the need to feel responsible for our actions out of fear that a supreme being will hold us accountable, we are still ethically responsible for our actions and their material consequences. Yet, despite our best thoughts and deeds, we still have to deal with the possibility of steely ripples hitting our lives.

The world does not necessarily conform to strict rules or morality, so we have to expect angst and despair, maybe even welcome them as we search for relevancy and create meaning out of our suffering.

Albert Camus (1913–1960), the 1957 Nobel Prize winner in literature and the frontrunner of a philosophical branch called absurdism, promoted the acceptance of a world devoid of objective meaning but the possibility to lead an existence of self-created purpose. An aim in which the brave and rebellious Camus excelled, but it should be noted that he opposed nihilism and that, in my opinion, his life and literary creations turned out to be the opposite of absurd. Camus illustrates the anguish individuals are bound to experience in *The Myth of Sisyphus*. It is based on an ancient Greek tale of a rapacious king Zeus, who punishes by having Sisyphus roll a rock up a hill for all eternity, again and again. Sisyphus is condemned to repeat this futile experience of seemingly never-ending misery without any purpose, reward, or termination. Notwithstanding, Camus' absurd hero Sisyphus isn't breaking under this punishment but, instead, creates his own meaning through his being and task and, by mastering this tragedy through the acceptance of his fate, dismantles Zeus' retaliative objective.

> *This universe henceforth without a master seems to him neither sterile nor futile. Each atom of that stone, each mineral flake of that night-filled mountain, in itself, forms a world. The struggle itself toward the heights is enough to fill a man's heart. One must imagine Sisyphus happy.*
>
> – ALBERT CAMUS, THE MYTH OF SISYPHUS

Let us end this section by sympathetically mentioning the premise of nihilism, a doctrine that takes the idea of purposeless humanity to another level. Here, we have a "belief" in absolutely nothing, not even shreds of anything, which means that no intrinsic value exists in the world. How does one believe in nothing, though?

In a meaningless world carrying empty existence to a hopeless "nomorrow," a notion of individual and collective human Destiny is pointless. Absence of God(s) is not the issue here. Our inherent nature will always seek and find import, with and without God(s), religion, and limiting ideologies.

CHAPTER 4

Affiliated Destinal Agencies[85]

Fortunes, Lucks, and Co.
—What Are the Odds?

In the beginning, our ancestors believed that, like the many other aspects and circumstances of life, all things lucky were decreed, designed, and dispensed by their respective Gods of Destiny as blessings from on high. Fortune and Destiny can be categorized as related concepts; hence, we find their divine representatives in our *Gods of Destiny* chapter. However, we are talking about two distinctly different ideas since luck and fortune are predominantly seen as autonomous, self-generating phenomena;[86] therefore, we notice the rise and enduring significance of those expertly standalone fortune and luck deities mentioned before, for instance, in Greece and the Roman Empire. The gracious gifts of celestial advantage are, per se, incredibly outstanding. Still, on top of that, these favors make us humans as genuinely special as can be by adding that crucial ingredient to any existence. Outstanding, sure. Superior, no.

Some are born great, some achieve greatness, and some have greatness thrust upon them.

– WILLIAM SHAKESPEARE, TWELFTH NIGHT

Luck is arguably one of the most important aspects in life, if not the singular *"it"* factor. Luck is the driving force behind many successes and failures, resulting from either an abundance or a defined lack of any one form of this energy. More often than not, we find that behind many stories of glory, fame, success, and material abundance, neither desert nor merit nor hard work always plays a major part. Not even the sharpest goal-focused human determination or talent alone rivals the boon that only fortune and favorable circumstances have to offer. That said, it should be noted that those of us capable of indeed bringing about any and even all of the above proactively and seemingly singularly are lucky in their own league for having been born with the necessary resilience, propensity, and *je ne sais quoi.*

The phenomenon of luck goes back a long time, and it was and is considered to result from impromptu acts of special intervention by an uncontrollable source. The Greek Tyche and the Roman Fortuna are enduring Goddesses representing luck and fortune. They were often depicted wearing a blindfold or holding a rudder. The ancients believed that these ladies were whimsically generating both merry and jinxy business.

Hindus revere Lakshmi, who brings wealth and good fortune. The Chinese culture relies on the celestial lords or Sanxing Fu, Lu, and Shou for everything auspicious and good.

And then we have the Pidgin/English-Chinese concept of Joss, which, depending on the trigger and occasion, can mean and produce positive or negative "fate" or luck.

We can find lots of other categories of luck beyond those dished out by the ancient Goddesses Tyche, Felicitas, and, especially, Fortuna. More folkloristic strands are headed by Western symbols like the horseshoe or the four-leaf clover. Globally, a great variety of good fortune-importing emblems and charms such as the Indic Om, the Chinese Ming, the lucky star, the wishbone, the piglet, the ladybug, fortuitous numbers, and the waving Japanese Maneki-Neko cat continue to attract millions of customers as they excel via their benevolent meaning as kindly-meant gifts.

There are many classes. We know the proverbial odds, good and bad luck, our fortune and misfortune, thin and thick luck, moral luck, brute luck, resultant luck, circumstantial luck, constitutional luck, determined luck, etc. [87]

Getting anywhere in life requires a deft amount of our topical phenomenal influence. It should be noted, though, that, traditionally, luck is said to have nothing to do with the laws of cause and effect, morality, desert, or even karma and dharma.

Not everything we achieve during our stints on this planet is deserved and down to our singular and own brilliant intentions and actions. Nor do we get wherever we may find ourselves on our own.

Equally, only some things or situations we must write off as unsuccessful are automatically our fault. Bi-directional fortune, especially a lack of luck and circumstance, has a heck of a lot to do with it.

Fortuna favors the brave.

– TERENTIUS

How can we get rewarded for courage by blindfolded, whimsy Fortuna, though? Could bravery be the great exception? Can we indeed entice and invite Felicity's special endowments through merit? Is showtime bravado meritorious, though, or just another lucky knack or personality trait? I reckon that, if any, the rather more subtle, demanding version of authentic, quiet bravery may win fortunate favor. Well, more on that in good time.

Being born spirited and valiant is top luck. Throughout history, many famous *"great and/or good"* were soldiers of fortune, partly and even majorly. Any factually, no just self-declared successful person will confirm this if they are honest. [88]

Malcolm Gladwell, in his 2008 bestseller *Outliers: The Story of Success*, states, and this is just a gist of it, that it is not the brightest who succeed and that success is not the sum of decisions and efforts undertaken on our own behalf, but that this success is rather a gift. He goes on that outliers are those of us who can muster the strength and mindset to seize given opportunities. [89]

Without intending to minimize anyone's achievements, it can be said that success simply is very, very often down to the not-so-secret good old luck sauce, external alignments, and serendipity. Aptitude, know-how, and strategy are undoubted elements of any kind of accomplishment; however, nothing beats being born fortunate or becoming an episodical or enduring fellow of the lucky bunch. Could it be that the fortuitous brigade is comprised of some kind of special elite, though? Definitely not, as classic luckiness is just what it is: a pretty-bowed-present from the unseen—nothing more, nothing less.

It seems only fitting that in 2021, one Mr. Elon Musk tweeted that *"luck is the best superpower."* [90]

The same goes for health, talent, charisma, looks, intellect, resilience, stamina, self-control, long-term thinking, and any constitutional special abilities and privileges, internal and external. We don't typically earn these—we get such goodies served, sometimes even in a package. Or not.

And no, the luck of the draw's got nothing to do with fairness or equality.

Examples:

We enter this world with a desirable upbringing in stable social conditions, accompanied by a privileged nationality and an emotionally and intellectually encouraging and prosperous background.

We have access to clean water, healthy food, a moderate climate, and a proper education in a somewhat functioning society with equal-ish rights for all.

We are born handsome, with a charming attitude and the gift of the gab. We find heightened intuition and a resilient disposition in our gift. We are natural organizers and problem solvers, maybe even with an ability for leadership.

How about some different luck? To go to sleep at night, somehow knowing that the next day may be demanding, yet our existences are cushioned against the severest hardships. And as the cherry on top, we aren't forced to leave our homeland and loved ones for a challenging, even dangerous, attempt to build a better life in another, rarely welcoming country.

Westerners are understandably coveted for their pole positions. However, the presumed happy pill of overt luck may cause justifiable side effects such as suspicion and resentment in onlookers on the opposite end of the scale. But that should be a natural consequence carried with grace and in the spirit of sharing any form of abundance by virtuously and voluntarily redistributing portions of such advantages. Because one day, someone may successfully prompt an ethical levy on blindingly apparent heaps of material luck anyway, so best to polish up our social karma by electing to do the right thing. The question *"Why them and not us?"* will remain as painful as it is unavoidable as long as there is too little luck and tolerant, supportive generosity abound. I wonder if we deal with fixed quantities of fortune and interpersonal goodwill, hence the obvious lack thereof.

And, we find ourselves equipped with moral luck, such as the gift of physical and mental strength, a tendency to be saved by the proverbial bell, or commanding a necessary pinch of strait-laced inner stability, discipline, and the ability to withstand temptation. In short: the art of saying *NO*.

Of course, it's not all just lucky. Whether genetic, epigenetic, moral, circumstantial, or any other human-styled luck variety, it also takes grit to make it and stay up there in any environment. Suppose we have the toughness and a sharply focused mind for such fortitude that, again, may be natural luck in the guise of self-determination.

And we haven't even started to talk about growing up being loved, acknowledged, respected, and cherished for all the right reasons. Having a caring parent or someone else who genuinely looks out for and supports a child's development—ideally encouraging compassion, tolerance, discipline, diligence, and yes, grit and universal virtues— plays its part. That's personal and, in a way, psychological luck. As is the capacity for critical and analytical thinking and a healthy degree of skepticism. And let's not forget the magic potion of veritable vim mixed with a touch of chutzpah to make it through a sub-optimal childhood if little of the above was to be had. That kind of luck can indeed be Destiny.

Aristotle offered intriguing views on who attracts luck. He thought that those who pursue the good in life might just generate a kind of virtuous magnetism towards the sweet spot in Tyche's books of lovely chances, which ranks above cleverness and wisdom. Maybe that is why we also have the phrase "dumb luck." The philosopher, who, on the one hand, saw luck as a natural if not divine benefit, also believed that mental clarity and sound decisions are vital (lucky?) elements of a life well lived.

As per time-honored and "official" definitions, the phenomena of fortune and luck have no connection to moral qualities, ethics, values, and even virtues. Fortuna grants her whimsical boon without the necessity to deserve such a celestial windfall from the horn of plenty. And luck is uncontrollable, with its category and occasion only rarely controllable. We can wish for a lucky star, and we may even pray for a gold-dusted wink and nudge from the capricious Goddess, but to no avail, as luck only offers done deals that deliver brightness or darkness, hitting us from out of the blue and without any reason.

So, as per the ruling perspective, sadly, we cannot deserve or earn our luck. Because the traditional view of the phenomenon of luck isn't karmic or dharmic. We cannot count on it either. We can't even duck from our luck or dodge it. And we have to accept that the nonmoral wheel of fortune often benefits recipients without any apparent merit instead of those worthy of a bit of a break, while bad luck can strike the cleverest of us. That said, the importance of good, or rather the tragedy of bad luck, speaks volumes through the attitude many of us develop toward those facing the challenges of misfortune. While we tend to tarnish misadventure as personal failure far too quickly and dish out blame too easily, we forget that many, if not most, elements of life are outside our control. Whatever happens to "them" can cut us down next, no matter how smart we think we'll be. This deplorable attitude is often prevalent vis-à-vis those poorer and more disadvantaged than ourselves. Best think again. Most of us, in difficult circumstances, are not the authors of these conditions but rolling with life's punches. Nobody should judge or belittle the less blessed. Next time we opine about or lecture anyone and even stoop to label others dense, at fault, and *undeserving*, let's remember that it takes only a sliver of contingency, a split-second event, to land us high-horsed moral posers in similar traps. Best internalize this passage from an impressive poem, often interpreted as a Native American proverb:

> *Take time to walk a mile in their moccasins.*
> – MARY TORRANCE LATHRAP, JUDGE SOFTLY

What this world needs is lots and lots of more equally (re)distributed good luck (and wealth) to lift those finding it impossible to better their situations and to update whoever is looking down their noses. And we lucksters should accept this gift's responsibility towards those less fortunate because maybe that's why we ended up favored in the first place: to set an example and help others.

What a suitable transition to the less exciting concept of *comeuppance*, an often-used American term that describes the consequential malaise of someone who has caused others harm. It was coined in 1859[91] by Harper's Magazine, signifying poetic retribution (the Greeks believed in a similar concept delivered by Nemesis & Co.). There is a growing trend to think of it as a quick turnaround kind of karma because of the proverbial decree of *what goes around—comes around*. The root of the word means that the perpetrator has to *come up* to, or rather stand straight in front of, a court or jury to receive their judgment and penalty. Comeuppance is a speculatory element of the already-discussed concept of just deserts.

I bet that there would be lots of takers if someone revealed something like a Comeuppance Button to enable a higher degree of, albeit perceptive, justice on this planet. It would work wonders for certain folks' dopamine levels for the simple reason that judgment and condemnation can lead to chemical rushes in some brains, so it is a good idea to keep the perilous Comeuppance Button away from mortal reach.

Serendipity is an extraordinary kind of fortuity. This phenomenon, named after the poem of British nobleman and first gothic novelist Horace Walpole[92] (1717–1797), was inspired by the Persian story *The Three Princes of Serendip* (Sri Lanka), based on *The Eight Paradises* or

Hasht-Bihisht by the poet Amir Khusrow *(ca. 1300)*. Serendipitous events happen when we find favorable circumstances we were neither expecting nor looking for. It's the unplanned discovery of something never on our agenda. Serendipity is also called accidental sagacity. In essence, serial serendipity is arguably another relevant ingredient of a successful, even happy, life. Serendipity also means "a lucky find" or "the accidental discovery." It's a seemingly contingent phenomenon that can occur when we stumble across anything fabulous lacking apparent reason. Without it, hard work and the iron will to succeed can shrink to the significance of mere details. It's an excellent example of thriving without controlling what happens to us beyond self-determination and human action.

It hits us nicely, straight from the lap of the Gods.

I'm just lucky to have been in the right place, at the right time. Another place, another time, I wouldn't have been as successful. Society enabled me to make my money, and my money should go to society. [93]

– WARREN BUFFETT

I've experienced serendipity time and again. It's the magic of constellations and conjunctions.

Providence is the idea that divine governance has a grip on the plan for everyone, and everything is happening according to this plan. It originated from the future-divining Roman deity and principle of foresight, Providentia, and it was even believed that anything important had been foreseen and provided by this essential pre-Christian imperial Roman Destiny principle. Romans accepted that an endearing, feminine Providentia would watch over the destinies of women and men, Rome, and the whole world like a guardian angel. She was often depicted holding a sphere, a horn of plenty, and sometimes a lightning bolt.

Providentialism was also an important element of Stoic philosophy.

The Stoics held Providentia in high regard because, through Providence, Destiny determines all events according to universal laws and necessity, so everything happens for a reason.

Providence also means using foresight and analysis to aid readiness for contingent outcomes and events that might occur. And foreknowledge, if and when available.

Perhaps far more providential energy is at work in this world than we are able to realize. We only go by what happens to us, even questioning life's fairness or labeling adverse events as fate. But do we ever consider enough whether something we cannot perceive, without our knowledge, may have invisibly intercepted, therefore preventing looming doom darkening our path? Do we ever ponder that what's been hitting us is just a small fraction of an incalculable enormity? That, no matter how terrible and hard it comes down, we still got away with a black eye as humanity and are still standing? Maybe something out there is still willing to humor our shenanigans with admirable lenience.

Chance and randomness are elements often, but not always correctly connected with Destiny. Chance is the probability of something taking place without any prior cause or reason. This physical phenomenon (or shall we call it a problem?) was also named the Law of Probability and Change in the past. So, since all is probable, everything is open to chance? What are the odds?

Randomness is the lack of order or predictability in a sequence of events. Both terms mean there's no pattern to whatever happens next— it could be anything, but it was never decreed!

How often do we say: *I'd love to get a chance to XYZ?* It means that we are hoping for something positive to affect us in a good way in the hope that a wish or aspiration will eventually materialize. And there it is the link to Destiny, serendipity, and providence. But chance is another out-of-the-blue phenomenon that can also result from our intense preparation, intelligent strategy, or simply coincidence. Chance also flourishes in the magic of an opportune moment. Someone who takes great risks or acts recklessly is not called a chancer for no reason.

Food for thought: Why do some seem to be often hitting it lucky while many others feel left out and overlooked by moody divinity for no apparent positive or negative reason? Could it be that good fortune, luck, serendipity, and co. are just different departments of a cosmic lottery? Could it be that no other explanation than the proverbial luck of the draw is relevant, and that's that? And would that not put a lot into perspective?

Yuanfen is a Chinese concept of destinal chance comprising the elements of Destiny, friendship, and preconditioned luck or relationship. [94]

It centers on ideal personal and business connections. Chinese culture was always heavily influenced by the order of Destiny and the importance of maintaining harmonious relationships that carry a celestial Destiny's touch. Here, the idea that selected people could be meant for each other creates a great sense of promise, if not commitment.

Yuanfen is comparable to Buddhism's karma. But it is *interactive* instead of *individual.* The actions we carried out during previous incarnations are believed to be the driving forces behind the Yuanfen we meet in this life.

Gareth Fisher [95] (born 1951) conducted a survey at Peking University, Nankai University, and the Temple of Universal Rescue (TUR) in China, finding that:

University students using Yuanfen for romantic relationships see it as the result of a pre-fated bond. That includes all real-life romances that started in the virtual space of an online chat room.

About 48 percent of university participants describe Yuanfen as *definitely* or *mostly* the cause of *all* relationships.

In contrast, participants from the TUR hardly ascribe romance to Yuanfen. Instead, they use it for *all* types of relationships. As many as 75 percent of these participants see Yuanfen as *definitely* or *mostly* the cause of *all* relationships.

Isn't that intriguing?

So, are the phenomena of fortune, luck, serendipity, chance, etc., actually autogenic and self-produced or variable, random, and bespoke departments within the Agency of Destiny?

In brief sum, they are both. Even cosmic, natural, and metaphysical marvels can cooperate from time to time, despite remaining non-dependent entities.

It is we who have to learn to align with our odds, though, since these independent branches tend not to see themselves as service providers to an increasingly entitled part of humanity. That said, there are options, yet we best talk about them in depth at another time.

Now we'll move on to another important idea: freedom. The ancient interpretations of Destiny meant that only a few occurrences in the world were entirely free. Humanity's place in the world felt supervised by transcendent, unfathomable forces full-time.

After a long time of living with the powers of decreed command, a new movement started questioning humanity's role and options in a world lorded over by an assortment of Gods. It was time to properly examine and explain how the aspects of the world worked. Where else could that particular bright spark have flourished among inquisitive Greek thinkers?

They were inspired, if not challenged, by their own and other cultures' cosmogonies, mythologies, and epic narratives. Swiftly, they began to critically examine the importance and impact of concepts like Destiny, values, liberty, truth, goodness, and justice. Logic and reason began to share the stage with mysticism. Sharply observing skeptic minds questioned the perceptions of the past and voiced doubt and contrasting theorem in their pursuit of figuring out our position within the universe and in Nature, followed by the birth of discussion and debate. The eagle of philosophy had officially landed.

The atomic philosophers Leucippus and his student Democritus were trailblazers of logical necessity and physical determinism, declaring existence to be anchored in the material realm, managed by the chain of previous events, yet absent of much hope of an eternal soul journey.

In addition to the already impressive pantheon of predestiners, the early Greek Nature philosophers of Miletus tried to understand governing laws of the universe and nature through the determining principles *pepromene* and *heimarmene*. [96]

Between ca. 624 to 546 BCE, this important thought school included beacons such as Thales and Anaximander. They focused on making sense of everything, seeking explanations through natural laws, causes, and effects.

An intriguing thought construct took hold; Plato called it *aitia*, Greek for cause, and Aristotle even proposed four different kinds of causation.

But the most famous monikers were later created in Latin:

Determinism—the predictable, causal law of Nature, Latin, stemming from the Roman *determinare*—to establish or cause, as in to determine something.

Fatalism—the doctrine of predecided and accepted inevitability, from Latin *fas, fari*—to speak, to predict, as in the Fates.

Let us look at these enduring, still hotly disputed metaphysical doctrines that continue to dwell in the spheres of Destiny.

Determinisms, and Co.—Doctrinal Simulation Games

In a nutshell: the deterministic universe is a unified system in which every event was and is determined by a preceding event. The world, therefore, proceeds from cause to effect in an ordered fashion. Things will pass from their causes to their effects, binding together all phenomena and events into a coherent universe. Everything is determined, but not all is predetermined. Let us clarify the connection and difference between Destiny and determinism. [97]

Both concepts may seem similar, and some aspects of determinism form part of the thought cosmos of Destiny's pervasive force and vice versa. Stringent determinism does not allow for free will, while the human preference for freedom is perfectly compatible with the empowering laws of Destiny. Life *can* be decreed by Destiny, shaped by determinism, yet lifted and illuminated by the gifts of human liberty.

Destiny is the seminal teleological and metaphysical principle that inspired various philosophers to ponder human freedom.

The design of a human's path can be predetermined—planned and even executed in every detail, yet the originator may or may not change the course to arrive at a similar or wholly different result. Determinism, though, is an iron law lacking flexibility no matter what.

Predeterminism is Destiny's or God's metaphysical or spiritual delivery of stepping stones, yet it also includes Nature's power to create and follow through on a chain of previous events, thereby controlling the outcome. While Destiny devises on a more personal level, determinism deals with the material framework.

Still, philosophically speaking, determinism could well be perceived as big sister Destiny's slightly more indifferent baby brother.

I like to compare my idea of Destiny to a cosmic crystal candy bowl abundant with various gems. It's held out to us invitingly, offering gifts, options, and obligations in many different shapes, colors, and flavors. Then it is up to us to pick and choose from this bowl of sometimes singular or multiple, bright or dark, shimmering or muted assets. And it's also up to us to hold on to, internalize, and even take them forward. The different gems or flavors can consist of excellence, artistic talent, resilience, remarkable intellect, qualities, and abilities such as persuasion, business acumen, patience, focus, memory, character depth, intrinsic and physical beauty, sex appeal, higher consciousness, integrity and self-determined ego-transcendence, luck, thoughtfulness, deep emotions, creativity, and pragmatism—basically, anything we must never take for granted and only use wisely. But they also come in the flavors of complication, tragedy, necessity, reluctance, procrastination, misfortune, challenge, dark thoughts, the sight, adverse conditions, non-belonging, idiosyncrasy, isolation, melancholy, and affliction—basically, anything uncomfortably helpful in practicing empathy and compassion.

Despite the kind of light-versus-dark appearance, we are dealing with a non-dualistic, non-meritocratic selection. All aspects run into one transcendent *beingness,* one set of experience training and preparing us for the achievement of knowledge and growing abilities.

Recap: Whereas metaphysical Destiny is open to mindful alterations provided by a metaphysical credo, determinism initially poses inflexible outcomes generated by the rules of material necessity, constraint, and causation.

How is free will defined again? Free will is available to a human agent when one or more options to *do otherwise*, i.e., to elect between different possibilities, are present.

Let's visit a few thought schools surrounding determinism. And yes, while it may be a little boring, it's necessary.

Destiny is the principle that co-designs the human journey in concert with our innate gifts.

Fate makes each event inevitable, as invisible forces dictate outcomes beyond our control.

Determinism holds that everything in this world results directly from previous events, regardless of our desires or actions.

Causal determinism harkens back to the old debate on whether humanity's acts are self-determined. Several schools of classic Greek and Roman philosophy already argued that previous chains of events even determine humanity's moral choices and actions.

Determinism simply teaches that all events are the result of prior events according to natural laws and without the significance or influence of free will. Instead, necessity, compulsion even, the universe, and Nature are in full charge, swinging inevitability.

Like fatalism on steroids, especially if it was ever officially declared to be a fact, this stern paradigm is still feared to cause us to abandon responsibility and aspiration, banish regrets, and live detrimentally without regard for the consequences of any actions. That's why we see no end to debating the relevance of determinism.

The famous Butterfly Effect is a deterministic phenomenon. Edward Lorenz (1917–2008), a meteorologist and creator of the chaos theory, coined this term when he discovered that small changes in previous conditions lead to notably different weather patterns, rendering long-term forecasts quite uncertain. The Butterfly Effect makes for an effective model of deterministic chaos, where systems follow strict rules and patterns, but their outcomes are highly exposed to prior states.

In the realm of determinism dwells fatalism, which is also seen as a direct consequence of a deterministic worldview. Fatalism is a religious and philosophical doctrine suggesting that any actions or events take place due to higher powers, certain Gods, Nature, or the law of fatum. Today, it is associated with a limp attitude of resignation, as everything in life is considered to be inevitable. Philosophically, fatalism implies that we are vulnerable and only entitled to experience the present moment, and that's that.

Not to be confused with Destiny. The Roman statesman Cicero wrote a book on fatum, i.e., fate—*De Fato*—in which he rejected the concept of fatalism in favor of selective human free will.

Logical Fatalism and necessity are closely connected. Events occur because they had to, and they did; thus, they must be necessary. All events are the result of what has been, what exists, and what will occur in the future.

Theological fatalism is the philosophical argument that all events have been predetermined by divine will, creating the historic dilemma we already discussed: Theodicy—an omniscient God's absolution from negative or evil outcomes, transferred to the causality axis of free will via wrong human decisions. Tendencies of theological fatalism, together with theological determinism, are present in Christianity (especially Calvinism) [98] and Islam.

Fatalism is also dubbed as counsel of despair. But whether we like it or not, scientists have found the belief that fate or God(s)' decisions led to a tragic event, for instance, the death of a beloved partner, may indeed help to cope when hardships hit. To consider a higher design and reason and accept that which is impossible to change or reverse can prove an effective mindset to soothe pain and disappointment. [99]

Not everyone has access to comprehensive information, counseling, and therapy, so I'm not knocking a somewhat fatalistic or external locus of control attitude if it brings about comfort and a sense of meaning. The same goes for the often necessary hope and solace religions provide. Considering the era we are approaching, we simply cannot afford to belittle or shun proven coping mechanisms. Pragmatists' lullaby: What works—works.

Both hard determinism and fatalism largely negate the idea of liberty to decide, but they differ in terms of the *why*. Both are seen as critical by those thinkers who insist on absolute human freedom to produce or uphold arguments to keep us morally responsible and justify the palette of consequences, such as blame, retribution, and praise.

It is called *desert-based moral responsibility*, meaning that positive or negative actions and their respective results—the desert—take place fully deserved by an agent—the deserver—due to their choice options. [100]

Our English terms deserve and desert originate in the Latin verb *deservire*, meaning good service and merit-based reward.

To carry moral responsibility, an agent has to exercise control in action to "justly deserve to be blamed and praised, punished, and rewarded for their actions." [101]

The models of basic and just deserts are the approach to moral duty and responsibility questioned by the contemporary philosopher Gregg Caruso. [102] He also criticizes the insistence on free will as an instrument to punish many too harshly, risking that *just* deserts turn into *unjust* deserts.

The idea of (just) deserts and whether we *deserve* praise, blame, rewards, or punishments is deeply embedded in our human psyche and culture. But is it just or fair enough? Would the theory of desert not require intense analysis and insight into individual or even collective circumstances? What about those that don't morally deserve their outcomes, be it in the forms of success or wealth? Like drug cartel bosses, unethical politicians, and inconsiderate billionaires? What if at least some of them, on top of a lot of hard or smart, even ingenious work, were simply born into favorable circumstances or met fortunate constellations, if not third-party deliberations, with resulting support, while possibly carrying genes and epigenetic enablers rendering them more focused, determined, and perhaps even more selfish and ruthless than the rest?

And what of the majority dealt a bad hand in life from the outset while doing everything in their grasp to cope with it and better their options, all with the best intentions and without knowingly harming a third party? Like poorer classes and countries, underprivileged ethnicities, and those of us who are hardworking, jumping through hoops to be good parents, and paying far-too-high dues while never getting anywhere? Desert, anyone?

Before quickly condemning anyone, we should consider what made, molded, and shaped them into who and what they are. Genes, upbringing, trauma, culture, religion, disorders of the mind and body, chemical imbalance, substance abuse, and lots more can be contributing factors to what we become. Many unchosen factors will remain out of our control; consequently, we should tread lightly and employ empathy before applying self-righteousness.

What if inevitability *is* at play when walking down or changing a presupposed path? Legend has it that once a future is decided, whatever the protagonist does or omits may lead to detours but won't alter their ordained outcome. This movie has already been wrapped.

Whatever challenges we attempt to circumnavigate only bring us closer to our predetermined destination since that script had been written and archived long ago.

Determinism also rose to popularity in the spheres of physics and formal logic. Many thinkers and scientists suggested that the universe operates based on fixed laws, including the physical world and all living beings. Humanity's thoughts, desires, and choices all happen under causation.

The Greek philosophers Heraclitus and Chrysippus advocated determinism early on. Their ideas influenced notable intellectuals, such as Baruch Spinoza (1632–1677), Sir Isaac Newton (1642–1727), and Albert Einstein (1879–1955).

Our freedom lies not in the self-determination of our physical body to seek our own destiny, but our understanding of the way the universe really is. To understand the workings of Nature is to find peace with it.

– BARUCH SPINOZA

The free will-skeptic philosopher Gregg Caruso suggests rather convincingly that human ideas of freedom are subjective interpretations produced by our different levels of consciousness. Simply imagining and desiring such freedom does not bring it into existence unless we subscribe to the Law of Attraction, which asserts that we can manifest almost anything into reality.

Compatibilism deals with the opposite concepts of free will and causal determinism. It neither insists that free will exists nor that determinism is true; it just maintains these two ideas can coexist to the extent that both or either apply.

For instance, the Stoics, David Hume (1711–1776), and our latter-day champion of compatibilism, the American philosopher and scientist Daniel Dennett (born 1942), all emphasize(d) the compatibility of determinism and human self-determination. Compatibilists are lovely—they always look for ways to reconcile two seemingly opposing positions, no matter how difficult.

Incompatibilism claims that free will and determinism are not compatible. If the universe and the human brain are deterministic, then humans can't command autonomy.

Incompatibilism uses two opposing concepts:

Libertarianism favors the opinion that humans not only have free will but that determinism is powerless over us. Libertarians expect ample capacity to want and do what they like. So we *can* have our cake *and* eat it?

Hard determinism argues that the human species operates under absolute determinism. No such thing as ethical or moral responsibility. Consequently, hard determinists don't credit benevolent actions of selfless and noble people.

Both views are thought-provoking. Is our will *really* free, uncrushable, and thus almost God-like? Or are we just remote-controlled bio-actors in a grand game, stuck in the iron chain of events and causation(s)?

What if we are a bit of both?

Even Daniel Dennett admits he goes left and right between the positions. Just like the Stoics, Dennett believes tight self-restraint to be a key to human responsibility, embedded in determinism that remains a fact alongside it.

Semicompatibilism, pioneered by the American philosopher John Martin Fischer[103] (born 1952), is a unique compatibilist direction holding that determinism and moral responsibility are not mutually exclusive. Professor Fischer outlines how determinism and lack of volition can get along with our moral values even if we lack the capacity to do otherwise, as opposed to the capability required in absolute free will, which is contradictory to determinism. In his case of semi-compatibilism, whatever is afoot, humans are morally responsible for their choices and actions, with or without volition or other options to choose from.

Fischer offers an instrumental aspect in maintaining any society and legal system running smoothly, even when determinism is proven to be true after all.

Modern societies just couldn't do without Fischer's interpretation. But is it always fair? Or realistic?

The time we live in, and the age ahead, would benefit from metaphysical generosity and flexibility, allowing for the option of *as well as* instead of the limitations of *one or the other*. Our deterministic universe won't mind anyway.

One of my main motivations for being a compatibilist is that I don't want our personhood and our moral responsibility, as it

*were, to hang on a thread or to be held hostage to the possible
scientific discovery that determinism is in fact true.* [104]
– JOHN MARTIN FISCHER

Sam Harris, neuroscientist and public intellectual who calls free will
an illusion, and Daniel Dennett famously debate this never aging puzzle.

Could it be that some members of the philosophical brigade are
far too busy with conceptual over-thinking in their proverbial ivory
towers while forgetting, or ignoring, neurobiological facts and the effect
of echo chambers concerning the workings of our brains and minds,
let alone other scientific factors of the human species in a vast cosmic
order? It would not feel too comfortable having to accept we are in
less control than we imagine if determinism is true. It may even boost
anxious ideations about the consequences if humans understand their
perceived abilities are weak. But what if it is just so?

Are we perhaps dealing with philosophical interpretations designed
to serve dogmatic, ideological, if not theological convenience? And if so,
would that be a first?

The philosophy of unhampered self-determination is far less
important to most people than those who govern or live in luxurious
thought worlds. Most humans have bigger fish from the seas of bare
necessities to fry than contemplating these and several other concepts
driven by arbitrary values.

A more practical and less ideological approach to human problems
and challenges wouldn't hurt, especially not when it comes to political
finger-pointing agendas exercised by total theoreticians.

The human species: just a bunch of loose cannons? We are trusted,
or instead told, to carry full moral responsibility, but we cannot be
what and how we naturally are. To protect whom exactly? The reigning
ideology or perhaps even us from… ourselves? Quite a negative view of
humanity, right? Let us take a little detour to visit the ripple effect.

In his time, Sigmund Freud contributed a lot to humanity—enough
that we should kindly ignore his several slip-ups. Freud is the father of
the unconscious mind—our inborn significant yet irrational *id* (Latin

for *it*), and the conscious departments of the sensible, rational *ego* and the *super-ego,* our moral processing and experience storage unit. He believed human behaviors to be irrational, driven by primal, if not primitive, instincts. Freud, suffering from cancer and misanthropy, fatefully sent his *Introduction to Psychoanalysis* [105] to one Edward Bernays, his nephew in America. Built on his uncle's theories, especially the thought that homo sapiens is predominantly led by the chase to satisfy cravings for various pleasures, he derived his strategy and verdict, condensed in portentous books such as *Crystallizing Public Opinion* (1923) [106] and the revolutionary tome *Propaganda (1928).* Bernays went on to cultivate and make gospel what he branded as *Engineering of Consent* with incredible success. We can all guess why Hitler's pernicious propaganda minister Joseph Goebbels was a fan and adopter of these mass-manipulation techniques, as Bernays claimed in his memoirs. I feel that his methodology is alive and kicking today, still throwing sand in the eyes of large parts of the public in numerous locations, particularly in support of ultra-conservative, nationalist, and authoritarian agendas.

America not only lapped up nephew Eddie's stratagem but followed the lead of his newly invented *public relations.* Bernays made smoking cigarettes desirable and patriotic for women. He pioneered the most successful campaign for the brand *Lucky Strike* when tobacco's deadly shadow wasn't scientifically proven yet. His campaigns also turned Americans to fat-laden breakfasts based on animal protein. Nonetheless, his endeavors exposed millions to industrial-greed-driven health risks, arguably contributing to innumerable sufferings followed by premature deaths from lung and other cancers.

It wasn't an official crime. Still, it was wrong all the same since it even started behavioral consumer patterns that led to far too many individuals living beyond their means on borrowed money. Yes, it always takes two to tango; however, manipulation techniques of the highest psychological order could hardly be resisted by a majority of unsuspecting consumers. Bernays' shenanigans, riding the waves of the ripple effect, also co-led to the future surplus undermining of resources, greater pollution, and the generation of mountains of toxic waste. And what for? All in the name of *more*. More seeming than being, more stuff, more business, more money, more corruption, more environmental damage, and much more debt. Well, China, the only former empire to properly come back from the shadows of history so far, rose again courtesy of the want for a lot of cheap stuff that's often unnecessary. So no point now moaning about the West's dependency on the Middle Kingdom but better contemplate why and how the opium wars were instigated. Thinking about it, Bernays likely had more than one chance to use his intelligence and insights to help advance humanity. Instead, he chose to feed greed.

Are we that shallow and predictable? Bernays' target groups had come out of the trauma of the Great Depression and World War II. That's how consumerism started—through the psychological reduction to *herd* desires and mentality. We are still experiencing these ripples.

Back to the question: Are we just built on wanting our superficial needs met? Some of us, probably. Yet, if all we sought was just thrills and pleasures, we would not be here today. We would not have social cohesion or the ability to exercise democracy. Humans have a built-in desire to pursue well-being, avoid pain and suffering, seek cooperation, and live safely, socially, and orderly.

Thankfully, not all of us are navel-focused hyper-individualists or responsibility-dodgers. In fact, most of us face the music every day. We enjoy working together under mutual values for the common good, desiring a positive tomorrow, a better world, and a shared auspicious Destiny for many generations.

By nature, homo sapiens is neither cynical nor nihilistic. We may be thoughtless, reckless even, gullible, and often selfish. We may get stressed by uncertainty, the rising demands of existence, and unabating concerns for safety and order. We are so far from being perfect. But humanity isn't a bushel of bad apples. Not at all. If anything, we're just a bushel of unripe ones, still green in many places with scattered adolescent phantasies of supernatural powers and illusions of exceptionalism. We are far too readily distracted and misguided, and we tend to be far too judgmental, forgetting that judging others does not automatically make us moral beacons.

Remember the Greek philosopher Protagoras (ca. fifth century BCE), who claimed that *man is the measure of all things*?

From the dawn of human history until today, it's blatantly obvious that he was way too hasty to arrive at such a conclusion. While we aren't just at the mercy of fate, our species has an important role to play and, if we play our cards right, an epic Destiny to fulfill. Nonetheless, our actions have a growing impact on the world around us.

Is it true that we're nothing more than data-processing machines, our lives determined by our genes and epigenetic factors influenced by the experiences of our youths, as some scientific theorem suggests?

Childhood and circumstances can make for both good Destiny and grim fate for sure. We know the jury is out on this one. Anyroad, let's not disregard the undeniable facts of science. Ignoring them would mean that, for instance, women would still be considered inferior to men, our planet Earth would be pinned to the center of the universe, and the concept of God(s) would still majorly be accepted as gospel without any evidence to back it up. Hold on a moment; all that *is* still ongoing despite scientific breakthroughs. Ah well.

Anyway, there are many truths, not just one and nothing, and no one can lay claim to totality. All these actualities take time to arrive. And land they will, eventually.

How about a few more philosophies commonly connected with deterministic Destiny?

Libertarianism, in the free will context, [107] is an incompatibilist construct emphasizing agent causation, arguing that a free person cannot live in a deterministic universe. Thus, philosophical libertarians claim that homo sapiens is not governed by determinism.

Amor fati is a deterministic philosophy or philosophical fatalism that interprets everything that happens as necessary and unavoidable yet, without a limp and inert attitude. *Amor fati* means love of fate or love of one's fate. The theory was observed by the Stoics, who focused on an accepting life perspective to make the best of immutable occurrences in life.

The German philosopher Friedrich Nietzsche's (1844–1900) famous extra take on amor fati can be associated with his other renowned notion of *eternal recurrence*, stating that everything recurs infinitely over a neverending cycle. Nietzsche desired to live the same life again and again for all eternity. A brave notion, considering that his life was anything but happy, healthy, or harmonic. Still, Nietzsche, who liked to refer to Destiny as *Fatum,* its Latin version, said he would not only accept everything as necessary and unavoidable but that he *embraced* his fate. Hence, his amor fati isn't fatalistic since it does not call to endure anything imposed by dark fate demurely. It creatively determines whatever happens to be proactively valued. It is reminiscent of the later quintessence of Albert Camus' *The Myth of Sisyphus* and Viktor Frankl's concept of a flexible attitude in the face of adversity. If it works—it works.

> *My formula for human greatness is amor fati: that one wants to have nothing different, not forward, not backward, not in all eternity. Not merely to bear the necessary, still less to conceal it... but to love it.*

> *We ought to face our destiny with courage.*

> *Give me today, for once, the worst throw of your dice, destiny. Today I transmute everything into gold.*
>
> – FRIEDRICH NIETZSCHE

Pragmatically dealing with and developing that which we cannot change can be a good idea, while loving it is a different matter entirely. The echo of amor fati reminds us to avoid falling victim to circumstances or third-party intentions by raising our resilience and not allowing ourselves to be crushed by internal negativity.

Historical determinism is applied to events that were historically determined and constrained by various forces. Following this line of thought, the future becomes an inevitable and predetermined result of the past.

Historical determinism, associated with nineteenth-century philosophers such as Marx and Hegel, had a resurgence in recent years. Jared Diamond also expresses this view in his 1997 nonfiction book *Guns, Germs, and Steel – The Fates of Human Societies*. W.W. Norton.

Economic determinism is the idea that economic conditions are the primary force behind all historical change, determining all aspects of society's structures. Karl Marx (1818–1883) was the most famous advocate of this theory.

Critics of determinism argue that, for instance, historical developments are complex and influenced by many factors. In their view, events are unpredictable, and therefore, the occurrences of history are not inevitable.

Biological determinism addresses human life from the point of view of biology. The concept is related to genetic determinism. Another definition suggests that biological factors (like individual genes of an organism) determine how systems behave and change over time. For biological determinism, cells of the human body are nanomachines that run on proteins. They cannot think and do not have free will. Since the body is made of cells, biological determinists point out that our actions and behaviors are driven by underlying processes and genetic factors.

While this bio-philosophical construct has not been comprehensively disproved, the debate is ongoing about the extent to which homo sapiens could be considered an overly complicated and vulnerable bio-machine.

Physical determinism assumes that we live in a material universe governed by physical laws. The brain is a physical entity. Thus, the same deterministic physical laws governing the material world also govern the brain and possibly even our thoughts.

This kind of determinism sports a fixed future, not for nothing, also called hard determinism. Hard determinists claim that we have no free will whatsoever and that their actions and choices just cannot be otherwise. Everything in the physical universe obeys the same physical laws, including us.

Environmental determinism is the idea that a physical environment shapes human behaviors, thoughts, and actions. An individual in a rainy, mountainous climate grows and behaves differently from an individual living in a desert. We have to adapt to our environment.

The physical world is a key factor in human history.

Location, climate, the shape of a landscape, and the abundance or scarcity of water and food are examples of deterministic elements that shape our history. They determine our behaviors and can empower or destroy societies.

Logical determinism is all about things and events, including the future, fixed due to absolute necessity and constraint. It deems that rational laws determine everything and that there are no fundamental truths that exist independently of these laws.

Critics of logical determinism mainly go with two non-deterministic approaches. One is to show that claims about the future have no value. The second is to distinguish between the necessity and the factuality of statements about the past and the future.

Let us remember the nature of all philosophical doctrines: A logical theory can be significant yet false or insignificant yet true.

Theological or divine determinism in the guise of divine providence and predetermination presents God as the sole power, creator, and foreknower of every event in the world. This view was also espoused by Augustine, John Calvin, and Thomas Aquinas.

Earlier Calvinists believed their God predetermines all human stories, eternally decreeing his high mystery of predestination and observing sin-laden human struggles. This idea is reflected in the Westminster Confession of Faith:

God from all eternity did, by the most wise and holy counsel of His own will, freely and unchangeably ordain whatsoever comes to pass, yet so, as thereby neither is God the author of sin, nor is violence offered to the will of the creatures, nor is the liberty or contingency of second causes taken away, but rather established.

And it goes on to say:

By the decree of God, for the manifestation of His glory, some men and angels, are predestinated unto everlasting life; and others foreordained to everlasting death.

These angels and men, thus predestinated, and foreordained, are particularly and unchangeably designed, and their number so certain and definite, that it cannot be either increased or diminished.

— Westminster Confession of Faith

Whatever happened to those angels?

Those chosen for good standing could not even ruin their *luck* through negative behavior, even if they tried, whereas those precondemned into God's bad book couldn't redeem themselves through good deeds or atonement since his fateful verdict was deemed eternal: the reprobate's Destiny.

Given some sympathetic understanding that the Westminster Confession of Faith was created during the horrid times of the English Civil War, I have little doubt why it became a main root of Protestant profit pursuance and even laissez-faire capitalism. This thought system is still present in today's self-righteousness of *deserving* devotees and holders of wealth in opposition to the *undeserving* classes. Moral high ground and human theodicy hard-coded in to berate the misbegotten. Was that the key concept of the man from Galilee? Is he not said to have stated that no rich man would ever enter paradise? And that, rather than getting there, a full-blown camel would fit through the eye of a needle?

Religious fatalism meets greed, exploitation, and co. without contradiction or inhibition. The Protestant John Calvin even promoted a form of double predestination, just like Saint Augustine, who thought even newborn babies were already morally compromised. He also peddled the idea that, on the one hand, God held mankind in the fully responsible state of human autonomy while he preordained everything, everyone, and their uncle, including their predecided fate, as either a good sheep or a reprobate. All this leads us back to the thought of newborn children being inserted into earthly life, fully morally mortgaged and indebted.

Psychological determinism rests on human behavioral patterns influenced by psychological processes and possibly even psychological laws.

In tandem with early life experiences, our resulting personalities, thoughts, and desires impact our choices and decisions and may just be what we sense as free will.

Neuroscientists can identify physical structures in the human brain responsible for decision-making in contribution to the field of neuroeconomics, which seeks to understand and predict the formation of decision-making processes.

And finally, we look at some spheres connected with determinism escaping me absolutely; or rather, we escape each other, these spheres and I.

Many different thought schools and scientific disciplines address the universe's nature and predictability, such as Newton's deterministic physics, indeterministic quantum mechanics, and the still much-discussed many-worlds interpretation.

As far as I can grasp it, this is the theory in a nutshell. How about either probability governs everything, and we are totally at the mercy of chance or randomness, [108] or a previous event determines each event, all our actions are predetermined, and we cannot escape that cycle? [109]

Quantum mechanics is a branch of physics that deals with physical phenomena at atomic and subatomic scales. Some of the most intriguing aspects of this field are the quantum states, their superposition, and Werner Heisenberg's [110] *Uncertainty Principle.* [111] If quantum mechanics were found to be accurate, it would rattle the idea of determinism because it proves the leitmotif of uncertainty in the universe. [112]

In contrast, the basic assumption of quantum theory suggests that physical processes in the universe and Nature are alternatively probabilistic.

This version of determinism only becomes significant when objects are tiny. In this sense, quantum theory deals with the rules by which the universe operates on microscopic scales. [113] If quantum theory is correct, physical determinism is real.

The many-worlds interpretation or MWI claims countless parallel universes coexist alongside our own, where certain events in Nature can lead to many possible outcomes.

The US physicist Hugh Everett (1930–1983) offers probabilities for each situation. The *quantum wave function* evolves in a way that reflects the entire range of possibilities. The MWI is a philosophical attempt to reconcile our understanding with the mathematical structures of quantum mechanics. MWI states that all observers and all possible worlds exist simultaneously. If the MWI is true, every single event that happens or ever will happen is going on and has already happened on alternate planes.

Determinism was and is a foundational belief in many cultures, from Greek and Chinese to African philosophy. [114] The ancient world already discussed philosophical determinism, which partly followed in the deistic footsteps of the different personified principles and Gods of Destiny we met earlier.

The idea that previous events cause all events, the so-called causal chain of necessity, has been with us since ancient Greece and Rome and is found in Hinduism, Buddhism, Daoism, and Islam. [115] And, with the emphasis on free will, it became another leitmotif of Western philosophy and science, fought in verbose word scuffles between determinists, indeterminists, and libertarians for more than two millennia now and counting. We still enjoy great thinkers passionately or condescendingly arguing determinism versus free will. [116]

Determinism entails that the good ship universe, with all of us on board, is designated to reach each destination, event after event. However, whether we're equipped well enough and find ourselves with or without a paddle on the journey up the creeks of continued occurrences, we're yet to find out. [117]

Destiny appears somehow related to determinism because the latter seems to represent a similar preordained course of events leading to set outcomes. Only it doesn't because determinism's ways are not preordained and expressly designed but the material consequences of predictable causes.

Destiny is a teleological, metaphysical phenomenon representing the laws of the cosmos and Nature as well. But the concept of Destiny can offer flexible options and alterable routes to get where we have to arrive.

Having said that, if determinism were proven an adamantine fact, Destiny would be the guest of honor at that material realm party. And vice versa.

More serious information is to be had from Robert M. Sapolsky's [118] (born 1957) book *Determined: A Science of Life without Free Will.* [119]

Whatever we may think, like, or reject, one point stands: the existence of the several forms of determinism versus free will remains under constant debate. After all, we are dealing with the many facets of philosophy, societal and legal needs, conjecture, debate, discourse, and a resounding laugh one sunshiny day.

So, tentative conclusions on how any of these philosophical concepts stack up against one another and how true or false they are can't be drawn from any of them since, clearly, no one knows anything for sure until that day when all will become clear. But that day is yet to be determined. If it ever will.

Philosophers' Darling

The metaphysical premium software running life and beyond is well-connected with similar principles. As we know, from likely before the Bronze Age and throughout our known history, outstanding bygone yet still relevant cultures revered and developed impressive concepts of the invisible designer. From Mesopotamia to Egypt, from Greece to Rome, there reigned magnificent incarnations of Destiny, fate, and fortune, and the first shoots of more or less divine determinism.

Philosophical and analytical aspects of the universal supra-power began to rise with advancing theories about predetermination and human free choice, courtesy of Greek philosophers such as Anaximander (ca. 610–545 BCE), Heraclitus, Leucippus (fifth century BCE), and Democritus (ca 460–370 BCE).

Philosophy is the Greek term for "love of wisdom." This unique affection was fostered in ancient Greece around 700 BCE. It could easily be called the art and craft of asking all the essential questions of life and thinking about finding reasonable answers to enhance the understanding of our existence and far beyond.

I know you won't believe me, but the highest form of human excellence is to question oneself and others.

– SOCRATES

Philosophy is one of the most eminent disciplines to gain insight into the workings for the betterment of humanity.

Many different, especially metaphysical perspectives orbit predeterminism, a paradigm that harkens back to the unseen force decreeing all occurrences in the universe, affecting our every move and step in the future. It's been a hot topic ever since humankind began wondering how the world functions and what, or maybe who, is in charge.

In philosophy, a majorly determining factor of what humankind's Destiny entails is free will. With the gift of considerable volition in our pockets, we mortals can rationalize our intentions, actions, and measures so that our destinies are co-shaped by interacting with the environment and the cosmos. Philosophers still argue for the existence of self-determination. If we are at liberty to make confident choices, is that freedom absolute with regard to what will happen in our future?

Our aptitude for self-determination can be interpreted as intention—decision—action outside and without the influence of other forces. Supposing our ability to elect and act to achieve a desired outcome, we are also capable of reacting to the consequences of our deeds, gaining access to a heightened sense of responsibility. But what about sin, praise, guilt, and other "judgments" that come with free choice? More on that later.

The ability to control our actions through conscious selection cannot be considered absolute. Different schools of philosophy, neurology, biology, etc., dispute how much authority we have over our options and to what extent we are free to choose. These arguments lead to varied challenges of the construct of free will, despite the strong sense of freedom we so like because of our rationality and that intuitive desire to make decisions by ourselves.

The question of how to gain insight into how humankind may act freely or not predates the birth of philosophy; the far-thinking ancients tried to understand whether their respective supernatural beings permitted independent thinking and freedom to act according to our mortal abilities. For this reason, certain creation myths present relevant yet compatible Gods humoring the freedom we hold so dear.

A commendable way of pondering our place and insight into the universe is called compatibilism, which states that determinism—the rules of pre-existing causal necessities—can work nicely with our freedom of choice. Compatibilism accepts that we are all driven by unseen and universal chains of causalities and events, with the exception, or rather a philosophical allowance, that certain decisions we make are actually signed off by our very own independence, resulting in a friendly "yes!" to determinism but with a self-decreed dollop of human responsibility. Not a bad concept. More on determinism later.

Back to the cradle of critical thinking.

Philosophy is believed to have officially started with a formidable astronomer and gentleman named Thales of Miletus (ca. 624–545 BCE), who was also a mathematician and then some. He pondered how natural occurrences take place and how the cosmos works, and he dared to question whether all that happens was indeed willed and instigated by Gods. He had a high opinion of the natural cosmic principle Ananke, though.

We'll look at a few philosophers who thought about Destiny in the grand scheme of things.

Heraclitus (ca. 540–480 BCE) declared the great plan as the universe's helm of reason. He also argued that Nature works under her own set of rules, and human beings can understand her if they strive to comprehend what causes natural occurrences. With this reasoning, his ideas later sparked the discovery—or rather an installation—of determinism, which also states that all things that happen in the universe, including human actions, are caused by a previous absolute necessity.

As a result, every effort, be it rational or not, would be logical and run in parallel with the rules of Nature. While determinism goes with and without the existence of supernatural beings pontificating the rules of the universe, the Stoic movement later suggested humanity's destinies be a product of our personal moral mastery of life while still being governed by ruling natural forces and the cosmos.

Some philosophers challenged the assumption that a set of rigid laws bonds Nature and humans. Greek philosophers began to add the element of free will to the mix of causal law and deterministic ideas, which declares humans responsible for many of the actions they take.

Speaking to us via Plato's written memory, and this is me paraphrasing Socrates—the bothersome contrarian, thought-provoker, and daemon-inspired genius of a gadfly [120]—who expanded early moral responsibility with his thought that no proper person would commit any wrongdoing as a result of a freely willed decision.

He also believed that self-controlled mortals would act only based on what they believe to be right and good and according to what they accept to be virtuous. Suppose full knowledge of what virtue entails is present. Socrates, whose cheeky examinations challenged the Athenian status quo, was declared an enemy of the state and convicted to die for rejection of Athens' official deities, among other fabricated accusations. The brave philosopher drank a lethal cup of hemlock, in keeping with his sense of virtue, likely reminiscing about the Delphic oracle's divination, destining him as the wisest Athenian. Here's to having the last word.

Be of good hope in the face of death. Believe in this one truth for certain, that no evil can befall a good man either in life or death, and that his fate is not a matter of indifference to the Gods.

— SOCRATES

He was succeeded by Plato (ca. 427–347 BCE), formerly an author of tragedies, who turned to philosophy and became a student of Socrates. Later, he founded the famous first-ever Academy in Athens. His school of philosophy also became an inspiration, if not part-foundation, of the largest religions in the world, as well as several schools of metaphysics. Plato emphasized a Destiny that is active in tandem with the ability of human choice and the proactive decision to practice self-constraint and seek just goodness, even straight over to and through the afterlife.

Plato's crypto-educational creations, such as the *Myth of Atlantis*, the *Allegory of the Cave,* and the *Myth of Er,* and his notions on the nature of the human soul continue to impress modern thinkers. He anchored his meditations in a metaphysical ideal: the cosmic Law of Destiny, and he saw the universe as good.

If in the order of Nature, and by divine destiny, a man were able to apprehend the truth about these things, he would have no need for laws to rule over him, for there is no law or order above knowledge, nor can mind without impiety be deemed to subject or slave of any, but rather the lord of all.

— PLATO, LAWS

Plato's student Aristotle (ca. 384–322 BCE) further challenged the rigidity of destinal determinism by stating that life consists of multiple elements that flow together. He also argued that a single factor does not cause everything that happens, and neither does any one supernatural being control all, pointing to the possibility of chance. If what is experienced in the world is a result of many options and prospects, human intervention could indeed influence the way the world operates.

Aristotle produced the idea of four possible causes for the events of Nature and humans: the material, the efficient, the formal, and the final, while also advising an emulation of the Gods as much as possible as the highest mortal goal.

Aristotle moved away from a solely mystical Destiny vis-à-vis human self-determination. He accepted Logical Fatalism, meaning the laws of the universe place worldly and human existence under the constraints of necessity (Ananke), while the future can also be based on what humans deem to be true in the present. In sum, Aristotle did not believe *all* occurrences are a result of necessity dictated by events of the past or inevitable need but that we do command a pretty degree of freedom indeed.

Aristotle's notion of chance and his breaking away from an all-determining causal chain brings about the idea that human actions depend on the individual characters that execute them. As an aside, and somewhat cutely contrasting: The proponents of human choice and certain freedoms— Socrates, Plato, and Aristotle—disliked the concept of democracy and even branded it as presenting anarchic tendencies. Uh-oh.

Well, you know, that's just like—uhh—your opinion, man.
> – JEFF LEBOWSKI (THE DUDE), THE BIG LEBOWSKI [121]

The philosopher Epicurus (ca.341–270 BCE), a kind of early-day agnostic, if not atheist, claimed that while there are factors that influence how the universe operates, its core nature is entirely random and moving in perpetual motion. This notion debunks any idea of strict determinism. It pushes the view of an altogether random actuality, which, in tandem with the forces of chance, supports humanity's ability to think independently. Epicurus was arguably the first philosopher to highlight the "free will versus necessity and determinism" spectrum and possible options.

The opponents of Epicureanism—namely the Greek school of Stoicism, also known then as Zenoism after Zeno of Citium (ca. 334–262 BCE), who founded this philosophy ca. 300 BCE—developed from the worldviews of the Cynics. These formidable thinkers emphasized life in virtuous harmony with the law of necessity in the natural realm, sidelining greed for power, wealth, and glory. The Stoics then cemented that natural laws have control over everything that exists, including the human mind. The cosmic *logos* breathes human Destiny into our spirit and our character. Stoic philosophy promotes the existence of an all-encompassing principle that plans and rules, also through Nature. It's humankind's job to fit into this world and get creative. With the introduction of the Stoa, a form of ancient compatibilism, humanity was determined partly by our actions but under an umbrella of Destiny. That means we can make independent decisions not purely run by natural necessity. As already mentioned, the philosophically enhanced divine embodiment of personal Destiny was called Pepromene—an individual plan embedded in the great authority's foreknowledge. Philosophers also revered another feminine principle: Heimarmene, determining the law of the universe and this world.

To excel at being a Stoic, a simple-yet-strict moral code seeking to be virtuous in all fields of life has to be followed. Stoics also believe in living with *eudaimonia*—Greek for being animated and favored by a spirit (daimon or daemon) of goodness. [122]

Eudaimonia is the state of mindful virtuousness in harmony with Nature through avoidance of distractions imposed by desires and wishful thinking. Stoicism focuses on what we can control, not on what is outside our control, and courageously accepts and optimizes what we cannot change. No wonder it became popular among later Roman Stoics to remind themselves of the inevitability of earthly demise: memento mori—remember that you'll die.

> *There are things which are within our power, and there are things which are beyond our power. Within our power are opinion, aim, desire, aversion, and, in a word, whatever affairs are our own. Beyond our power are body, property, reputation, office, and, in a word, whatever are not properly our own affairs.*
>
> – EPICTETUS, GREEK PHILOSOPHER

Stoics embrace mental balance with *that which is* at the very moment in time. Notable Stoics were Epictetus (ca. 50–135 BCE), the statesman

Seneca the Younger (ca. 1–69 CE), and the Roman emperor Marcus Aurelius (121–180 CE). Roman Stoicism also introduced the notion of *amor fati,* Latin for loving one's Destiny to excel in the face of both adversity and serendipity.

Further reading tip: *The Enchiridion* by Epictetus. [123] You can find it online for free.

Marcus Aurelius was a proponent of the Stoic belief that all human actions and decisions were guided by a grand plan created by a divine force while giving individuals self-determination.

To feel grief, anger, or fear is to try to escape from something decreed by the ruler of all things, now or in the past or in the future.

– Marcus Aurelius, Meditations

All circumstances following a human decision would have been already considered and coined by causation and necessity. The Stoic movement extended its significance far beyond the reign of Marcus Aurelius. In fact, Stoicism is highly popular today for more than one reason. Some modern Stoics still use the phrase "if the Fates allow" [124] in their communications, which I find utterly charming.

Stoic thinking is built on the foundations of a strong character, discipline, and steadfastness in the face of misadventure, in harmony with the guiding principle. Character, actually, is Destiny. [125]

Stoics, especially the "top management philosopher" Epictetus, featured his version of compatibilism (free will within a determinism), including personal virtues in concert with liberty, possibility, and action, a kind of rational harmony of human freedom and Destiny. [126] He believed the world worked under the laws of necessity and chance while mortals could act responsibly.

Stoic philosophy is ideal for those with well-connected left–right brains and oodles of self-restraint, plus a high-functioning executive prefrontal cortex, an important part of the brain residing behind our foreheads. It basically runs our most complex mental and moral processes and, if developed well, is an executive gift of factual good fortune.

The Epicureans (ca. 307 BCE), that plucky philosophical movement that originated from the ideas of their founder Epicurus (341–270 BCE), cheekily denied mortals the option to blame fate for what may go wrong in their lives. For these seekers of balance and grounded sensible hedonistic pleasures and freedoms, everyone should be capable of voluntary action, so long as they do it logically and rationally. Epicureans argued that perceiving Nature and existence on an atomic level would, at some point, explain life and the world around them. They also stood tall for their views that mortals should prioritize a peaceful life, avoiding pain but filled with joy, kind of "while it lasts." The highly tolerant Epicurus taught that, likely, the Gods existed but that they weren't interested in the mortal world (too busy being absolutely divine). According to him, the atomic universe created itself by necessity and chance, without a creator-God(dess), and there was no eternal journey or an afterlife of the soul to be had.

> *Is God willing to prevent evil, but not able? Then he is not omnipotent.*
> *Is he able, but not willing? Then he is malevolent.*
> *Is he both able and willing? Then whence cometh evil?*
> *Is he neither able nor willing? Then why call him God?*
>
> — Epicurus

We need to briefly visit the so-called Idle or Lazy Argument (*De Interpretatione* by Aristotle and notions of Chrysippus) the Roman statesman and orator Cicero (106–43 CE) tried to refute in his book *De Fato* (On Fate). He built a case against Stoic views by emphasizing the existence of human freedom to act ethically on the grounds of moral principles outside a total diktat of fatum but within certain "co-destined," natural-necessity-determined causations. The Idle or Lazy Argument poses an interesting philosophical paradox since it is both a confirmation and a denial of fatalism. [127]

It is fascinating to see that both sides still argue today, getting, well, nowhere. More on that later.

Are we able to control our destinies and carry through with free actions? Are we even at liberty to exercise volition and do everything we want to do? There will always be internal and external circumstances that prevent us from doing so.

Thomas Hobbes (1588–1679), a British philosopher who believed in the compatibility of free will and causal necessity, held that to experience liberty, we must be able to act without regard for external factors—provided there are no impediments. According to him, freedom is our capacity to choose between action and inaction within limits set by our capacity.

David Hume (1711–1776), a Scottish Enlightenment philosopher, added to this compatibilist view, noting that human liberty rests upon the fact that so long as someone isn't in prison or bound by chains, they have the freedom to decide whether they should or shouldn't take action on something they desire—all within a deterministic world.

The laws of causality do not negate human agency to a degree.

Free will and free action are two different concepts. The fact that we cannot reach our goal due to events beyond our control does not render our intentions to achieve what we wanted redundant. Our aspirations remain valid even if they never come to fruition. We are also free to tweak our ideas and adjust our plans in such a way that we may yet reach our destination despite obstacles, just perhaps slower and in different ways. The gift of savvy thinking and flexibility will never cease giving, even if we cannot reach our desired destination due to events beyond our control. Let's see what the German philosopher and compatibilist Arthur Schopenhauer had to say:

A man can do what he wants, but he cannot will what he wills.

Der Mensch kann zwar tun was er will, aber er kann nicht wollen, was er will.

– Arthur Schopenhauer, On the Freedom of the Will

Freedom to will is the main component of moral responsibility. When a thunderstorm destroys the roof of our house and devastates all its contents, we believe this happened as an act of Nature, a totally random occurrence. Unpleasant, but what are we going to do? Yet, if some yahoos break into our house to steal and vandalize our belongings, their actions will result in moral blame, and the demand for the culprits to be found and punished will arise quickly. If a person dies by lightning, not much judgment will occur. Yet, outrage and condemnation are the norms if a drunk driver terminates a person's life.

Destruction and death occur no matter what, but the human source of both makes all the difference concerning acceptance and demand for consequences.

Pondering control over our destinies and the degrees of responsibility that come with it, we will see why it is essential to care about the available level of freedom—and to understand the high degree of accountability via ego-reduction necessary for the portion of choice we can control. Equally, (ab)using the principles of Destiny recklessly as reasons for certain events such as war, power obsession, withdrawal of human rights and liberties, etc., is highly problematic due to the misleading and untrue nature of the claims.

To declare society's problems, personal or political schemes a predetermined course of a country, or even humankind, seemingly destined even, only to blame the resulting woes on unseen agents in the universe, is yet another fall from grace. That corrupt, if not dangerous, worldview must be thwarted as an absolute necessity. Destiny is never the reason nor the instrument for any mortal's or government's naked ambitions. Caveat emptor, for there'll await massive dragons.

The Cult of Free Will and Ego

Socrates believed humans will always wish for that which is good and beneficial over what they believe to be inferior or bad. Plato and Aristotle stated that once humans encounter "the good," they never stoop to do anything evil.

Free will. There are those who claim it to be an illusion we humans operate under to make us feel better, and then there are those of us who believe that free will is a question of character and honor, while there are quite a few thinkers maintaining the golden middle path. Let's imagine free will as a cute, rustic girl or boy reclining in a field of wheat or rye, enjoying a cheeky sunbath instead of toiling like the rest, playfully chewing on a straw, humming a cheerful little melody, blissfully convinced of inhabiting the top of our game. But what if we aren't?

Wishes and intentions are uniquely human specifics. And human home rule *is* a compelling concept. But what if we live in a deterministic universe, after all? And, even more interesting, what if the fatalists, atheists, existentialists, absurdists, and even the nihilists have a point or two?

Nutshell recap: Free will is present if we're in control of our choices and actions without any third-party or outside involvement and if alternative options are available to us to do either or otherwise, with the resulting consequence of full moral responsibility. The notion of free will alone is accepted as sufficient to render us ethically competent.

The concept of autonomy is crucial for the consented functioning of our personal, societal, and legal interactions, and the more humans populate this planet, the more individual volition is a desired social construct. Without it, God(s) and humans would carry too much or too little responsibility. Would religion become less attractive due to the lack of theodicy and rising reasoning that no God is all-powerful in the face of the towering universe and Nature? And in our daily lives, would we all descend into gaping chaos?

Let's remember: Free will's philosophical champions on Earth are libertarians, while the agents of free will negation are determinists.

Understandably, independence has been on humanity's bucket list from the early days of the Greek philosophers. At first, themes of finding meaning in existence, followed by the growing spheres of virtue, ethics, and morality, were the main drivers behind this perennial debate. We discovered we could not be reduced to rudderless boats on Poseidon's sea. But then, and before long, free choice was declared an excellent tool to exculpate God(s) from originally claimed authorship for everything that's ever going to happen, which includes horrible events and natural acts. So, to delegate full responsibility for all things uncool, we were granted fully-fledged autonomy, both under the divine and the worldly law, to address our sins and questionable acts. To this day, certain systems fear implosion if redoubtable evidence is delivered that our absolute freedom may just be a wish and willful thinking, a symbolic instrument, a myth.

As already discussed, the ongoing skirmishes between the moral complexities of determinism, let alone Destiny versus varied degrees of human free will, show no signs of abating.

Nutshell recap: Determinism refers to situations when, due to a natural or previously instigated chain of cosmic causality or the will of an unseen force, no other options are left open to any intentions, decisions, and actions we might wish to take. The cookie always crumbles the way it does because said cookie had already crumbled in advance. If freedom is with us, so are alternatives and diverse routes to our unhampered decision-making processes and actions. But what if the array of options is just another form of caused occurrence and thus determined, or maybe even destined?

For centuries, predominantly Western civilization has been led to believe we come with oodles of inbuilt free will and ample control as icing on the cake, plus a giant cherry. It's become an expected, accepted, and agreed social construct of reality. But does that make it necessarily true? Does human self-determination exist, or is it just another item of conventional wisdom? Could we be far more manipulated than we want to believe? We are ever so busy thinking about how free we should be, what we want, and, more importantly, what we don't want. Our one-of-a-kind, brilliant personalities must count in every way, specifically in grander contexts. Maybe, just maybe, we forget how remote-controlled we might be and that our craving for freedom is just a fun feature embedded in our determined programming.

The once purely metaphysical debate about free will versus determinism is almost as old as me, with no one being the wiser regarding proving or disproving free choice.

Also, not everyone has liberal access to the fine concept of choice. Poverty, illness, and religious or social challenges are more than sufficient to disable the whole construct and turn it into a mirage for far too many of us. Exceptions and outliers don't count in this sad human equation, for not all are born resilient and perseverent. Or lucky.

But, over these last 100 or so years, change is in the air since several philosophical schools claiming mortal autonomy and different versions of compatibilism are increasingly challenged by the findings of neuroscience, neurobiology, and even quantum physics.

Is free will a fact, or are we preordained and predetermined by covert forces and events? Does everyone have more or less free will, or is just a group of *chosen* or even lucky ones vested in fully autonomous volition? And if so, why and how?

Is the concept itself a fact or a Fata Morgana, a mere handy mirage? Do we command it, or are we just told we must have it? Just like the other must-have ideation of a special purpose in life?

It has to be noted that living under full-blown determinism would not deny humans the unique wish for cake, but the proverbial eating *and* keeping it might become an entirely different matter.

But perhaps we can be both: selectively free-willing agents in a partially determined universe?

Philosophically, the school of compatibilism—the doctrine of soft determinism supporting sensible responsibility in a deterministic cosmos—offers a take on bridging this ideological rift. John Martin Fischer's idea of semicompatibilism claims that determinism and moral responsibility for human actions are not mutually exclusive but compatible.

But even this harmonic stance continues to be a hot potato, thrown about between the scientific opinions of, as already briefly mentioned, the neuroscientist Sam Harris and the philosopher Daniel Dennett on several occasions. Same old song, just the band is new. It is all online.

While early humanity accepted supernatural guidance rather willingly, the dawn of ancient Greek philosophy inspired a particular kind of human independence and a good portion of mastery of human Destiny. Free will means uninfluenced liberty to opt in or out of various choices and alternative routes. It also implies the acceptance of responsibility for our deeds, inviting governments, religions, and society to expect and demand us to bow to any ruling ideology. Exercising unrestrained free will also leads to the logical consequence of enabling said bodies to cast verdicts on our behavior, often on moral grounds. Many see absolute autonomy as a human *conditio sine qua non*—a total condition and prerogative. Quite a few others feel that this freedom might just be a mirage. And science has one or two things to say about that, too.

Take Benjamin Libet's paradigm: *Humans don't have free will.* In 1983, he and his colleagues discovered that human decisions are preordained by the unconscious and executed by our brains, a good deal *before* we think to have acted deliberately through our presumed free will. Their *readiness potential* is highly debated. In 2012, neuroscientist Aaron Schurger published his findings that many decisions are preceded by *random neural noise.*

Sam Harris, the author of *Free Will* (2012) and other thought-provoking books, suggests the concepts of free will "cannot be mapped onto any conceivable reality."

> *Free will is an illusion. Our wills are simply not of our own making. Thoughts and intentions emerge from background causes of which we are unaware and over which we exert no conscious control. We do not have the freedom we think we have.*
>
> – SAM HARRIS

The philosopher and determinist Gregg D. Caruso agrees and wrote an eminent book on the same topic—*Free Will and Consciousness: A Determinist Account of the Illusion of Free Will* (2012)—in which he questions absolute human liability vis-à-vis all those many factors beyond our control. Fortunately, the majority of us are inclined to feel and practice moral responsibility.

No matter how thin you slice it, there will always be two sides.
– Baruch Spinoza

We sometimes have the ability of even full intent and purpose to selective action self-determination, given necessary or favorable internal and external conditions and circumstances. As we may have noticed, bleak fatalism is not an option in the realm of Destiny.

So, why do I call this chapter The Cult of Free Will and Ego? Because, IMO, far too much insistence on what we will and what we want, fueled by oodles of ego and entitlement, is at play.

Most of our actions aren't driven by our glorified self-determination but are caused by facts and patterns we've inherited, learned, experienced, and internalized. We remind me of children who mirror and resonate with parents or caregivers. Ego will always insist on control based on what it, often misguidedly, believes to be a direct expression of its uniqueness, freedom, and personal choice. The proper *self* does not rest on the ego. Healthy selfhood is anchored, accepting given bounds while embracing the challenge of exploring and expanding opportunities. No wonder the principles of Destiny and karma never harmonize with excess ego.

There it is, the old but golden paradox of absolute liberty. We'll likely never be able to control our wants and desires because the unaware or subconscious part of our mind takes charge way before we may blissfully convince ourselves to have made a conscious choice. It's understandably hard to accept for some, but the unconscious mind runs around 90 percent of our echo chambers and experience-based thoughts and behavioral patterns. Our self-image predominantly consists of some kind of wishful thinking and the stories our brain tells our mind to compose and produce our perceived reality, or rather realities, for there appear to be plenty. Just like a studio project. Humans need to create beliefs to make sense of being alive. One of these beliefs may just be the idea of absolute free will and individuality, for example, yearning for a slice of omnipotence and the illusion of a smorgasbord of liberties. That is rather cute, as long as we are not wrongly influencing or harming others with dogmatism and ill-advised ideology. Another fun bit: We even lack access to the data we process, so hey!

The philosopher Parmenides of Elea (ca. 515–450 BCE or 530–470 BC) wrote a revelatory poem, sadly only preserved in fragments, now called *On Nature*. He narrates his journey to the gates of Destiny, where the Goddesses Ananke and Moira enlighten him about the untrustworthiness of mortal opinions and their perceptions of the world. [128] An ancient hint to the difference between sensory and rational validity?

For Aristotle, a naturally ethical and conscious person is holder and keeper of virtues [129] like dignity, honesty, fortitude, and fairness. Such an excellent being would hardly be negatively affected by philosophically limited autonomy since they would understand and act on her determinants of ethical intentions and behavior. And they would know the importance of decent human interactions, not because of rules, but because they've internalized proper sense, probity, and consideration for others as well as themselves as their best way to live. Not for the laws of anyone or anything, not human, God(s), or government induced, but as a consistent, reliable part of their self-possession and self-actualization.

It's just like with love and loyalty: Ideally, we don't remain faithful because we are told to but because that's what we *want* to do, as per our intrinsic values. We don't steal just because a text says it's forbidden; we don't steal because we don't want to take away what belongs to others. This innate knowing and resolve can result in exercising personal integrity with a good portion of free will. It's self-accountability, built on necessary principles to keep the world around us stable. We can follow our standards or personal code of moral sense before any third-party rule, quietly and dignified, holding ourselves responsible. And the bar is set high; the proverbial ante can't go up any further. Tough but terrific. And it's the opposite of popular abundant lip service and moral signaling, claiming to be a person that plays by the book but doesn't.

If in the order of Nature, and by divine destiny, a man were able to apprehend the truth about these things, he would have no need of laws to rule over him.

— Plato, The Republic

Self-accountability and restraint remain major factors in exercising the gift of liberty and maintaining responsible excellence. Emphatically speaking, anyone unlucky enough not to have been born with or to have developed inner resilience and authentic integrity may require a lot more understanding before applying prejudice or judgment.

Not everyone is strong. Not everyone can handle responsibilities and consequences well. Are most of us highly functioning self-determiners? If we were and could, we'd already have reached a form of transhumanism. Those born without or with too little empathy often fail to understand what it feels like to grow up in a desperate precariat or to be stressed by mentally challenged parents. We need a heck of a lot of compassion to rise above that problem-blindness to understand what it feels like to grow up under such circumstances. Most cannot relate to situations they've never experienced. It takes courage and tolerance to overcome the boundaries of ignorance, while it is easy to judge and discard.

Life is not just all down to volition, let alone human control, and no one is either good or bad. We are complex, feeling, not always primarily analytical and conscious, often unaware travelers on a rather deterministic plain. Conditions may lift or befall us, good or bad, and mostly undeserved. We can be at the wrong place at the wrong time or hit a serendipitous spot running. We can be born into an environment that leaves traces on us, either a protective layer of sane love, character-building, and empowerment or emotional scars from deprivation and mental and physical abuse. It's not all our fault. We aren't born sinners, and sin is an arbitrary concept anyway. We are human, warts and all. We *can* learn. We *can* even overcome obstacles and, sometimes, ourselves. We are able to rise above the parapet and achieve wonderful and horrible things. What matters is that we don't give up trying to act responsibly within the framework of our inner and outer determinants.

Or, as my grandmother said, paraphrasing Plato:

Ignorance is not a disgrace, but to deliberately stay ignorant is disgraceful.

Building bridges is vital. Again, credit is indeed due to the American philosopher John Martin Fischer's elegant and sleek theory of semicompatibilism. [130]

We *can* think, feel, and act responsibly, even in a deterministic universe. And we can learn to muster the ability to discover and internalize the options. That is part of our Destiny.

Knowing how, why, and when to do the right thing can result in a (semi)compatibilist balance between *what is as it is* and what we actually can pull off. Because we intend to. Because we can *choose* that as our schtick, M.O., or thing as often as possible. Common sense and compassion are the leading buzzwords here.

How much do we know, though?

Albert Einstein's theory of relativity enlightened humanity with his idea of the unity of acceleration-gravity, time, and space, providing his time with a new way to mirror humankind in the many eyes of the universe.

When we observe the wealth of his work, we begin to fathom that it also explains how Mother Nature is likely sharply organized despite her seemingly apparent chaos and diversity. By creating theories of unity, Einstein laid the foundation for generations of scientists to come up with fancy concepts like superstring theories. To him, life was about our sense of being and natural potential.

Everything is determined by forces over which we have no control.
It is determined for the insect as well as for the star. Human
beings, vegetables, or cosmic dust—we all dance to a mysterious
tune, intoned in the distance by an invisible piper.

– ALBERT EINSTEIN

The idea of our *self* as the sole source of our destinies is commonly found in existentialism and other beliefs that reject the idea of a supreme power that assigns and guides human beings. Fair enough, as long as no cult of the ego is found at the center of some of these ideologies, vindicating selfishness with a nifty excuse. Much milder, this is also valid in some ideas of the New Age, where we are essentially souls with bodies on a journey to discover higher spiritual essence that may unlock hidden strength.

By putting ourselves at the center of the quest to find purpose, followers of the New Age often support independent self-determination, which isn't all too egotistical.

To the more self-involved faction of egoism—the puffed-up fancying of personal significance, or even the more negative egotism that lends total focus on ourselves—often neither a caring divinity nor a beckoning universe plays a role in that human experience because who or what could be greater than the empty *moi*? It may work for a time, but never forever. That said, egomania is also found in ardent followers of varied dogmatic systems or individuals because it just suits the me-obsessed agenda. However, any of these ego-tripping "isms" are neither vice nor virtue but, to an extent, deserve sympathy because we don't know what pushed us into these poor human versions. Selfishness, one of humanity's banes, isn't a prerequisite for lasting success and is never a classically destinal trait, arguably not driven by our genes but by early experiences that could have turned wounds into distorted hyper-selves.

When placing individual whim into the absolute center to gain self-optimization through navel-orbiting only, we set ourselves above all others, craving and claiming a sense of special meaning for everything we think and do. That's how we can become delusional. We will only listen to those telling us what we want to hear. An overinflated ego is often a red flag for an underlying affliction or personality challenge. So maybe we need to behold the growing portion of ego worshippers with more understanding and even compassion instead of just downright judging them.

Putting self-interest above all else can help us feel pretty special and our existence less banal. But life is not a case of accomplishing the next fad to tickle our fancies to unlock unknown, undiscovered potential. No wonder self-centeredness is an increasingly popular and disturbing trait observed in the likes of politicians, including hubris, self-righteousness, and vainglory to boot. Doesn't the path appear more enticing if comrade ego walks with us?

Naked selfishness is self-deception, and often, the more ego-involved we feel, the less affection we have for ourselves. It is a dark Destiny, a fate even to be unable to inspire unadulterated respect and loyalty in others. On both sides, ulterior motives, materialism, and lip service may seep in far too quickly.

> *From this same fault springs also that universal conviction that one's own folly is wisdom, with its consequences that we fancy we know everything when we know as good as nothing, refuse to allow others to manage a business we do not understand, and fall into inevitable errors in transacting it for ourselves. Every man, then, must shun extreme self-love and follow ever in the steps of his better, undeterred by any shame for his case.*
>
> – PLATO, LAWS

Grounded self-respect, self-possession, and acceptance, in combination with generosity and compassion towards others, is the epitome of goodness. I suggest reading Aristotle's *Nicomachean Ethics* (especially Book 9), one of Western philosophy's most influential texts on moral choice. It explores what it means to live virtuously within eudaimonia (Greek for being animated and favored by a daemon of goodness). Aristotle states that humans possess the capacity for moral choice and can only be held responsible for their actions if two conditions are met: control over them and explicit knowledge about what they're doing.

He acknowledged that ethically sound people often choose the right thing out of a sense of goodness-inspired duty. Plato understood that not all actions are predestined, yet an honorable life can be lived through acts of integrity, kindness, and care for those around us. What a great goal to pursue if we are born with such philosophical insight and moral superiority or lucky enough to be tutored in these values early in life! But what if our environment at birth doesn't auto-foster Platonian, Aristotelian, or Kantian ideals? Even then, it remains our spiritual responsibility to defend such standards while also surviving; yet, to always do so, we'd need a wonderfully whispering daemon by our side to keep us out of trouble and defeat evil while maintaining our superior moral standing.

We better cut ourselves and others some slack since too many world children aren't exactly born into ideal philosophical conditions, and those lovely daemons are few and far between these days.

Greek philosophy promoted a somewhat healthy sense of caring for the self. They originally named it *eudaimonia*, which from Greek translates to the art of living well. Altruism, caring for the well-being and happiness of others, i.e., less talk and theory but more investment of practically applied time and coin, played a significant part in the Stoic views of virtues and values. Aristotle was a fan of eudaimonia.

Some more recent perspectives, like the famous Law of Attraction, point to our wishes as the source and goal of all meaning, enticing the universe to conspire the materialization of favorable, especially materially enriching, circumstances.

Except our own thoughts, there is nothing absolutely in our power.
                                        – René Descartes

So here we are—the world of thoughts versus the deterministic realm.

Is free will just a human idea and thus only in our anyway subjective heads?

Modern psychology and neuroscience stipulate we are capable of achieving high potential through consistent learning and experience, seemingly suggesting the idea of the *tabula rasa* or the blank slate proposed by the philosopher John Locke. A person, essentially, is seen as an empty canvas endowed with experience. Innatism is a theory expanded by the philosophers Plato, Descartes, and Leibniz, postulating that a soul can enter a new life with an inborn, hard-wired recollection of certain mindsets, knowledge, and even a spiritual memory, ready to be released and improved upon. To me, it is a form of Destiny, be it carried forward from a previous life or given to achieve forethought results.

And why should many of us not be born with an innate capacity for doing the right thing? Why should it be impossible that, through the process of acquiring insight, we can follow our inner voice or elect to consider any belief that could provide meaning to our existence and assign it as an additional source to our Destiny? While we know systems of faith and control that provide moral dogma to prescribe thoughts and actions as the ultimate goal for humankind, it is still up to each of us to elect those systems as guidance or reject them. It is exactly this quiet inner ability and freedom granted to us human beings to listen to our inner voices.

Governmental systems like free will almost more than codified religions do. Indeed, a healthy sense of self-actualization can be one of the personal forces to emphasize the necessary determination. While many of us feel more secure and even well provided for under the wings of a state or an organized belief system, it should not mean that being part of a collective equates to signing over individual aspirations and ideals. Throughout history, humankind fought for liberty and increasingly resisted oppression, which is likely the best kind of collective self-actualization available.

I would like to convince biologists that a belief in free will is nothing other than a continuing belief in vitalism (or, as I say, a belief in magic).

– PROFESSOR ANTHONY CASHMORE [131]

I reckon that our authentic selfhood can only thrive by sticking to our intrinsic values. That alone makes for a lot of luxurious freedom. When we're in sync with our personal and even our collective Destiny, things begin to shift! We can see ourselves, the future, our relationships, and even the planet in a whole new light. Tricky bit: We still need to discover how consciousness works or how we form our beliefs. The whole free will versus determinism debate is ongoing and without one clear answer in sight. All we can know for sure is that many ideas, different motivations, and loads of vested interests are out there.

Best keep our toys in the pram and be grateful to have those options to subjectively choose from in a world that will, or so I still expect, retain tolerance for different ideas, results, and perspectives. Our innermost essence as human(e) individuals is complemented by genetic and epigenetic precursors managed by neural and biological processing that influences our perceptions and personal interpretations of ourselves within our realities and environments. A manifold lack of control just comes with being human. We process our experiences mainly subjectively. Over time, or as a response to psychological stressors, we can even construct them into our own truth concepts. On top of these homemade narratives, we have a tendency to go by what we're told to accept as gospel by the agents of dogma and ideology. How about two unpopular but regardlessly necessary questions? Does objectivity even exist? Or is it just another dream state or self-generated certainty surplus to the factuality of birth and death? Maybe an objective and absolute reality, let alone *the* truth, dwells far beyond limited human grasp? And will we ever be added to the mailing list?

We should not split hairs and believe we are smarter than the next wo(man). Everything exists, and all is either kind of right or not. Likely both. Infinity is uncontrollable, no matter how much we mortals desire shreds of leverage while worshiping our obsession with sovereignty.

Whether determinists, compatibilists, or libertarians are right, the fact is that all our lives are interconnected to create one shared human Destiny. It's humanity's job to balance this world between the given and desired pillars. Probably, all is somehow natural and fluently complementary.

Considering the challenges ahead, many perspectives need to be reviewed. As so often in history, we may just have to gracefully accept the natural maxims of the *as well as* instead of the *either this or that.*

And given how our current information age develops—with all its perks and growing top-down control technologies—we may not be too concerned with the question of whether we are the managers over our lives, perceptions, wishes, and decisions or not, since right now it is all going in just one direction.

> *Free will without Fatum is no more conceivable than spirit without matter, good without evil.*
>
> – FRIEDRICH NIETZSCHE, FATE AND HISTORY

When Science Meets Destiny

Science has always been and will remain invested in the future, spurring scientists and mathematicians to investigate how our shared human Destiny may unfold. Different branches of science, such as physics, neurobiology, and biochemistry, make remarkable advances toward unraveling this mystery.

Is the universe moving in an orderly, predictable direction? If so, all possibilities within the cosmos might already have been determined because all particles would behave along a single trajectory, including our human minds.

Sir Isaac Newton's theory of motion strengthened deterministic opinions due to empirical evidence of causality. With Newton's classical mechanics, it became possible for empiricists to shift away from codified theories of origin.

Gottfried Leibniz (1646–1716), a distinguished German philosopher and mathematician, already pondered humanity moving away from religious dogma in the light of the explanation of the universe's origin and that, as a consequence, scientists could attain Godlike knowledge.

It is not that things happen to each of us according to his fate, but that he interprets what has happened, if he has power to do so, according to his sense of his own destiny.

– SIR ISAAC NEWTON

Later and in contrast, Charles Darwin (1809–1882) challenged Newton's mechanistic view of the cosmos with his revolutionary theory of evolution. Recognizing the diversity of human genes, Darwin proposed the unpredictable nature of future developments.

Neuroscientists argue that we adopt certain habits resulting in choices according to our upbringing and environment, which seems to question the idea that we are born with full-blown self-ordination and perform uninfluenced actions. Biological breakthroughs also champion the notion that chance or randomness in Nature is a necessary enabler of human evolution.

Quantum mechanics introduced a new understanding of free will. Formerly, most philosophers and classical scientists tried to reconcile determinism, human freedom, and even Destiny. Yet, with the fact that the quantum theory perspective of the universe may work in indeterminate patterns, the debate about human freedom is ongoing. Have earlier scientists been asking the wrong questions about the destination of humanity? If the universe can only be calculated according to statistical probabilities of larger objects, chaotic and random from the atomic perspective, would we humans even participate in deciding its Destiny?

Science is increasingly concerned with the idea of a cosmos changing at rates not yet measured, while some scientists, instead, focus on the vision of how far humankind can possibly go. World-renowned theoretical physicist Michio Kaku is one of the thinkers behind the (Pythagorean) musical vibration-based String Theory. He is the author of *The God Equation* (2021), bridging the gap between science and faith. In 2012 and 2018, he envisaged how humanity could approach and find its technological, universal, and cosmic destinies in two groundbreaking books. [132] [133]

What signifies being destined? When we first set eyes on the love of our life, win success and acclaim, or are unexplainably invigorated to fulfill our aspirations and achieve our loftiest goals, should we not wonder how much of this could be actual Destiny? Easy enough because it's all good stuff. But equally, what about those of us without sunny paths, seemingly condemned to endure lives of struggle lacking even the slightest chance of improvement, riddled with poverty and illness perhaps, or oppressed and limited by the culture born into and consequently trapped? Are such predicaments destinal, or are all complex outcomes merely the result of randomness or "fated" bad luck? Would that not declare Destiny a class phenomenon reserved for the chosen only, the special ones, the outliers, and the proverbially favored agents of pluck and ministers of bravery, the designated agents of Destiny, the ones with so much if not all in their gift? And no, again, we're not talking about karma here

More on that in the next book.

For many centuries, we ascribed life's great opportunities and memorable moments to the edict of Destiny's supra-powers. This belief is ingrained in sayings such as *what will be, will be,* or that things happen because they are *meant to be* or a *twist of fate.* Yet, of late, contrary to the classic narrative of a mythological and metaphysical plan of supernatural origins, the world is being presented with scientific facts that, to some, are perhaps unwelcome.

In 2019, Dr. Hannah Critchlow released *The Science of Fate: Why Your Future is More Predictable Than You Think*. In her book, Dr. Critchlow, a respected neuroscientist with a background in neuropsychiatry and a Fellow of Magdalene College, Cambridge, explores the deep programming of a person's future due to their genes and environment. She's been proclaimed one of the top 100 scientists in the United Kingdom, addressing the possible myth that humans have total control of our lives and fortunes. Can we be reduced to mere marionettes simply held and driven by the strings of our genetic inheritance, brains, and habitats, vulnerable, neurotic, thin-skinned bio-machines devoid of transcendence? As per the latest science, human genes and environments compose uniquely woven fabrics in the brain that could be responsible for the predictable outcomes of our lives in the future.

Through research and understanding the roles our genetic and epigenetic markers play in our physical journeys, we can begin to decode the options in some, if not many, areas of our lives.

Destinal Psychology

Human liberty presupposes conscious decisions and habits. With this argument, the ability of a human being to be open to different views on Destiny through psychology offers a striking polarity necessary to understand ourselves and learn who we (think) we are.

> *Eros and Ananke (Love and Necessity/Destiny) have become the parents of human civilization.*
>
> — SIGMUND FREUD

Austrian nineteenth and twentieth-century psychiatrist Sigmund Freud made one of the earliest attempts in psychology to remove the concept of Moira from sheer mythology. According to Freud, our actions are based on desires *and drive destinies* craving satisfaction. Dr. Freud defined the reasons for behavioral patterns stemming from the conflict of these instinctual longings. And our behavioral Destiny, according to Freud, is woven by three constants in a person's life—the conditions of our ego-controlled self-preservation, an erotic life drive, and death. And our parents, of course.

> *It would be very nice if there were a God who created the world and was a benevolent providence, and if there were a moral order in the universe and an after-life but it is a very striking fact that all this is exactly as we are bound to wish it to.*
>
> — Sigmund Freud

Freud was an outstanding, special kind of atheist with spectacular achievements. Yet he also saw homo sapiens as driven by fear and desire lurking in the subconscious only to lead us astray, which paints us quite irrational and aggressive. And he stated, *"Destiny is anatomy,"* meaning that our gender practically decides our fate, voicing the sad facts of patriarchal and religious prejudice, judging women as inferior to men.

Furthermore, theorized by the good doctor, women are envious of males' few swinging extra centimeters. Well, science and society progressed and more or less debunked the otherwise quite brilliant Dr. Siggi several times over.

Early psychoanalysis argued that the ladies were more susceptible to mood swings because of their physical nature, rendering them unreliable regarding the more serious stuff, such as politics, philosophy, or science. Misogynistic views made biological facts redundant, such as PMS, since even learned scientists of those days were ignorant of hormonal influences on both sexes, resulting in misguided conjecture. According to some worldviews, women are still judged as less valuable for various reasons. According to those cultures, women are also feebler than men, thus, weaker and less productive. Well, tick-tock.

The misconstrued concept that *destiny is anatomy* sadly also helped to undermine ethnicities.

Cultural minorities were often expected, if not pushed, to believe they'd never have the power to escape the yoke of racist prejudice. In the past, that may have meant being enslaved, forced to live under the exploitative rule of foreign colonizers, having next to no rights, and being pressed to serve under unacceptable conditions while barred from higher education and careers. We were simply expected to know and accept our place and resign ourselves to a white-man-made pseudo-fate that self-styled supreme systems insisted on being true.

At the same time, ethnic minorities were coerced to identify with the made-up inferiority of their race and subscribe to a hopeless notion of oppression, which also meant deprivation of personal aspirations. Identifying with such manipulated ideas of discriminatory, counterfeit Destiny can lead to deep feelings of weakness and resignation, even resulting in a painful mentality of victimhood, a disadvantage easily abused by the unscrupulous.

Fortunately, times were and are changing, and, at last, we are slowly but firmly moving in the only direction.

Swiss psychoanalyst and psychiatrist Carl Gustav Jung (1875–1961) held unique personal views on the relevance of Destiny that seem to originate in personal experience.

From the beginning, I had a sense of destiny, as though my life was assigned to me by fate and had to be fulfilled. This gave me an inner security, and, though I could never prove to myself, it proved itself to me. I did not have the certainty, it had me.
— CARL JUNG, MEMORIES, DREAMS AND REFLECTIONS

Jung believed that each psyche or soul consisted of different yet connective strands: the ego, the personal, and the collective unconscious.

A person can transform through self-development and create their future through self-actualization.
— CARL JUNG

The now ubiquitous, simplistic, slightly doubtable, and rather binary Myer-Briggs Type Indicator or MBTI,[134] also dubbed *Astrology for Businessmen,* was originally developed based on Jung's book *Psychological Types* and his credible ideas of human personality traits.

Carl Gustav Jung also created the concept of synchronicity that deciphered what he called *meaningful coincidences*, which, just like his archetypes theory of the self, the persona, the shadow, and the Animus/ Anima, remains prevalent.

The ancients devised magic to compel fate. They needed it to determine outer fate. We need it to determine inner fate and to find the way that we are unable to conceive.

– Carl Jung, The Red Book

Individuals who believe they are masters of their fate are as a rule the slaves of destiny.

– Carl Jung, letter to Valentine Brooke

That which you do not bring to consciousness comes to you as your Fate, that which you do bring to consciousness, whether it was what you thought you wanted or not, is your Destiny. The right way to wholeness is made up of fateful detours and wrong turnings.

– Carl Jung

The Viennese psychiatrist and neurologist Viktor Frankl (1905–1997) survived the ordeals of four of Nazi Germany's infamous concentration camps, only to learn upon liberation that he had lost his father, brother, mother, and wife to the brutality of the Third Reich. During his captive years, Frankl never gave up trying to encourage his fellow prisoners who, like himself, were challenged to breaking point, understandably losing hope and giving in to despair. He asked them to remember precious personal memories and stories and hold on to these happy moments. Frankl himself didn't break, not even when learning that he would not see his beloved wife again in this life. Based on his tragic experience, Frankl developed *Logotherapy* (healing through meaning), which he built on the purpose of life and even suffering, the latter to be counteracted by mindset and attitude, and wrote the eye-opening world bestseller *Man's Search for Meaning.*

When a man finds that it is his destiny to suffer, he will have to accept his suffering as his task; his single and unique task. He will have to acknowledge the fact that even in suffering he is unique and alone in the universe. No one can relieve him of his suffering or suffer in his place.

> *The way in which a man accepts his fate and all the suffering it entails, the way in which he takes up his cross, gives him ample opportunity – even under the most difficult circumstances – to add a deeper meaning to his life.*
> — VIKTOR FRANKL, MAN'S SEARCH FOR MEANING

The American existential psychologist Rollo May (1909–1994) believed that if we want to be free, we have to affirm ourselves. This understanding of the self and how to attain freedom allows us to find significance in Destiny—accepting the purpose of our life, the calling, and the ability to reach set goals. May argued that the very construct of Destiny—a given string of seeming circumstances—is almost impossible to control. Freedom, though, is not entirely random and arbitrary. While the concept of invisible design may seem to carry many deterministic elements, it is also the core of being self-conscious and free. May's ideas of utmost freedom and Destiny are indeed interconnected and even dependent on one another in the intentional creation of meaning and personal growth in the face of adversity.

Rollo May, just like the ancient Greeks with their Moira—the personified principle, and I never distinguished between Destiny and fate but perceived both entities to be elements of the one cosmic principle, defined as different concepts.

Cosmic Destiny—unforeseeable forces of Nature we cannot control.

Genetic Destiny—manifesting as biological aspects inherited from our ancestors.

Circumstantial Destiny—events like war or a pandemic over which we lack direct influence.

Cultural Destiny—the unchosen societal constellations we are born into, like family, nationality, religion, and early upbringing.

> *It is the design of the universe speaking through the design of each one of us.*
>
> – ROLLO MAY

It takes a seriously self-actualized individual to approach, accept and fulfill a factual Destiny with an open mind and eyes. And what is freedom without necessary constraints?

Leopold Szondi (1893–1986), a Hungarian psychiatrist and professor of psychology, taught that human Destiny was predetermined unconsciously by human genetics. He observed how hereditary conditions greatly influence our lives, our environment, and the health patterns of the generations before us.

To Szondi, even romantic decisions like whom to marry and have children with are controlled by genetic and familial circumstances. He proposed that humans have a set of possible traits that stem from recessive genes they carry, and these traits influence our behavior for life. But he did not say that humans are incapable of making choices independently.

When we look at Szondi's notion of Destiny, it comes across as neither predetermined nor wholly based on free choices. Between 1944 and 1963, Szondi published five volumes of his *Fate Analysis*. He also created the *Szondi Test*—a non-verbal projective personality assessment. To Szondi, genes and selective other factors form the vital plan within an individual's unconscious. [135]

The US psychologist Abraham Maslow (1908–1970), who invented the *Hierarchy of Needs,* [136] based on his theory of fostering psychological well-being through prioritization and fulfillment of human needs leading to self-actualization, found *metamotivation* to be at the core of…

...dedicated people, devoted to some task "outside themselves," some vocation, or duty, or beloved job.
   – Abraham Maslow, Farther Reaches of Human Nature

The ever-sanguine Dr. Maslow explained further that such a vocation could even be interpreted as our *Destiny* and that *"such people are particularly talented in their field and could be called naturals."*

Metamotivation is a next-level aspiration available and advisable to those who perhaps successfully managed or achieved Maslow's originally five pyramidal [137] tiers of human needs with the goal of self-actualization from the lowest, broadest level to the top:

Physiological needs—water, food, sleep

Safety needs—security

Love and belonging—emotional/sexual relationships and friends

Esteem—regard and respect

Self-actualization—personal growth toward full potential

Self-transcendence—(intrinsic) meaning and values

And finally, let us look at *The Locus of Control*. This concept was developed by the American psychologist Julian Rotter (1916–2014).

This presumed seat of self-evaluation is a term based on his theory that those of us who operate from an *internal* locus of control command proactive power over our lives, making us more successful than the ones believing in an *external* locus of control, meaning that events in their lives are caused by outside forces like a deterministic universe, natural restraints, God(s), or Destiny.

The interesting difference is that if we acted from an internal locus of control, we'd interpret eventual results—good or bad—as emerging from our own convictions and actions under personal responsibility.

Sounds kind of easy, right? I am oversimplifying here, but can we flip our settings and change gear from external to internal, considering all the elements and factors that influence our human beingness? And what about millions of underprivileged people who have to go with the flow or trust in God(s) to decide their paths? Let's forget singular destinies for a moment. Would anyone, especially collectively, have better options to rise from the shadows of disadvantage and poverty if they ditch their worldview to switch to an internal locus of control?

Theory is one thing, challenged and practical hands-on life another.

What right do we have to presume our way of life is superior, leading to more progress, material wealth, and happiness? And even if individuals or whole cultures find strength in thinking that certain aspects of life are pre-decreed and even unavoidable—it is their right to seek and find equilibrium with whatever works for them.

Political Destiny

History vividly narrates how we view our individual and collective futures, depending a lot on the mainstream perception of public Destiny. This perception can be heavily influenced, if not controlled, by the reigning powers in any civilization. These *powers that be* include the state, the officialdom, the political caste, and respective religions. While ruling bodies create and control policies for implementation in societies, the type of rule we fall under greatly impacts how we view our freedoms and how we are expected to deliver moral responsibility. While anyone may believe in free will and the capability of free action, citizenship will always affect the amount of freedom available, depending on many factors, such as location, urban or rural habitat, and social position. In a discourse about pursuing Destiny, the government and the political situation of our country of residence will likely affect our perspective and reality of the range of acceptable liberties, beliefs, and possible actions.

The Greek philosopher Plato classified political regimes according to personal attributes and virtues of a ruler and those that exert influence over society.

Virtue is the desire of things honorable and the power of attaining them.

— PLATO, MENO

In his classification of different types of governments, Plato illustrates the kind of society that could be created out of the predictable sets of policies and the ability to implement them.

Integrity is your destiny; it is the light that guides your way.

— PLATO

Aristocracy-led societies were governed by a small, advantaged elite group exerting total control while most citizens were excluded from any participation in policymaking.

The autocratic rule dictates that only one person decides and imposes laws.

The democratic administration involves the majority of a population through the capacity to vote on how the state should be run, ideally influencing decisions made by policymakers and implementers.

All the gold which is under or upon the earth is not enough to give in exchange for virtue.

— PLATO, LAWS

In a democratic society, we can perceive ourselves as individuals capable of making decisions on how we enjoy our lives, of course, limited by certain constraints of the law and the expectations of society. Autocratic and aristocratic governments, though, may or may not consider personal liberties and the rights of the people. When we look at individual and collective Destiny in the context of political ambition and government rule, a large part of the future of us citizens is beholden to the type of policies in place until changed. Governments control a certain amount of freedom and access to resources, often putting a cap on the material wealth we accumulate, mainly through taxation and shunning any alternative options outside regulation. It also has the administration to control our behaviors, primarily exercised by penal law, governmental and societal observation, and peer pressure. Human Destiny, within and under dogmatic political governments, can often seem bleak and largely dependent on suppressing various liberties. We must never stop being vigilant. Do political governments compromise and hamper human independence? That is in the eye of the beholder. More often than not, political ambition, lack of virtue, and the chase for power of a rulership-obsessed caste always try to rein in the actual amount of freedom of choice in us. Ideally, a well-principled political system representing us and our diversity, beliefs, and lifestyle choices would be critical to protecting collective and individual rights, safeguarding the pursuit of social justice and self-actualization, to enhance our shared Destiny.

> *Good moral character is not something that we can achieve on our own. We need a culture that supports the conditions under which self-love and friendship flourish.*
>
> – ARISTOTLE

Red Thread of Civilizations

Destiny has proven to be an eternally popular term when talking about great aspirations, exploits, love, and a reason to exist; hence, entire civilizations from both hemispheres of the planet elected its meaning. It remains a pivotal argument in fields such as romance, career, and higher mission but, sadly and wrongly, also for waging war or justifying colonization.

Chinese and Japanese dynasties believed the continuation of the family's supremacy to be a part of their Destiny. Many monarchs conquered and ruled their kingdoms based on a clever mix of ruthless ambition and religious virtue signaling. But nothing beats the prophecy or legend that someone is destined to spearhead a cause or movement, let alone lead a nation. Many kingdoms and their rulers profited from nurturing the rumor that their elevation was willed and brought about by the supra-principle. And by the time a long-awaited child was born to a noble house to fill the role of the heir apparent, it was often murmured that the Goddesses of Destiny determined them to be a great hero or sovereign.

The shrewd Athenian on-off tyrant, general, and early PR expert Pisistratos (ca. 600–527) had the magic of being deity-devised down to a fine art. When it became necessary to convince the citizens of Athens to accept him back into office, he hired a tall lady to dress up as the Goddess Athena in a shield and helmet. Then he sent messengers ahead to condition the Athenians that Pisistratos was riding into town in his battle chariot towered over by Athena herself. It worked a treat. Pisistratos also excelled as an interesting prototype of a social warrior since he took from the rich and redistributed their wealth to the poor, which made him popular with the latter target group, yet with the fat cats, not so much.

Ideas about the importance of a meaningful life became progressive when philosophy introduced the concepts of virtue, justice, liberty, and ethics and values.

As a side note: The ancient Greeks were the first to develop the notion of hope in humans. The writer Hesiod records in his mythological poem *Works and Days* how Zeus punishes humanity for using the gift of fire, stolen by the titan Prometheus, by sending the beautiful Pandora among the mortals for an unboxing session of assorted evils and curses.

Another version points out that Zeus's favorite son, the amiable God and divine messenger Hermes, quickly slipped in *Elpis*—the spirit of hope—and hid her at the very bottom of the box to ease humanity's woes, just before his peeved Papa shut the calamitous container and sent Pandora on her tragical terror mission. Yet another version reports that when Pandora opened said box and launched a myriad of pains on humanity, all took flight apart from Elpis. Hope remained trapped within at Zeus's command to deprive the mortals of this last and sole recourse. It wasn't Papa's finest hour.

But the amazing and ever-so-human phenomenon we call hope made her way to us after all and has stayed with mankind ever since. Not even Zeus could hamper that.

Hope is an extraordinary power that can influence the unchangeable as long as its expectations are managed sensibly. It can even bring down a dictator, topple a corrupt government, or deal with toxic dogma. Hope counteracts and soothes despair; it lifts us to take necessary action. Thanks to Hermes, hope became a vital gift of human Destiny.

Our ancestors, like quite a few modern contemporaries, had a penchant for being God-like. Throughout antiquity, Egyptian pharaohs, Sumerian kings, and Roman emperors were given the privilege of being pronounced deities by a declaration at birth, during their lifetime, or after their passing.

Many civilizations practice(d) the tradition of ancestor worship, which gives us yet another idea of the desire to follow and deliver on our reason for being by attaining a Godly status in becoming a venerated ancestor and role model for generations to follow.

The rise of the Holy Mother Church in Rome introduced the concept that humanity's Destiny should exclusively be decreed as per God's will.

Sadly, the same holy institution cursed the world with its brutal crusades, the Inquisition, and then some. It was a gift that our ancestors rediscovered classic and especially stoic philosophy during the European Middle Ages, also prevalent in early Islamic philosophy. Thankfully, they were given center stage during the glory days of the enlightened Muslim kingdom of Al-Andaluz in Spain.

We should always remember that Islamic scholars translated the almost forgotten gems of Roman and Greek philosophy, thus re-gifting them to a darkened Europe in dire need of a few torches through a splendid revival. Greek and Roman scholarship and philosophy then returned yet again with a gentle-but-effective vengeance during the turbulent, inspired era of the Renaissance. Wisdom can never be concealed or kept down for long.

Europe began to restore the intellectual gems of the ancient Greeks, Romans, and Hebrews. The human being began to move into the spotlight of the thriving arts. With a refreshed acquisition of the teachings of Socrates, Plato, Aristotle, and Co., philosophical and political discussions were focused on the idea that humanity should aim at better destinies while upholding higher principles. This trend ushered in a radical paradigm shift in treating each other per a just law, a golden rule, and the ideal that everyone should be able to achieve a worthy life.

Fast-forward to new stances about homo sapiens' Destiny and life's purpose. As contemporary philosophy flourished, a part of humankind became slightly dubious about the existence of a supernatural power with certain levels of control over humanity. Later, modern takes on our future emerged to challenge the perspective that Destiny was a locked concept when it should also depend on our experience and rationality. We can indeed freely choose our values.

We want and need standards of virtue, our Destiny being the desired outcome of life achieved through the quest for knowledge and conducting ourselves according to our ethical standards.

A concert sounds extra marvelous with an empathetic conductor's added talent and experience. Still, the corps d'orchestre features many gifted instrumentalists, vocalists, and sounds. A harmonically, *symphonically* cooperative orchestra can still play well without a star conductor, but nothing beats the performance of both entities in concert. The term symphony comes from the Greek *symphonos* for an agreement or concord of sound. Unity is human Destiny's glimmering thread.

Since I am neither nihilistically nor religiously inclined, I salute Plato and his views in *The Republic*, where he shares that humans incorporate souls to be sagacious and that happiness is achievable through inherent virtue. Copy that.

Golden Laws of Cause and Effect

Fate and free will both play an equal role in destinies.
As people go their own way, destiny goes with them.

– INDIAN APHORISMS

Karma is often construed to be a kind of Destiny we earn, i.e., self-created from our erstwhile actions. If we are kind, we will earn fair karma, resulting in a well-walkable path in our next life. If not... not. The karmic notion originates in the Indian philosophies of Hinduism and Buddhism, and many of us in the Western world adopt it as a reminder that good deeds are rewarded, while unsavory acts lead to unfavorable consequences.

In Indian thought schools, original karma is ambivalent and not predominantly about enforcing the dualistic concepts of good and bad, let alone vengeful. It also isn't a simplistic motivational or disciplinary doctrine to inspire a moral life but to learn to live with the balancing consequences of our respective attitudes and measures. It also suggests why and how evil may come to exist in the world.

In a 2019 research study conducted in the US and published by the Statista Research Department in 2021, 31 percent of respondents said they strongly believed in the law of karma, while 10 percent said they did not believe in it at all. [138]

In a 2017 poll conducted among Britons, approximately half of the respondents confirmed their belief in karma (51 percent). [139]

The paradigms of karma and dharma go back thousands of years. They are mentioned to everlasting effect around 3130 BCE in the Vedic *Mahabharata*, including the *Bhagavad Gita* (The Divine Song). Both Sanskrit terms are extensions of Rita or Rta—the natural Destiny-form mother law and order of the universe that runs everything and everyone on every level—cosmic and human.

Karma means action, deed, and rule of cause and effect, while dharma is that which is just, the natural and established principle and law, the aim of living. The karmic notion of cause and effect teaches that our past actions influence our future lives.

Its maxim is also a splendid factor in Buddhist and Jain philosophy.

Karma is interpreted to work in three ways: as the sum of our deeds, as an autonomous force created by our own actions, and as a natural principle of underlying causality.

Karma is the disposition of a soul, self-managed through pre-settled and flexible components affecting life from before birth through reincarnations. Its components consist of the environment (family, friends, society, and culture), third-party spiritual significance, temperament and temperance, self-determination, personal capability, energy, choices, and responsibility. Karma could not operate without human volition as well as moral and ethical accountability since it determines how life develops with respect to the person's intentions and actions. Here we have an impressive example of compatibilism—the harmony between a great force and the human ability to make responsible choices. The law of karma rests on the idea that whatever we put out into the world will return to us. This theory can also help to shape our lives according to our own values.

The English-speaking world knows a most befitting proverb:

What goes around comes around.

While karma cannot be called Destiny, the law of karma creates educational forces that return to us in the form of individual Destiny.

Through positive actions, dharma is the soul's path to freedom from karma, thus earning the great goal of *moksha* or *mukti*—freedom from the wheel of karmic rebirth—*samsara*.

It is the path of granted and chosen life purpose and calling. We get as we give.

In Hinduism, we have to find our dharma and live it proactively, leading a life that pleases the Gods, while in Buddhism, it refers to personal responsibility for reaching enlightenment. In Jainism, dharma emphasizes living a pure life by following benevolent rules.

While originally a concept that affects our life after reincarnation, in contemporary urban trends and on social media, karma is often invoked for either reaping the rewards for right deeds or just "getting it" for wrong activities, ideally instantly. And yes, there may be quite a bit of confirmation bias involved here. Furthermore, karmic effects have nothing to do with revenge since the great ordinance exclusively leads to self-generated consequences.

Ambivalent or moral, it is advantageous for everyone to adhere to ethical responsibility and goodwill toward others and hold right back on misdeeds and the old ego. The contemporary interpretation of karma is almost on par with the Christian belief led by the words of Jesus in his Sermon on the Mount:

Only do unto others what you would want them to do unto you.

After all, this principle is not called the Golden Rule for no reason. Like karma, Jesus' wisdom remains a timeless, leading principle.

The German philosopher Immanuel Kant gave us these three existential questions:

What can I know? What must I do? What may I hope?

Arguably, these are the most poignant questions we should ask and answer ourselves. Kant's categorical imperative isn't far from the Golden Rule:

Act as if you want all people to act toward all other people. Act according to the maxim that you would wish all other rational people to follow as if it were a universal law.

Any incentivizing system can, at its core, become too self-involved. Ideally, we should not do good or abstain from low stuff just because of the proverbial *something in it* for us. Doing the right thing should never be considered just for the brownie points alone. But we live in the so-called real world. After all, even religions operate with spiritual goodies and promises of a pleasant and secure hereafter to condition desired behavior in their followers.

Utilitarianism, a school of thought that evaluates potential outcomes by considering what will bring about the highest benefit for society, is another valid perspective; however, it may also foster social prejudice while discouraging empathy and compassion—two of the necessary superpowers to achieve an individual and collectively sustainable human(e) Destiny. Utilitarian philosophy traces back to British reformer Jeremy Bentham (1748–1832) and classic liberal economist and thinker John Stuart Mill (1806–1873). Pursuing success and even happiness with healthy self-interest is an effective way to encourage responsible choices. But is that helping those who need more than an abstract right to wish for or pursue happiness, and is the majority of those in need ever adequately provided for?

> *The greatest happiness of the greatest number is the foundation of morals and legislation.*
>
> – JEREMY BENTHAM

But is the idea of happiness more important than those of parity, equality, or social justice?

I recommend the universal views of the liberal American political philosopher Professor John Rawls (1929–2002), who, in 1971, published *A Theory of Justice*. His principles—*Equal Liberty* and *Equality*—preserve the dignity and justify the needs of any individual as a prerequisite to fair treatment, especially for the economically and otherwise less fortunate. Yes, you read that right: *less fortunate*. Rawl's efficient methodology of *Reflective Equilibrium* helps us arrive at proper evaluations and decisions from an intuitive direction. It remains highly influential and is my tip for anyone interested in solidarity and the social contract. [140]

What is "good"? Should the notion of good be universal to all? Does the good come with a specific standard like the laws of cause and effect and the Golden Rule, prevalent in Hinduism, Confucianism, Judaism,

Christianity, Islam, and Buddhism and embedded in Kant's categorical imperative? We, as humans, want to be treated well by others. Consequently, we are seeding this desired effect by behaving kindly, with our fairness acting as a trigger to be reciprocated by others.

> *Give to every human being every right that you claim for yourself.*
> – ROBERT GREEN INGERSOLL, THE GREAT AGNOSTIC

We often are far too transactional—trading goodness, deeds, values, and rewards via an over-heightened sense of self-interest. Kant's supreme moral principle rested on his rational belief in an ethical code that should voluntarily be practiced among human beings. A golden mean between Aristotle's and Kant's philosophies seems a positive way forward—individual volition and collective commitment in one fluent concert.

A Question for Destiny, God(s), and Karma

Guilty as charged, I advocate altruism and humanitarianism. Regarding Destiny and karma, I sometimes wonder if when we intercept and improve someone's negative trajectory, the support we offer translates to meddling with their preordained path. Are we disturbing an allotted predicament dispensed by Destiny, God(s), or karma without an invitation or mission to accomplish? What if their past or actual life renders this troubled existence a karmic necessity to learn from it and develop their character? But if we swan in and help or even lift their current circumstances, are we perhaps softening the direct consequences of their potentially harmful deeds or the order of a supernatural or cosmic preordainment? Could those in need, distress, and even mass poverty indeed "deserve" their current station in this life? And, would it consequently mean that those idiosyncratic and more or less erratic billionaires, vainglorious public personae, dangerous dictators, reckless politicians, crony capitalists, or pseudo-profound guru-hucksters were all prima personalities in their former life performances?

By extending a hand, are we just hitting the karma *pause* button only for the comeuppance to come around and hit *play* when we aren't present? What does it mean when large parts of whole nations live under privation and distress?

And what if we are diddling with a harrowing experience, destined and necessary for the process of forging a future hero(ine) or mover, only to send them back to square one in the cosmic game? Not cool.

Are they all just exercising their karma? Or God's will? Or are they Destiny's agents-in-the-making? And what about animals we humans far too often treat with disgusting brutality or, in contrast, with overarching, *ersatz* love? Are these sentient co-beings we so brutally exploit and slaughter for our gusto guilty of what exactly? And were those cute kitties and plush puppies celebrated online "good" in their past existences now being rewarded?

What about the suffering majorities? To let them struggle and perish—is it Destiny's direction, God's command, or just the karmic consequence they themselves prepared earlier?

Well, I, for one, don't think so.

It is our Destiny to help others; it is *not* our Destiny to ignore the challenges and sufferings of others. It is destined to step up with empathy and civil courage and help those in need to get at least a slight chance to rise from their predicament and support them to learn to help themselves and each other. It is Destiny to understand and improve ourselves, but it isn't Destiny to look down on and mistreat others. It is Destiny to be generous and cooperative, but never destined to conveniently ignore and disregard third-party misfortunes.

After all, we fortunate ones have just about enough free will to lead a benevolent, tolerant, compassionate life sharing a portion of whatever we can temporarily call our own with those who don't.

Human Destiny is the result of complex interplay, but it is neither a lottery nor down to blind Fortuna's mood nor a payback or brownie-point operation.

Destiny isn't the same as luck; however, luck can be an important element of a destinal existence, as it is a substantial arrow in our quivers.

It comes with an auto-updating clean slate, time and again. Developing human competence for provident forethought is one of its goals. Know and grow is the motto.

Who wouldn't prefer positive, responsible, caring actions undertaken with just the right amount of "what's in for me?" Nothing wrong with a healthy level of self-care and self-benevolence without using warped third-party personal perspectives as an excuse to be mainly about the proverbial me, myself, and I. In my book, and no matter what anyone thinks, altruism is a necessity, although a highly volatile one that belongs in good hands. Caring and looking out for others beyond personal interest and payback is an absolute requirement for a positive human Destiny.

> *If you care about other people, that's now a very dangerous idea. If you care about other people, you might try to organize to undermine power and authority. That's not going to happen if you care only about yourself. Maybe you can become rich, but you don't care whether other people's kids can go to school, or can afford food to eat, or things like that. In the United States, that's called "libertarian" for some wild reason. I mean, it's actually highly authoritarian, but that doctrine is extremely important for power systems as a way of atomizing and undermining the public.*
>
> – Noam Chomsky

We should salute the manifold and efficacious options of giving practical pro bono support to those in need by becoming a proponent of Effective Altruism—the art of earning to give. [141]

Should our happiness always be the main, let alone the leading goal? Meaningful characters don't just chase and hoard material surplus, praise, and attention. Even striving for a high degree of personal happiness isn't always a necessity in the knowledge that the nature of happiness is often temporary, fickle, and feeble.

Happiness remains a lovely aspiration. But we may find that, soon, there will be bigger fish to fry, and we'll have to graciously accept far less and share a lot more while still putting our best foot forward. Talking of superpowers, that's likely as good as it gets for the human species.

Designated Exceptionalism

The ancient Greeks and many other cultures believed the forces of Destiny controlled all aspects of the universe. Even their legendary heroes avoided fighting the callers of all shots to not be perceived as cowards since the highest moral courage had to be mustered to harmonize our ambitions with the cosmic plan. A hero(ine) was someone who accepted their Destiny, whatever it meant, period. But times change, and so do role models.

The modern world has a different idea of heroism. We believe a hero is someone who nobly and selflessly defends the weak and the needy while standing tall for the moral code they believe in against all odds. Self-discovery is undoubtedly an induction tool for heroism, next to life's stressors, pressures, necessities, and circumstances. Reluctant heroes frequently muddle through mediocrity until they get sent on the lightful path. Many great characters that went to see a presage may also have self-delivered their destinies unconsciously through self-fulfilling prophecies (Neo in *The Matrix*).

Here we have it again, the eternal mythological theme of the chosen one: Neo is The One. That's his Destiny. Except he insists on maintaining control over his life.

The Oracle even puts the irony to Neo that he does not even believe in *"this fate crap."*

His "free" decision for the perilous red pill of troublesome veracity instead of the blue version designed to hold him down in the forced illusional status quo happens in concert with and as per his Destiny. Neo's long-foreseen "choice" for the red pill enables him to escape and combat a generated dream world of artificial faux fate instigated and orchestrated through the antihuman Matrix. By becoming The One, Neo is at one with Destiny. But wasn't that always a foregone conclusion?

This arch points to the likelihood that internal and external expectations, whether chosen or not, can condition our mindsets and behaviors until we reach these destinations and meet our individual or third-party prospects.

Let's look at the Pygmalion effect. [142] If someone we trust believes we have the self-efficacy and ability to meet what is expected of us or what is necessary, we can rise to the occasion, grow wings, become leaders, fight evil and win the day, and go beyond our potential and even our wildest dreams or ambitions.

History, my personal experience, and the HIP/Heroic Imagination Project by Dr. Philip Zimbardo [143] suggest a hero(ine) in all of us. Mankind is seen as a bounty of heroic "sleepers" waiting to come to the fore if we dare to get over ourselves, identify with authentic heroism, and act with civil courage. This everyday heroism underlines a new, democratic, and inclusive status no longer reserved for legendary beings, military contexts, absolute outliers, or twentieth-century supernatural character tropes of non-mythological surrogate messiahs like Superman, [144] Skywalker, and Co.

We all carry the potential for greatness in us and rise beyond ourselves in one way or another and shape our and others' destinies.

All that the circumstances of your birth can ever grant you is potential, but your destiny is yours alone to see completed.
  – Gregory V. Diehl, The Heroic and Exceptional Minority [145]

Deathstiny

Outwitting, if not beating the powers of death, has always been atop the mortal agenda since the word go. God(s) represent(s) even more supernatural significance due to the sheer fact they are "deathless." We are jealous of their immortality without the slightest clue what it means to be unending; thereby, physical expiration and all surrounding uncertainty remain a big problem.

How well are we dealing with the mortal options of a Destiny beyond our material sell-by dates?

In 2011, researchers at the University of Oxford found that incredible numbers of us across many nations naturally expect a form of hereafter. Furthermore, despite the fact atheism, agnosticism, and independent spirituality are on the rise across the globe, we display a strong tendency to believe in the existence of supernatural entities. [146]

That legendary Faustian longing for immortality never went out of fashion. The trouble with death is that, no matter how far advanced we are as humans in the so-called developed world, possibly the less we are inclined to accept our natural perishability in comparison with our fatality-fearing predecessors way back when. To them, death was life's regrettable, immutable direction and destination. Their anguish fueled the success of religions that promise either a conditional realm of forgiving ephemeral forms of eternal life to their devotees or even sensual delights to those who, for instance, condone that their weaponized deaths are instrumentalized for dogmatic agendas.

This deeply human *angst* spans many faiths and, in my experience, is surprisingly prevalent in those who claim to be surest of and closest to religion. Across many civilizations, in literature, philosophy, and science, death is the top spiritual and intellectual challenge. Humanity's struggle with death as the ultimate fate played a belief-shaping role throughout all cultures. Ancient Greece responded with classical epics and the invention of tragedy, often featuring the woes of human Destiny, offering cathartic treatment to tormented souls long before the days of psychotherapy.

With the evergreen hope of escaping death, self-preservation and self-prolongation won importance beyond almost everything else. In all the different ways humanity has tried to explore, avoid, or at least delay dying, we are still wrapping our minds around the big question of whether something or someone awaits us after we leave our frail frames behind. While this question is as old as Destiny, innovations and new perspectives about the universe continually transform our ideas about death and the value of human life.

Many beliefs acknowledge the fragility and relative shortness of life, but the inevitability of our physical sell-by-date remains a considerable burden. Escapism is a perennial literature theme, and it is discussed repeatedly. Since time began, many humans and even philosophies have reckoned that death was the maximum Destiny. Greek mythology has moving accounts of mortals pleading for the lives of their loved ones, such as Orpheus asking to be allowed to go to the underworld to bring back his beloved Eurydice or of caring Gods intercepting the danger of imminent death.

Mesopotamian epics, Greek myths, and later, Christianity painted vivid pictures of what horrors may await us after physical demise, some of which excel in intricate details of what's to be endured unless we walk in line while alive. These scenarios are not exactly helpful to calm our nerves. They were, and still are, adding to the general fear and panic about leaving this plane. The brilliant Dante Alighieri's highly theological *Inferno* did an excellent job, too, but not in just that regard.

Our visions of a hereafter are not all a matter of concern. The idea that we'll meet our loved ones in paradise, heaven, or a less-defined afterworld is a beautiful notion offering solace and hopeful expectation. Some narratives tried to shed light on the possibility of being snatched away from the clutches of illness, pain, misfortune, or even an early death through the intervention of miracles and supernatural agencies. When it comes to gaining direct insight into the hereafter through eyewitness reports, limited accounts exist of those who have successfully cheated death or returned to this side from the beyond to tell all. We are not talking about near-death or out-of-the-body experiences here but proper broadcasts from the realm beyond physical human expiration. Despite much modern interest and medical research, most statements and ancient stories still crystallize death's absolute certainty to humanity.

We find a tantalizing exception to this rule in The *Myth of Er*, the final part of *The Republic*, written by Plato—the Greek titan of philosophy— around 375 BCE.

Plato tells the story of Er, a princely Pamphylian (Armenian) soldier who gets himself killed in a war. He journeys to the invisible world to witness how the other side of the veil works.

Without going into too much detail here, since that is for another book, let me just say that Er beholds the realm of Destiny and watches Lady Necessity (Ananke) and her three daughters—Clotho, Lachesis, and Atropos (the Moirai) singing the Law of Destiny in one cosmic harmony. He observes the meaningful casting of the lots of future lives (lottery) and the assignment of personal daemons (spirits, echoed later by the Roman concept of Genii). The waiting souls are offered to choose, for themselves, to migrate from the ethereal realm into a new frame of material existence to live again with a portion of guided yet self-decided responsibility. To cut this outstanding story short: After being dead for nine days, Er slips back into his mortal costume on the living side to tell his mourning companions, now breathlessly listening, about the afterworld and the Spindle of Destiny.

Poetry, religions, and many schools of thought have done their best to give insight into the concepts of mortality. In different philosophies, the fact of dying also reminds us that life has intrinsic value, and we should add to it by leading a caring existence. To us fragile yet logical and rational beings craving control throughout our physical sojourn, death remains our most challenging stage.

Modern humanity has a hard time accepting our lack of handle on so many levels and still being at the receiving end of Nature and circumstances. I marvel at today's cuddly ideology that we would be the protectors of a gossamer-spun idyllic Nature. Just like the final French queen Marie Antoinette, we are increasingly idealizing ourselves romantically as wannabe-bucolic keepers and preservers, hence the flood of glossy, cute country life magazines and shows. While that is all quite understandable escapism since it takes the mind away from urban harshness, it is also odd considering the majestic ambivalence around us. We amplify Nature's response, if not retaliation, through our polluting ways while we swarm this gem of a planet. The memo is in the mail.

The thought of an inevitable Deathstiny does not have to be an ominous threat, only a constant reminder—a *memento mori*—to use our limited time as optimally as possible and focus on living a decent life in the here and now without forgetting the beyond. Because life—be it just a one-hit-wonder or an evergreen— is our Destiny, not death.

CHAPTER 5

Prisms of Arts and Love [147]

The role our seminal force played for thousands of years in all formats of emotional and thus artistic creation deserves focused attention due to its enduring impact on human development.

Literature—Destiny is Written

To discover how the concept of Destiny differs from era to era, literature is always a good reference point since books, poems, and journals enable us to decipher prominent feelings of a specific period or society swiftly. Literature offers us direct access to the ideas and ideals circulating during a particular time and how humanity's past, present, and future Destiny was valued.

According to anthropologists, we mapped our place in Nature and the universe long before creating a writing system. The introduction of alphabets provided tools to preserve memory and information by recording accounts of daily life, experiences with the universe, and the beliefs that amplified cultures.

Fate shuffles the cards, and we play.
— Arthur Schopenhauer

Literature, per se, is designed to educate, entertain, enlighten, and provoke critical and independent thinking. These characteristics are crucial when opening different conversations about our varied experiences of existence. Just like art, literature reflects the respective

199

generations' thoughts, hopes, and views on our world's ever-changing themes carrying ever-changing perspectives about the voyage to our destination.

Antiquity

Ancient, Classic Greek and Roman literature shone with masterpieces featuring destined heroes, like the *Epic of Gilgamesh*, Homer's *Iliad* and *Odyssey,* and Virgil's *Aeneid*, or, more instructively, focusing on human Destiny, as in Ovid's *Metamorphoses*, Seneca's *Letters from a Stoic*, and Marcus Aurelius'*Meditations*.

> *The thing ordained for you, teach yourself to be at one with those.*
> *And the people who share them with you, treat them with love.*
> *With real love.*
>
> – MARCUS AURELIUS, MEDITATIONS

The Middle Ages

We remember medieval fiction for its fairies, kings, dragons, knights, princesses, and idyllic realms. Wales and England excelled at creating timeless masterpieces such as *The Mabinogion* and the much-loved Arthurian legends reflecting exemplary agency. Religious texts also rose in relevance.

Destiny and fate once more became popular themes, courtesy of the Roman philosopher Boethius (ca. 480–524 CE), who reintroduced the Greek/Roman Goddess Tyche/Fortuna and her wheel to medieval Europe and beyond with his classic book *The Consolation of Philosophy.*

Things went wrong when the Holy Catholic Church fed into greedy instincts all over Europe. Enter the bloody Crusades. These military exploits, blessed by the pope of Rome, were not so much a spiritually motivated measure but predominantly a low-minded, profit-grabbing exercise. During the bleak times of the main eight Crusades (1095–

1270), nations desperately looked for lightful meaning in their lives. Eventually, the Ottomans tore away Constantinople (today's Istanbul), the pearl of culture, and stripped dominance from the Eastern Roman Empire, also known as the Byzantine Empire (ca. 330–1453). Overall, the amazing Byzantium ruled for a good 1,123 years, making it the longest active regency to date. Jerusalem was also captured, and the city sacred to all three book religions became a conflicting addition to Muslim treasure troves. Under the pretext of freeing the Holy Land, Christian war campaigns then set the Near East even more on fire, thinly veiled as a pilgrimage. More and more Europeans felt their faith had to prop them with divine solace and reassurance. For this reason, most of the literature available during this time focused on promoting the cause of the Church to keep the flock and their support in line.

Christian beacons such as the animal-loving Italian friar Francis of Assisi (1181/82–1226) and his Franciscan brotherhood authored serene material symbolic of peace, harmony with Nature, and modesty.

> *Keep a clear eye toward life's end. Do not forget your purpose and destiny as God's creature.*
>
> — FRANCIS OF ASSISI

The Bible was still only available in Latin. And we must not forget that books were written, illuminated, and produced by hand, often in monasteries. Texts illustrating different scenes from the Bible were also published. Courtly love became high fashion, and troubadours roamed Europe singing of the ideal feelings and eternal devotion to an idealized lady. In England, Geoffrey Chaucer (1342–1400) presented *The Canterbury Tales* and translated a part of the *Roman de la Rose,* both bestsellers of their time.

Italian star author Dante Alighieri (1265–1321) even welcomed the Goddess Fortuna as a representation of Destiny in his very Christian *Divine Comedy,*[148] with the slight adaptation that in his cosmology, Fortuna was declared a power created by God to "guide the destinies of man on Earth."

Do not be afraid; our fate cannot be taken from us; it is a gift.
                              – Dante Alighieri, Inferno

Europe suffered under the Great Famine and Black Death pandemic, reducing the Western population dramatically. It is often claimed that a contributing factor was the stupefying fact that the Catholic Church demonized cats and brutally decimated them in perverse numbers. With not enough felines left to control millions of plague-infested fleas and lice-carrying rats, the Black Death could spread uninhibited. Very sad poetic justice?

The Renaissance·

Our current age reminds me of this era. We are surrounded by so many improvements and innovations, enjoying new options and ways to learn and achieve our goals. And still, too many fields seem somewhat fragile, increasingly insecure, and adversely controlled.

Starting in the fourteenth century, the Renaissance extended into the sixteenth century. It began in northern Italy; horrific wars and local feuds tore the country apart. It is said that the greater the pressure, the greater the achievements. That's also how Nature creates diamonds. Our ancestors craved alternative sources of wisdom to nourish self-awareness and added orientation they required to make it through these culturally enriched yet merciless, restless, and demanding years.

Despite its comforting notion, our Italian forebears would not stay exclusively caught up in the realm of religious revelation, nor did the vision of salvation suffice to answer all questions about the Destiny of humanity. Minds demanded expansion only to find rejuvenation in classic, eternal ideals, courtesy of Muslim kingdoms and their commissioned intellectuals that rediscovered and regained access to antiquity's lost philosophical and metaphysical treasures during the Middle Ages. And so began the subsequent rise of classic philosophers such as Plato and Aristotle, enabling the onset of the age of humanism, placing us at the front and core of everything. But this great age was far from being the perfect place it tried to become. The unconventional, trailblazing philosopher and scientific theorist Giordano Bruno (1548–1600) was burnt at the stake by malevolent ignorami of the Catholic Church for rightly stating that planet Earth, contrary to Aristotle's outdated but then still Church-accepted theories, was anything but the center of the cosmos, while the universe was, and remains, infinite.

Thanks to the German innovator Johannes Gutenberg (ca. 1400–1468) and his invention of the printing press (however, techniques of printing per se were pioneered in China way before the Common Era), processes and products of publishing turned the world upside down. Then, books were equivalent to the benefits and disruptions our Internet continues to cause—an eye-opening, liberating, yet also disconcerting and cord-cutting evolving sensation. Western civilization finally entered the era of multiplied ideas and words, and the literacy rate rose. Poems and dramas became the most popular forms of literature and entertainment, turning the spotlight on English playwrights like Christopher Marlowe (1564–1593), William Shakespeare (1564–1616), and John Milton (1608–1674), who often addressed mankind's capacity for free will in correspondence with the Protestant age, which was co-shaped by the doctrine of predestination, a kind of *ersatz* Destiny.

Our wills and fates do so contrary run, that our devices still are overthrown; our thoughts are ours, their ends none of our own.
— WILLIAM SHAKESPEARE, HAMLET

The Renaissance, what a game-changer.

He who has access to the fountain does not go to the water pot.
— LEONARDO DA VINCI

Gripping stories, like Kit Marlowe's *Dr. Faustus,* inspired to dare and think, while the theater taught enchanted audiences how to dream and aspire to different destinies.

Hope and imagination remain indomitable powers, especially when we allow ourselves to be encouraged to learn how to fight for our ideals and dreams to face and dismantle what stands in our way.

Enter the Reformation, one spirited German ex-priest named Martin Luther (1483–1546), and his long-overdue translation of the Bible. Again, views on the face of a predetermined future shifted big time. Some folks even embraced their Christian faith *and* the wisdom of the classics while using their system of scholasticism to increase the amount of meaning in their existence. Still, even the revolutionary Luther promoted stiff predestination and denied free will.

All things whatever arise from, and depend on the divine appointment; whereby it was foreordained who should receive the word of life, and who should disbelieve it; who should be delivered from their sins, and who should be hardened in them; and who should be justified and who should be condemned.

– MARTIN LUTHER

Christian scholars, such as Dutch humanist Desiderius Erasmus (1469–1536), wrote guidebooks on how to reach salvation despite a burning interest in the Greek and Roman classics. Erasmus believed the best and most legitimate path to achieving and fulfilling our Destiny was choosing the road to salvation. Political works during these times were also quite a treat. With the rebirth of Hellenistic and Roman philosophy, especially Stoicism, books such as the Italian humanist Francesco Petrarca's (1304–1374) *Remedies for Good and Bad Fortune* were published as an aid in dealing with the best, the middle, and the worst luck, following in the tradition of Seneca.

The thought school of skepticism re-emerged. Florentine political philosopher Niccolo Machiavelli (1469–1527) wrote the quintessential management bible for the silk and velvet-clad top of the upper Italian human(ist) food chain, based on the behavioral example of the ruthless pope–son and statesman–warrior Cesare Borgia (1476–1507). *The Prince*, an everlasting world bestseller, fortified the idea that "the end justifies the means," i.e., permitted effective rulers to get away with whatever it took. For the betterment of society, of course.

> *Nevertheless, that our free will may not be altogether extinguished, I think it may be true that Fortune is the ruler of half our actions, but that she allows the other half or a little less to be governed by us.*
>
> – NICCOLO MACHIAVELLI, THE PRINCE

Instead of just sticking to theories of the classics and Holy Scripture, mortal destinies were increasingly entrusted into the hands of science and empirical confirmation.

The German–Polish astronomer Nicolaus Copernicus (ca. 1473–1543) discovered the Earth moves around the sun, contrary to centuries of doctrinal belief that God made our planet the center of his creations.

Europe's egotistical claim to a guaranteed privileged and special Destiny got slightly rattled when Portuguese explorer Ferdinand Magellan (1480–1521) circumnavigated the world to discover that Europe wasn't right in the middle of the globe. Christopher Columbus (1451–1506), an Italian captain in Spanish service, rediscovered America only to open the floodgates for the greedy and destructive ambitions of Spain, England, and Portugal.

The Age of Enlightenment

Jean de la Fontaine (1621–1695), the famous French author of *The Fables*, said:

> *A person often meets his destiny on the road he took to avoid it.*

Revolutionary thoughts about monarchy, faith systems, and economics landed. The religious predestination we've talked about earlier, especially the brand baked into Christianity, raised philosophical and intellectual eyebrows and was increasingly seen as problematic for patronizing and disenfranchising devotees. Jean-Jacques Rousseau

(1712–1778), an immigrant from Switzerland who moved to Paris to become a musician, was one of the most intricate thinkers of his era. In his thought-provoking book *The Social Contract*, he challenged the divine right of kings, preferring to put political authority in the hands of the people. He also thoroughly managed to upset the Church by proclaiming that all religions are equal because they are all instrumental in bringing good to everyone. In his late autobiographical work, Rousseau vividly described his deep understanding of the meaning of *destinée*.

Voltaire (1694–1778), who once wanted to follow in Shakespeare's footsteps, turned out to be an exemplary satirist thanks to his acerbic wit. He, too, attacked the Church and questioned the authorities of the most potent French establishments. He took issue with religious and metaphysical doctrines, including most folkloristic interpretations of Destiny; therefore, he wrote *Zadig—The Book of Fate*—a philosophical trailblazer for detective tropes.

The philosopher Denis Diderot (1713–1784), who was almost obsessed with the concepts of the great primordial design, gave us the satirical novel *Jacques the Fatalist*. Diderot teamed up with polymath Jean Le Rond d'Alembert (1717–1783) to publish the first *Encyclopedia (A Systematic Dictionary of the Sciences, Arts and Crafts)*. They encouraged a change of thinking through knowledge in the "common" folks, *et voilá*, just in time for the French Revolution.

Things were slightly different over in America during this time, where the Puritans were mainly in charge of literature. The English Puritan and later governor, William Bradford (1590–1657), wrote the *Plymouth Plantation,* which describes the settlement of the Pilgrim Fathers. Clergyman Jonathan Edward (1703–1758) wrote *Sinners in the Hands of the Angry God.* This book focuses on how God punishes anyone unwilling to follow his prescriptions. The instructive and straightforward style in which these works were written was deliberate to effectively instill the authority of their Christian faith in almost any area of human life. After all, Puritans believed salvation to be the only possible Destiny and still called religious predestination a comforting doctrine. They were also heavily into magical ideas of witchcraft, etc.

The Romantic Movement

Meet Sir Walter Scott's (1771–1832) heroes and heroines in *Ivanhoe, The Lady of the Lake, Rob Roy,* and *The Bride of Lammermoor*—and their dramatic destinies.

> *Teach self-denial and make its practice pleasure, and you can create for the world a destiny more sublime that ever issued from the brain of the wildest dreamer.*
>
> – SIR WALTER SCOTT

In Germany, the *Sturm und Drang* (storm and need) (1765–1790) and Jean Paul's (1763–1825) creative *Weltschmerz* (world-weariness) movements marked exceptional times of creative emotion.

In her novel *Middlemarch,* British writer Mary Anne Evans (1819–1880), better known under her masculine pseudonym George Eliot, transposes a strong sense of Destiny and even fate in the form of a natural-yet-principled equalizer. French author Victor Hugo (1802–1885) said he felt inspired, if not compelled, to write *The Hunchback of Notre Dame* when he saw the word ANANKE inscribed in Greek letters on a wall when visiting Notre Dame after a fire.

There is will in the thought; there is none in the dream. The dream, which is completely spontaneous, takes and keeps, even in the gigantic and the ideal, the form of our mind.

> *Nothing springs more directly and more sincerely from the very bottom of our souls than our un-reflected and indefinite aspirations towards the splendors of destiny.*
>
> – VICTOR HUGO, LES MISÉRABLES

In America, writer Nathaniel Hawthorne (1804–1864) featured his views on the invisible agency in *The Scarlet Letter* and *The Fairy Legend of the Threefold Destiny*.

Published in 1845, the autobiography *An American Slave* by Frederick Douglass (ca. 1816–1895) revealed the horrific experiences of the ex-slave who became an influential lecturer and politician who removed mountains from the road to emancipation and the abolition of slavery. Its author was one of the most exceptional activists of his time.

The destiny of the colored American is the destiny of America.
— FREDERICK DOUGLASS

And in 1852, the American author and campaigner Harriet Beecher Stowe (1811–1896) published the global bestseller *Uncle Tom's Cabin*. Her *"narrative of the life and sufferings of Uncle Tom"* tells a gripping story, painting a gruesome picture of slavery. The book condemns the inhumane treatment of African Americans and directs awareness to the inhuman conditions Black Americans were forced to endure as cruelly and wrongfully imposed false Destiny. *Uncle Tom's Cabin* became an important catalyst for the abolition of slavery.

Life Among the Paiutes: Their Wrongs and Claims was published in 1882 by the first Native American woman to write a book. Native American rights activist Sarah Winnemucca Hopkins, or Tocmetone (ca. 1844–1891), tells her life story as a member of the Paiute tribe, describing her family's struggles against encroaching European settlers and the resulting injustices inflicted on her people.

Over in the United Kingdom, Thomas Hardy made his protagonists' inability to control their lives (for instance, in *The Mayor of Casterbridge, Tess of the d'Urbervilles,* and *Far from the Madding Crowd*) a recurring theme, as in his countryman Charles Dickens' (1812–1870) stories often challenging inequality and the status quo in the likes of *Great Expectations, David Copperfield, Our Mutual Friend,* and *A Tale of Two Cities*.

*Under an accumulation of staggerers, no man can be considered
a free agent. No man knocks himself down; if his destiny knocks
him down, his destiny must pick him up again.*

       – CHARLES DICKENS, THE OLD CURIOSITY SHOP

American cult author Edgar Allan Poe (1809–1849) stated:

*If it is meant for you, you won't have to beg for it. You will never
have to sacrifice your dignity for your destiny.*

Meanwhile, Ralph Waldo Emerson (1803–1882), head of the
Transcendentalist movement, said:

If you believe in fate, believe in it, at least, for your good.

Over to France. Stendhal's (1783–1842) *Le Rouge et le Noir* and
Gustave Flaubert's (1821–1880) groundbreaking *Madame Bovary*
portray troubled destinies in a way that the Irish author Oscar Wilde
(1854–1900) summed up terrifically:

*Each man lived his own life and paid his own price for living it.
The only pity was one had to pay so often for a single fault. One
had to pay over and over again, indeed. In her dealings with man,
destiny never closed her accounts.*

Crossing into the modern era, let's salute the German novelist
Hermann Hesse (1877–1962), one of the world's influential, critically
acclaimed writers of *Siddhartha* and *Steppenwolf.* He received the Nobel
Prize in Literature for *The Glass Bead Game* in 1946. Spiritual growth
and Destiny play a vital part in his timeless literary creations.

*Siddhartha stopped fighting his fate this very hour, and he stopped
suffering.*

       – HERMAN HESSE, SIDDHARTA

If what matters in a person's existence is to accept the inevitable consciously, to taste the good and bad to the full and, to make for oneself a more individual, unaccidental and, inward Destiny alongside one's external fate, then my life has been neither empty nor worthless.

— HERMAN HESSE, GERTRUDE

Solitude is not chosen, any more than destiny is chosen. Solitude comes to us if we have within us the magic stone that attracts destiny.

— HERMAN HESSE

Let us end our brief visit of only a few examples of the role of Destiny in literature over time with the words of an eminent twentieth-century author.

Almost nothing important that ever happens to you happens because you engineer it. Destiny has no beeper; destiny always leans trenchcoated out of an alley with some sort of "psst" that you usually can't even hear because you're in such a rush to or from something important you've tried to engineer.

— DAVID FOSTER WALLACE, INFINITE JEST

Art and music, just like literature, are not just born out of creative acumen but are also dependent on the social and philosophical norms present at the time of their composition, serving as a reflection of hopes, beliefs, ideas, and human experiences throughout all ages. Early art and music were parts of religious rituals—dance and rhythm echoed the earth's vibrations. Getting in sync with Nature brought young civilizations closer to the fabric of the cosmos, accompanying our ancestral relationships with ancient Gods and flourishing spirituality.

Art, from cave signs to Caravaggio (1571–1610), was always instrumental in creating and emphasizing myths, legends, and symbols through a visual representation of narratives passed down from one generation to another.

Why should we look to art in search of humanity's concepts of Destiny? Because, along with our beliefs, artistic notions about our role in the universe are reflected in the visual arts.

Fortunately, art does not just aloofly reside in museums, galleries, and exhibitions to be enjoyed by collectors and the upper classes.

Western Art's Changing Notion
of Destiny

Classic Greek art possesses unbeatable balance and aesthetics, bringing back dreams of a golden age. Many philosophers were fans of spiritual perfection and achieved an idea of humankind's Destiny with benevolent supervision from the "world invisible." To the Greeks, beauty was an external sign, if not a confirmation of goodness and virtue. This notion might appear discriminative to us today, but it does reflect actual human nature, not just a bygone era during which this exclusive ideal of attractiveness was cherished. Bluntly put, it is still valid today, no matter what we are told to think or to reject. Need I mention social media, the entertainment industry, and our cultivated biases?

Giants of sculpture like the Parthenon's mastermind creator Phidias (ca. 488–431 BCE), Polykleitos (ca. 490 BCE–unknown), and Myron (ca. 480–440 BCE), celebrated the human form and breathed life into marble and bronze, portraying Gods and exceptional mortals.

The Romans later insisted on the continuation of this artistic strata by proclaiming and displaying the deep roots of their belief in a Destiny-led Rome. To this day, their spirituality, art, and architecture—echoing Greek symmetry in combination with ambitious yet more down-to-earth designs—are still dominant in representative buildings around the world, such as the US Capitol.

Medieval art focused on visual storytelling and Christianity. There were knights in shining armor and lovely ladies to be sung to, but it was also a troubling time of political turmoil, the Black Death, and several wars.

Arts became essential in reassuring belief in the mother Church, the lives of saints, and the Christian version of the afterlife. Absolute license to dictate conviction allowed the Crusaders to beat the infidels and snatch back Jerusalem from Islamic rule, doing God's bidding to prevent the spread of anything differently inclined.

This need for control was also displayed in the lavish and ornamental architecture of cathedrals and churches, symbolizing the might of Christendom. Though many illustrious gems of Christian masterpieces of worship we still admire today in Italy, Spain, France, and the United Kingdom often copy brilliant Islamic architecture and design. [149]

The Catholic Church was shocked by challenging reformers like Luther and Calvin. Both cord-cutters pushed the concept of predestination, i.e., God had already determined lives for better or for worse and in an unchangeable fashion. Catholic styles, devotional paintings, and lavish church ornaments were deemed idolatrous and superfluous, ornamental overload.

To this day, Protestant places of worship are built and equipped practically and in a minimalist way, being much less luxurious than the gold-plated temples of their older Catholic siblings in faith. Reformation led to Counter-Reformation. Protestants and Catholics submerged each other in decades of horrid war—the worst way to claim revelation and attain salvation.

Bringing Back Philosophy Through Art

The Renaissance of philosophy and art was born in Florence, northern Italy. This culturally fruitful yet tough and demanding age celebrated the pursuit of knowledge and a more refined life instead of just existing to aggravate neighboring states and trying to win wars. A more systematic way of banking was created, which brought wealth to Florence, allowing the House of Medici—with Destiny written all over the family—to become the rulers of this epicenter of culture and commerce.

Unsurprisingly, the three Moirai or Fates and the Goddess Fortuna were popular motifs in all art forms of the Renaissance.

Cosimo de Medici (1389–1464), known as the Father of the Nation, encouraged and materially enticed artists to try daring new styles. Humanist philosophy flourished among the intellectual class, supporting a new focus on the meaning of human life outside religion. Renaissance artists directed the spotlight again to the human form, led by master sculptor Donatello (ca. 1386–1466). Leonardo da Vinci's (1452–1519) universal genius discovered the importance of physical detail and expression, evident throughout his magnificent body of work. He also invented and designed the odometer to measure distance and came up with portable bridges, the rack-and-pinion system, and the continuously variable transmission. And this:

> *I have always felt it is my destiny to build a machine that would allow man to fly.*
>
> — LEONARDO DA VINCI

Michelangelo (1474–1564) was applauded as the master of fresco and sculpture. His contemporary Raphael (1483–1520) became famous for manifold paintings and depictions of the Madonna, a replacement for the ancient motherly Goddess Isis. While the Renaissance was mainly about natural ideals and meaning, Mannerism, the art movement that followed, focused on exaggerated features, leading to the Baroque and the Golden Age of Dutch and Flemish painters. The rise of the must-have fashion to have our portrait taken, if we were members of the nobility or rich merchants, became as unstoppable as the breathtaking paintings of Caravaggio.

These buzzwords fast-forward us beyond the Baroque (ca. 1625–1700) and the Rococo (ca. 1699–1780) to align with the era of Classicism and Romanticism, the American fight for independence for freedom from the British Empire (1775–1783), the French Revolution (1789–1799), the war-ridden Napoleonic era (1799–1815) and its ensuing political struggles. Ailing humanity began to yearn for the simplicity and honesty of Nature since many felt a sharp sense of purposelessness. The Romantic era (ca. 1790–1850) featured human emotions, sensations, and individualism instead of bleak intellectual and moral values. It underscored equality and universality in the world, the longing for a new style of human destination. We began to focus on our innermost emotions, realizing their need for a fulfilling Destiny and that there was more to life than focusing on a promise of an after-the-fact paradise. They began to discover the fallibility of their theological and worldly leaderships and went on to ponder change.

Realism

The modern period in art went along with significant shifts in technology and politics and changes in the pursuit of meaningful purpose.

We felt abandoned and sold out by our nobles and kings, and the idealist perception, once popular during the Renaissance, began to wane. With this attitude and outlook, the Realist movement emerged, focusing on the ordinary, leaving the traditions of opulent art behind for a more progressive and authentic feel. People were painted as they were, no longer tarted up, but presented in the unflattering light of day, warts and all. It sent waves of discomfort through the middle and upper classes and even the intelligentsia.

What does Realism as an art movement say about human Destiny? Like the shock value it provided in the early 1900s, it also blew away the covers of the once oh-so-secure political and social classes. It was high time to figure out the value of life and go on the quest for our reason to be.

All changed in sharp contrast to the Renaissance and Romanticism. Realism almost brutally pushed out idealist topics. Around 1850, individualism (the notion that a person is important) was discredited in art and replaced by objectivity. Standards rose without distortions or subjectivity.

Art then became concerned with new ideas and social responsibility. Gustave Courbet (1819–1877), the leading man of French Realism, left behind the staged portraits and ideal scenes to paint the bland expressions of everyday toil, banality, and in-your-face nudity, all with a generous pinch of visceral anarchy. During the time of Realism, perspectives gravitated toward rationalism.

In contrast, the English Pre-Raphaelite Movement 1848–ca.1900) revived classic motifs, arranged in sumptuous colors and spiked with tasteful drama of storied Destiny, a touch of histrionics, and lots of lush escapism. Dante-Gabriel Rossetti (1828–1882), John Everett Millais (1829–1896), William Holman Hunt 1827–1910), Edward Burne-Jones (1833–1898), and William Morris (1834–1896), to name but a few, believed in the mission of their art and human values. For example, one of their most eminent members, John William Waterhouse (1849–1917), painted the enigmatic *La Fileuse*—fate spinning the Destiny of man.

Twentieth Century and Beyond

Impressionism and Art Nouveau conquered the young twentieth century, followed by Expressionism and Surrealism.

The twentieth century was arguably one of the most turbulent times in history so far. Futurism became an international trend in the arts. Then Dadaism. Artists during this time embraced the anti-art movements to defy the hierarchy and conventions set by their predecessors. They battled both individualism and universality, as opposed to objectivity and subjectivity.

Enter an almost karmic act of Destiny: Colonialism was dismantled at last, while despots and fascists wreaked havoc and dragged the world through several wars. It was the time when photography and film took over.

After World War II, twentieth-century art movements encountered a new future with liberties, machines, and marketing. Like other eras in art history, this transition didn't happen overnight but was the product of many societal changes due to modern technology's introduction. Pop artists such as Andy Warhol became icons with idealizations of the American Dream that emerged following wartime economic hardship. Consumerism and television took an impressive and game-changing hold, followed by the computer-generated virtual revolution and the Internet, both of which only affected our lives by less than ten percent so far. That's right, mere foreplay. The vast remainder, including the A.I.-driven Fourth Industrial Revolution, is yet to take over in a fashion we cannot comprehend today, if we ever. Digital Destiny, anyone?

The Soundtrack to Human Destiny

Music seems to be a more fleeting expression of feelings and desires than other art forms. Yet we all know how easily and intensely a song or melody can stay with us forever.

Music is intangible but one of the most emotional and philosophically complex artistic expressions. It is around and within us; it can be heard, felt, interpreted, and understood from many angles. Performance, production, recording, and composition add facets to this art form.

During the Bronze Age and antiquity, according to musicologists, dance and music became integral in human activities, especially in performing rituals, a popular method to communicate with higher beings. And, apart from prayer, there hardly exists a better way to emphasize our devotion, desires, and dreams.

Philosophy Maestros Plato and Aristotle agreed that music represented human character and emotions were the creations of melodic images of the senses. Confucianism introduced the idea of music as a metaphysical expression of ethereal quality, furthering harmony between heaven and Earth.

Our human species always understood and cherished the benefits of a great song. The Greeks revered music as an essential gift granted by the nine Muses, prompting the outstanding philosopher and mathematician Pythagoras of Samos (580–500 BCE)—who was mentored in wisdom, ethics, and philosophy by the Delphic Pythia Themistoclea—to reveal harmonic ratios and musical concords for this special delivery from Mount Helicon (the residence of the Muses).

There is geometry in the humming of the strings; there is music in the spacing of the spheres.

– PYTHAGORAS

And for good measure:

Know that death comes to everyone and that wealth will sometimes be acquired, sometimes lost. Whatever grief mortals suffer by divine chance, whatever destiny you have, endure it, and do not complain. But it is right to improve it as much as you can and remember this: Fate does not give very many of these griefs to good people.

– PYTHAGORAS

Classic mythology also offered creative ways to communicate with the Gods through their divinely preferred instruments. The charm of the Muses became integral in the recital of poetry. Since poems were traditionally read and accompanied by the lyre, words accompanying music are called lyrics.

Music and Christian Worship

No surprise that Catholicism invested heavily in the development of music for worship and church rituals. Early Christians attended synagogues and learned to appreciate and emulate the beauty and meaning of Jewish hymns.

Music played an intense role in propagating religion. Most believers lacked access to the holy scriptures due to their inability to speak Latin and general illiteracy. Sacred narratives and prayers were set to music for the listeners to remember. Thus, like in the visual arts, the church became a formidable patron. The treasure chest of songs of praise also helped to develop classical and, later, the wonderful gospel music we cherish today.

What has music got to do with Destiny? Everything.

Did you know that classical music even has its own Destiny and fate motif? It prevails from Beethoven's *Symphony No. 5* to Wagner's *Walküre*, Verdi's *La Forza del Destino*, Mahler's *Symphony No. 6,* and Shostakovich's *Stalingrad Symphony*, to name but a few.

When we think about classical music's link with the artistic perceptions of cosmic design, the Olympian creations of composers like Johann Sebastian Bach (1685–1750), Franz Joseph Haydn (1732–1809), and especially Ludwig Van Beethoven (1770–1827) and his *Symphony No. 5 in C minor On Destiny* come to mind.

But it was Pyotr Ilyich Tchaikovsky (1840–1894) who possibly dealt most personally with the heavy notion of fate. He created one of the most dramatic orchestral pieces, entitled *Symphony No. 4*, darkly inspired by an illicit affair that led to the failure of his marriage. This composition, simply dubbed *Fate*, transposes his struggles to escape these circumstances. When his world disintegrated, he admitted that shaking off the Great Design was impossible.

Mournful and yet grand is the destiny of the artist.

– Franz Liszt

Another special musical experience is embedded into *The Song of the Fates* by Johannes Brahms (1833–1897) based on Johann Wolfgang von Goethe's (1749–1832) version of the Greek play *Iphigenia in Tauris* by Euripides (ca. 480–406 BCE). [150]

Brahms also composed another captivating piece for choir, this time set to the poem by Friedrich Hölderin (1770–1834) from his novel *Hyperion—The Song of Destiny*.

Classical music essentially taught us to delve into a vivid connection to their dreams and, thus, to their desired destinies. Music is a profoundly individual experience relaying how it feels to be human. And music is universally democratic. We do not need to belong to anything or anywhere; we don't have to know how to read or understand the foundations of fine art to catch the most simple, most beautiful, and the harshest and most painful realization encapsulated in the magnetism of melodies and rhythms.

Their utilization substantially changed when broadcasting and recording technology entered the stage. Classical music was still the most popular genre, but by World War I, the tune changed.

Humanity required themes to fit the horrendous circumstances they endured, and composers like Maurice Ravel (1875–1937), Edward Elgar (1857–1934), and Gustav Holst (1874–1934) delivered big-time triggering compelling responses to the debilitating human conditions during those times. The tragedy of this era forced composers like Holst, Elgar, and Vaughan Williams (1872–1958) to create music that served as eulogies for all war casualties.

The world needed a return to a more positive outlook, and it appeared: jazz, heralding affirmation of life, hope, joy, and faith in concert with personal action.

Rock 'n Roll and Civil Rights

It's the Destiny of music to evolve constantly. Rhythm and blues, famously led by African Americans, took over at last, followed by rock 'n' roll, well placed in the company of genres like folk, gospel, and blues. Rock 'n' roll was a culmination of all genres at that time, the post-World War II equivalent of today's pop music. Protesters used the influence of both gospel and folk music to underpin the black American movement, resisting racial oppression and social inequality. Eventually, these styles inspired the evolution of beat, punk, grunge, alternative, disco, and way beyond into our manifold genres of beloved pop music.

Destiny is impressively evoked in pop and rock songs like *Hand of Fate* by The Rolling Stones (1976) and *Definition of Destiny* by Billy Talent (2009).

Music was and will always be highly influential in reminding us to look beyond a seemingly meaningless existence and refuse to be easily absorbed by existential angst and, instead, seek their Destiny.

Wrapping the Mega Maxim

Like in art, music, and literature, Destiny was and is a core theme of movies and television. Screenwriters and soundtrack composers are fascinated with the dramatic avenues of myths, an inescapable future, and whether humankind can run this show alone. The vision of transcendence and the significance of our lives run as a red thread through many movies and show scripts.

In the fantasy genre, invoking Destiny and even fate brings out internal conflicts and often addresses the war between right and wrong, playing with abstract ideas such as human desire versus a higher power or chaos versus order.

Films featuring the invisible architect also make us think about the value of our emotions since this theme often kindles the subconscious and the unknown, with subplots such as luck, the presence of the supernatural, and options for control in life. Audiences across all cultures are moved by the uncertainty in their lives as opposed to the degree of clarity dramatic Destiny seems to offer, albeit at a price. So many productions carry the cosmic force as an undercurrent in one way or another.

Gods, Goddesses, and Supernatural Beings

What makes the realm of the supernormal so important in connection with Destiny? Why, who would not want a little help from a currently unseen dimension to deal with life's issues, stand out from the crowd, and even become a heroine? Who would not want to be trusted by a higher entity that sees something beyond the ordinary in us? And who would not like to bring hope and change the world for the better, no matter whether we're acting winged, caped, or dressed plainly?

> *The call to adventure signifies that destiny has summoned the hero.*
>
> – Joseph Campbell, The Hero with a Thousand Faces

Whatever anyone may think about Campbell's political orientation and personal sentiments, his lasting impact on storytelling is undeniable. And, in places, his work can make any destinal agency far more interesting, especially when our antagonists command superpowers as well.

> *With great power comes great responsibility.*
>
> – Uncle Ben, Spider-Man

And that's the case with predetermined superiority—the more demanding the calling, the higher the expectations of the agent's abilities and virtues. There is always a price tag attached to standing out. Being chosen by Destiny can turn out to be a sword of Damocles, even. Consequently, proper heroes are almost always reluctant and reticent to follow a clarion call, rarely rating themselves as the champion they are meant to become. Heroism does not require praise or limelight. Knowing it is rather enough, sometimes even too much, to bear. The meta-human heroism we see in movies differs a lot from real-life heroism. To me, real-life heroes are "ordinary" people who care for others empathetically, inspire fortitude, and go about doing what is necessary, especially when no one is looking.

Finding the center of strength within ourselves is in the long run the best contribution we can make to our fellow men. One person with indigenous inner strength exercises a great calming effect on panic among people around him. This is what our society needs — not new ideas and inventions; important as these are, and not geniuses and supermen, but persons who can be, that is, persons who have a center of strength within themselves.

— Rollo May, The Courage to Create

Designated Heroes, Special Powers, and Moral Codes

The Hero's Journey is by no means purely a Campbellian concept. The champion of the oppressed and misbegotten, the inspiring leader of thought and (wo)men, and the bringer of change is a vital theme not just of movies, shows, and books but going back through thousands of years of mythological and inspirational narratives. The longing for role models and moral guidance is a positive human trait, as is the yearning for transformation.

We find it in *The Lord of the Rings, Dune, Superman, Highlander, Star Wars, The Matrix, Harry Potter,* and *The Hunger Games.* Quite a few of these plots cross over from literature, signifying not only the mysticism of being born special but also the magic that develops in the act of designated *becoming,* a sigil step on Destiny's agenda, making for grand story arcs.

For when the heart insists on its destiny, resisting the general blandishment, then the agony is great, so too the danger. Forces, however, will have been set in motion beyond the reckoning of the senses. Sequences of events from the corners of the world will draw gradually together, and miracles of coincidence bring the inevitable to pass.

— Joseph Campbell, The Hero with a Thousand Faces

Another successful, long-standing concept is that of the destined, transformative, if not resurrected, *chosen one*. It goes back several millennia. We find it in the myths of Egypt, in the epics of Mesopotamia, the poems of Greece and Rome, in the epics of the Egyptian Horus, the Indian Lord Krishna, the Zoroastrian Mithras, the Greek Orpheus, the Trojan-Roman Aeneas, and the Abrahamic Jesus.

One flourishing undercurrent in many films involves heroic interceptors abiding by a moral code they refuse to break, no matter what. But aside from great action scenes, humanity also craves heroes who do not need to injure or kill others to achieve their goals. Where do we find the answer to another deep human desire—that of a world where superheroes are no longer required because this version of the earthly stage is just and kind, so all extraordinary vigilantes can finally relax and write their memoirs? Chosen ones often rise to the requirement for a fixer. Take the original Batman's Gotham. Yet even Batman hopes for positive change. But then, Batman is a vigilante archetype, representing a branch of modern Destiny personified, in his case, in the guise of fateful ferociousness behind a rubber mask. But he is nonetheless a reminder of higher justice and reassuring certainty, a grandson of Nemesis.

Actual heroes often lead a double life and hide behind a kind of vizard, cloaking their abilities in obscurity, unable and unwilling to gain from their gifts. That's where fairly inconspicuous day jobs come in handy.

But now to the most complex exemplars: the antiheroes. These guys are more-dimensional, often achieving the desired result through unusual, unconventional, and sometimes broody and cynical stewardship of necessity, sometimes amplified by night-colored traits and not-so-shining motivation. Still, they are Destiny's pets, and somehow, they know it. We do not have to be a pure Sir Galahad or a noble Sir Percival to get the job done and restore order. The grand principle prefers a maverick.

Necessity's desire to designate and activate slumbering heroes cannot be better explained by anyone other than Joseph Campbell, the original *ersatz-daddy*, mythographer, and defender of crumbling manliness.

However, I salute the more mindful take on The Hero's Journey by the psychotherapist Dr. Miles Neale. In his 2018 book, *Gradual Awakening: The Tibetan Buddhist Path of Becoming Fully Human,* he combines neuroscience with a compacted approach to the twelve stages of Campbell's concept. Three plateaus are meant to help the seeker leave behind self-centeredness, emotional burdens, biased ways of (over) thinking, and compulsive behavioral patterns to walk a path of finding wisdom and enlightenment as a fully actualized human being, ready and able to enrich the world. Neale also addresses the issue of guru adulation and offers a grounded, perhaps less mythical, spectacular, and dramatic option to the often self-indulgent pseudo-heroic path. His approach is timeless-modern, balanced, and aligned with the ideals of the greater good.

Intercepting Destiny

Time traveling can provide certain options to change a perceived or, indeed, a looming future fate. This science fiction movie trope enjoys enduring popularity. Think of the *Terminator* franchise. Or *X-Men: Days of the Future Past*—Wolverine's task is to prevent the Sentinels from eradicating humans and mutants.

The possibility of foreknowing the future is another rich topic. Predictive power comes with the absolute maximum responsibility resting on the shoulders of the seer, such as on *Doctor Who, Sliders,* or *Quantum Leap.* The 1997 show *Crime Traveller* also allowed its protagonists to use a time machine to review past crimes to solve in the present.

In *12 Monkeys,* Bruce Willis' character goes back in time to prevent a deadly virus from spreading, threatening to annihilate the majority of humans in the future. But is his mission just the product of projected fear of an absurd future? Or even schizophrenia?

The ability to divine the future, see the past, and even unveil hidden events of the present was, is, and will always be a tough job.

The movie *Edge of Tomorrow* introduces the concept of repeating failure over and over to become more resilient with each defeat. *The Butterfly Effect* shows that altered experience comes with a price and that our mere existence can play a part in the Destiny of others.

Precognition, Premonition, and Prophecy

We have already talked about the role of divination, foreknowledge, and prophecy in the realms of Destiny.

Precognition, or the ability to know the future, is a screenwriter's feast across all genres, from science fiction to comedy. And why is it such an important theme? Because it transcends the ego and changes the perspective. It may even dwarf our selfhood until we understand that it is not down to us alone to shape the future and our destinies. In the 1944 film *It Happened Tomorrow*, a news reporter gets a paper with tomorrow's headlines. Still, instead of preventing the next day's scenario, the protagonist unwittingly brings about tomorrow's events.

The 90s show *Early Edition* makes a superhero out of an ordinary man who is visited by an orange tabby cat presenting a copy of tomorrow's newspaper, turning the guy into a game-changer. *Early Edition* argues that precognition and knowledge of what is bound to happen can enable us to do something about it. The movie *It Happened Tomorrow* suggests that knowing the future may just be clairvoyance, and despite the presence of this arcane ability, nothing can be done to alter the course of what is meant to happen.

Looper shows what time traveling and knowledge of the future can do to those seeing what lies ahead.

In *Next*, Nicolas Cage's character uses magic to foresee a terrorist threat. *Minority Report* features future crime determination technology, which enables law enforcement to apprehend offenders before they can strike.

And what does this tell us about Destiny? Again, everything because the future is not always open to negotiations. *Final Destination* provides a backdrop of the predetermination of death in the characters where they all try and fail to avoid it—*déjà vu* or not.

> *Respect your curses, for they are the instruments of your destiny.*
> – JOSEPH CAMPBELL

Prophecies in films fall into a different category—divining the future through prophecy, i.e., acquired information through a supernatural force or God(s). In *The Lord of the Rings*, several story strands pertain to the mesmerizing effects of foreordainment.

Taking Charge of Destiny

Productions featuring British monarch Henry VIII, such as *The Other Boleyn Girl, Anne of the Thousand Days,* and *The Tudors*, offer opulent insights on how love, hubris, and the pressing need to produce a male heir. Henry VIII divorced his pious but reproductively dysfunctional first queen, Catherine, to marry the young, charming, intelligent Anne Boleyn, hoping for a son to inherit the throne. When this endeavor only resulted in a little girl, Elizabeth, and no male heir materialized from his union with his second queen, Anne Boleyn was swiftly and falsely accused of incest and got herself beheaded. Her dismissed daughter, who was even officially declared a bastard, became one of the most powerful monarchs of her time, the Virgin Queen, who symbolically gave birth to England's golden age—last words, laughs, and so on. Misguided ambition can be so fruitless. Henry married six times, fathered one sickly son, and eventually failed in his plans to secure the male Tudor bloodline.

All his struggles came to nothing; Destiny had a different aim, and a shunned little girl rose as the celebrated Elizabeth Regina. Finally, her wrongly accused mother Anne Boleyn's dream came true after all—yet, with a twist, since her daughter became the then most powerful woman in the world, not her.

Apart from presenting what is good or right, films featuring Destiny also foster hope and inspiration to change the world for all the right reasons.

The King and I tells the story of an Englishwoman who, as a governess, changes the mindset of the traditional King of Siam, thus improving his children's outlook. *The Pursuit of Happiness* follows an African American who changes his family's fortunes through the survival of a series of hardships as a homeless man, only to have a great opportunity land in his lap, enabling him to become one of the most successful traders on Wall Street. The *Star Wars* franchise is steeped in the principle of being chosen for a high purpose and agency of Destiny, just as in Ridley Scott's *Gladiator*, where the actual mover is writ large all over the script and movie. Protagonist Maximus' painful journey of self-transience is a reminder of the fact that one person can dismantle large frameworks of life and society and that, sometimes, one (wo)man can indeed change the world.

Games of Destinies

In spite of not being a gamer myself, I salute the fact that interactive games can come quite close to the proper idea of Destiny. They offer direct involvement vis-à-vis our passive consumption of impressive yet mere third-party experiences that we follow when reading a story, watching a movie, or internalizing the narratives of religions and dogmatic ideologies.

As in all other creative media, the grand cosmic plan is often a leading factor in video games. One of them stands out like a beacon, often called the best video game of them all, with a wonderful soundtrack and lasting message of hope.

The Legend of Zelda, 1986 (Nintendo EAD) and its 3D follow-up *Ocarina of Time*, 1998 (Nintendo) are exceptional open-ended, third-person game creations featuring the concept of a complex, challenging, and thought-provoking Destiny. Link, a young boy declared "Child of Destiny," is tasked with the rescue of Princess Zelda from the clutches of the evil Ganondorf while utilizing and battling multi-layered dynamics and highly psychological twists in his time-traveling attempts to regain the Triforce of Power, Courage, and Wisdom and bring peace to the land of Hyrule.

In *Majora's Mask*, 2000 (Nintendo), Link has to prevent an apparently inevitable catastrophe of darkest-fate proportions by overcoming recurring nightmare-style obstacles with his braveness and ability to co-influence the not always iron thread of Destiny. This sequel also allows for a first-person perspective.

Ōkami, 2006, (Clover Studio/Capcom) is a third-person adventure where a white she-wolf regains the sun-goddesses' power fighting the forces of evil. It is based on heroic Destiny in the tradition of Japan's rich mythology.

Life is Strange, 2015 (Dontnod) is based on the ripples of Edward Lorenz's deterministic Butterfly Effect, which we looked at in the chapter *Affiliated Destinal Agencies*. In winding back the strand of time via the third-person view, questions arise about the importance of human choices pertaining to the free will and predetermination debate.

Despite it not being philosophically connected to the notion of Destiny, I like to give an honorary mention to *Destiny*, 2014 (Bungie), a top-rated interactive, originally first-person shooter open-world game. It takes place in a post-apocalyptic world ruled by an oppressive regime called the Red Legion.

Seemingly boundless developments in machine learning like natural language processing, computer vision, and deep reinforcement learning of A.I. are generating a new generation of games, inviting players beyond all those already fascinating options since the inception of video games in the early sixties of the 20th century. At the time of writing this, we are migrating from the already existent option of multiple to uncountable, unlimited outcomes for human players and uncontrolled non-player characters (NPC), including dialogue.

Digital Destiny, anyone?

A Love That's Meant to Be?

From every human being there rises a light that reaches straight to heaven. When two souls are destined for each other and find each other, their streams of light flow together and a single brighter light goes forth from their united being.

— Rabbi Israel ben Eliezer, known as Baal Shem Tov

We've made it to the most requested chapter to explore some of the popular concepts of the two great phenomenons that make the world spin, separately and in concert: love and Destiny.

But is destined love even relevant?

Can a significant other be our Destiny, or can we be theirs? Is getting our emotional, romantic, and passionate ideals and needs to meet a metaphysically envisaged and apportioned path in its own right? Just for us to live happily ever after? Seriously? Is that not a bit entitled to expect? And where is the Destiny in that? Or is there a special purpose in finding the perfect partner, a mission even to transcend the here and now and create meaning and more for the benefit of others?

We know this phenomenon under quite a few different monikers: soul mates, twin flames, divine union, heavenly match, intertwined souls, and companions forevermore, even beyond the gates of death and back, time and again, even if theoretically speaking, we'll have different Destinies each time around unless we are on a prolonged or perpetual assignment.

Therefore, *Destilove* is the ultimate life goal for many of us.

It can be a bewitching, if not surreal, experience to feel that we've met "the one" when our heart begins to race the moment we gaze upon or speak with someone who makes our pulse and our common sense perform somersaults.

And if we go on to believe we have known this person for much longer than we do, something seems to tell us this may just be the kind of designated magic we have been waiting for all along.

Love and the yearning to become and stay as one with another person come effortlessly with the idea of Destiny. A few thousand years of history, literature, art, and ballads are full of stories of lovers, detailing how their emotions inspired them to do whatever it takes to be with the one. Love, like war, makes us do the most extraordinary things.

We live in a time when falling in love is made almost too easy. In the past and in some cultures, forming a romantic bond was and is a highly observed and convention-bound affair. Today, many of us can create representations of who we are or how we want to be seen online, on social media, and through various apps to assist in the pursuit of attention. Sometimes, although all those tech tools are at our command, and we master many ways to make ourselves appear desirable, we still hit obstacles in finding authentic, sincere, and lasting love.

The idea of crossing the path of the person we are destined to be with is as much in favor as, if not more, than ever. Not to everyone, though, since Destiny isn't always given importance when it comes to sincere love or whether a person or a relationship is worth giving our everything. Several directions of popular research [151] question, if not negate, the idea that we stand a chance of ever finding the ones we may be scheduled to be with. And for those who do not see human Destiny as a factor of life, albeit chosen by incredible numbers of us worldwide, being meant for a specific person can appear either like an absurd notion or a highly desirable yet impossible ideal. Some sources even claim that believing in destined love or concepts like soulmates makes it harder, if not ruinous, to our chances to ever embark on a lasting relationship due to unfulfilled mystical expectations.

We are here to find a golden mean between different perspectives. But before it gets interesting, I pause for an important point. Let's take a tiny detour to the ancient Greeks again, who knew seven different ways to love, rarely active or present all at once, but often, each of them in good time, which is fine when we come to think of it without wearing those rose-tinted glasses humans can be so partial to.

> *Agape*:   selfless,   all-embracing,   charitable,   and compassionate devotion.

Storge: familiar and limitless emotion.

Pragma: loyal and companionate fondness.

Philia: genuine, virtuous, and faithful affection.

Philautia: wholesome and realistic friendship and self-appreciation.

Ludus: coquettish, flirty, and high-spirited enchantment.

Eros: ardent, sensual, and physical passion.

Romantic love wasn't on the cards for the majority of our foremothers and fathers. Marriage was there to generate heirs for the more fortunate and providers for the less affluent. There was no security system in place, not for old age, misadventures, or ill health. Keeping land and other possessions together and using arranged marriages as strategic tools was the norm. Love stories were the exception to the rule, and these narratives for idealists and daydreamers became popular tropes in literature and song. For men, it was deemed permissible to look for an *affaire du cœur* and get lots more out of life wherever their fancy took them. It is not that our forebears were generally horrible or irresponsible. Let's give them the benefit of the doubt and consider male DNA in tandem with the effects of a patriarchal society, an international norm then, still fully operative today in many parts of the world. Understandably, "real" big love stories were the exception to a global rule. Not getting into a marital union for predominantly pragmatic reasons but expecting a love match only became en vogue in the Western World courtesy of the Romantic Movement (ca. 1780s–1850s) via literature, art, music, and many other expressions. It was when our predecessors began to feel fed up with the overexposure of religious and cultural dogma and their far too many limitations. So, instead, they celebrated feelings and freedom. Women wanted to be treated and do better in every department. So going forward, sensitive and sensible expectations made way for growing entitlement to sweet love, hot sex, sincere intentions, and enduring fidelity, all rolled into the relationship du jour. And that's when our increasing divorce rate was firmly added to the menu in the Global North after WWII, and it's not only a lot now but stuck there ever since, for better or worse. At least girls now cheat almost as often as guys. Is that strictly necessary to balance the books? No, but it is unsurprising all the same. Too low or high expectations will always fail or at least fall on their faces. A significant connection to another spirit dwells in the invisible realms of shared character, empathy, solidarity, wisdom, and values, making for a stable, beautiful meant-to-be unity. And yes, there could be an objective to conquer. All else could just turn out to be cosmic sugar dust.

That brings us to the concept of partners in Destiny: rare and precious as the legendary bond over time and space.

We are looking at a phenomenon that should neither be mindlessly expected nor taken for granted because it may just land the way we hope. Destiny does not necessarily only mean for something to be pre-decreed, so guaranteed to occur. It can also result in the opposite—even in the bitter fact we don't get what we think we want.

Before we delve deeper, let's address an increasing problem: when overly proclaimed love isn't real.

Genuinely loving someone is an outstanding experience. And to be loved this way ranges far above all else. Yet, not all loves are created equal. There are countless examples of modern-day lovers who look for their next true soulmate whenever the previous model has been let go for not being "soulmatey" enough. So, a new soul flame must be found under the fashionable tagline that *"he or she is out there."* So no wonder more and more of our contemporaries now try to use the object of their desire as an emotional supply. We have two kinds of love to look at. The first example—enduring love—is ideally unconditional and without grand expectations, healthfully growing from pure emotion, authenticity, sincerity, and the absence of neediness, because this rare state is predominantly about the beloved. Unrequited love comes to mind, along with complex relationships and the many variations of loss.

I hold it true, whate'er befall; I feel it, when I sorrow most;
'tis better to have loved and lost, than never to have loved at all.
— Alfred, Lord Tennyson

The second and problematic example, a less classic form, is rife in persons with selfish tendencies, focusing on possible benefits gained from the other's affection, seeking their reflection in the eyes of the perceived incarnation or external ornament of our ego. Some personality afflictions can lead to expertly seeking emotional stockpiling, stemming from a constant drip of neediness to be adored to imagine being in love, basking in the other's care and attention.

A conjured, fervently branded soulmates' agenda may be rolled out after just a few weeks, or even days or hours, of first contact. Some fake folks go to great lengths and even throw around that Destiny or karma has a hand in their current relationship agenda. It is time to run if we hear or read any of this. Fast.

Why are so many of us like that these days? Before we judge, we should not forget what we talked about earlier. Not all behaviors and traits are intentional or "willed." We are in much less control than some of us want to acknowledge. So we should always also ask *why* an increasing amount of us are displaying such disturbing emotional patterns. Their genetic composures and life experiences may have pushed them into one or the other corner, emulating, replicating, and dishing out only what they learned and knew, possibly in early mental self-defense or as a coping mechanism.

No one is just good or bad. Nobody is perfect, and that includes our precious and vulnerable selfhoods. Walking away is the best route, but judgment isn't. A little tolerance and empathy also avoid being drawn into a vindictive vortex of disappointment-driven injury, even hatred. Not worth it, next to the fact that we are not here to do Nemesis's job or bring about instant karma.

Rising above, cutting the cord, and moving on is the healthiest strategy, even if that feels unfair to our wounded feelings. And there may be distinct reasons why a franchisee of the Narcissus brand targeted us in the first place. Perhaps we are too inclined to dependencies topped with a sliver of gullibility? Too easily love-bombed and hoodwinked? A bit of self-reflection and humility goes a long way. Also, here is a little comfort: Luckily, we will have gotten away before everything becomes unhinged.

No matter what magazines and rom-coms claim in their hyperbole tropes of whirlwind romances, rapid awareness of infatuating soul connections *being out there,* genuine, enduring love seldom happens at first sight, and it neither idolizes the beloved nor puts them up on a plinth or a pedestal like a God(dess).

Actual love is rarely rapid. Sincere love takes time. It's not being blown in by a whirlwind and it does not fall prey to emotional craze, peppered with delusion, obsession, infatuation, or projection. Love does not expect the constant provision of thrilling sensations. Nor does it demand non-stop good vibes to lift the needy part from an otherwise drab and mundane existence devoid of any meaning. If encountered—run! Fast. Sadly, I've seen too many good persons suffer from this kind of fake love. Fortunately, more people are getting aware of these negative and often destructive traits of the "too good to be true love interest" and are on their guard, no matter how thick the love bombs are raining down far too soon.

Attitudinal values, however, are actualized wherever the individual is faced with something unalterable, something imposed by destiny. From the manner in which a person takes these things upon himself, assimilates these difficulties into his own psyche, there flows an incalculable multitude of value potentialities.

> *The only question is whether the failure to achieve love is really imposed by destiny and is not a neurotic failure, one for which the person has himself to blame.*
>
> – VIKTOR FRANKL

We need to talk about infatuation. It may sound attractive, but it isn't. This state has nothing to do with feelings sent by the often Destiny-replacing term fate. Infatuation was coined in the 1600s to describe an almost instant amorous behavior bewitchingly blinded by magnetic entitlement, acute dependency, eros, and stupidity. The term harkens back to the Latin word *fatuus,* meaning silly, from which *infatuatus* developed, translating to making a right old fool of ourselves. [152]

Try not to let that happen to our feelings and longings and retreat if we or a romantic candidate display infatuation symptoms.

Sadly, another way to fall into the trap of imagined Destiny beckons. When we feel lonely, left out, and deprived of affection and companionship, we interpret deep and foreordained meaning in someone's words or actions. Here, it's not the other party that plays the tricky part. In this case, a seeker may exclusively listen to their inner yearning, looking for tangible signs of having been *made for each other*, leading to false positives of Jungian synchronicity. Flirtatious and seemingly spiritual phrases and buzzwords like soulmates or "fate brought us together" don't signify the hand of the Great Aim. It is more important to double-check the validity of our own and the other party's desires and possible manifestations before we take anything for granted, and this is true for almost all areas of life.

Destined love or anything worth our while will not appear in the guise of easy catchwords or ulterior motives. If it's Destiny, we'll know. Not just because we want it so, but because it's happening.

The Idea of Preordained Love

You don't find love—it finds you. It's got a little bit to do with destiny, fate and what's written in the stars.

– Anaïs Nin

Our modern world is circled by romantic concepts like magnetic satellites. Is finding perfect love a must-have from the mystic realm of "meant to be"?

Terms like soulmates, twin flames, twin souls, and twin spirits inspire the romantic side of the Internet, the book world, screen productions, and social media. Many definitions and interpretations of the origin and genesis of these time-honored, hope and desire-inducing views are about. The most mesmerizing narrative was gifted to us by the Greek philosopher Plato. In his *Symposium* (an academic banquet), the playwright Aristophanes (446 BCE–386 BCE) talks about a legend from the time when there were female, male, and androgynous beings— the original human "two in one" souls. They were split into separate parts by a seriously disgruntled Zeus. He even condemned the drifting halves, already severely incomplete as is, to feel compelled to longingly seek reunion with the missing parts in the hope of becoming whole again.

According to idyllic interpretations of this myth, we can only comprehend the state of completeness if we find our missing half or if they find us.

> *And, when one of them meets the other half—the actual half of himself, whether he be a lover of youth or a lover of another sort—the pair are lost in an amazement of love and friendship and intimacy and one will not be out of the other's sight, as I may say, even for a moment.*
>
> – PLATO, THE SYMPOSIUM

Plato went on to dispute this perhaps oversimplified idea by not taking the mythical tale all too seriously. But he stated that *true love* seeks only those significant others who are good through and through, being good to all sides. So while Plato is largely credited with introducing the concept of storied mystical love and ideal union by design in a philosophical, if not an abstract, setting, he makes a point that we should only ever love a person who is positive for us—a lover with whom, together, we can achieve the best proactive good. And beyond romantic and sensual love, the famous Platonic relationship invites us to share a pure but non-physical, non-selfish connection defined as loving one another in the highest and purest form.

Destinal love would never require validation from the visible world since it is meaningful in itself. And this kind of attachment does not require the expectation of being completed via an idealized amorous alliance. First, it just does not work like that, and second, there are more significant avenues to seek.

The idea of a designated other is not exclusively confined to intimate liaisons. A destined partner can be a person we feel a deep affinity with—we may feel simpatico, compatible, and like-minded. We may feel inclined to protect and comfort each other or turn shared aspirations into actual deeds, and we may experience a mutual feeling of complete trust and loyalty.

Emotional or other forms of dependence aren't playing any part in being meant for one another, nor ulterior motives like seeking to fulfill easy, materialistic ambitions. All of that betrays the very notion of good love. It is not a destined partner's job to furnish us with what we lack outside the spiritual and emotional sphere. It would uncloak us as the antithesis of the idea of *meant to be*. We can build a life together and care for each other in every way, yet in fair exchange for mutual growth on all levels.

Why do we feel the need to be completed, even to have been designed for each other? Without the intention of trivializing, it could come over as a bit entitled to expect a cosmic match only to get our romantic, let alone material, requirements met. Ethical and honest partners should empower and bring out the best in each other by supporting and even reinforcing complete acceptance and, together, developing who and what the two characters bring to the shared path, but not like saviors, fixers, mentors, or coaches, let alone therapists, no matter how tempting and flattering that idea may be. That, apart from a lack of qualification and experience, would, again, defy the original objective of two intended spirits accepting each other wholly without arbitrary remodeling. The likes of Pygmalion, Svengali, or Professor Higgins need not apply, and if they do, it's time to let them go before they try to fulfill their fantasies.

The calling is to sincerely and responsibly love significant others while not trying to change them into what we believe to be perfect. We do not want this beautiful, ancient notion to end up serving as a crutch, lending consequence where otherwise we find insufficient substance.

Finding a destined other is a gift, while being one is often a challenge, but the romantic side is not the main reason we exist.

> *When love has fused and mingled two beings in a sacred and angelic unity, the secret of life has been discovered so far as they are concerned; they are no longer anything more than the two boundaries of the same destiny; they are no longer anything but the two wings of the same spirit. Love, soar.*
>
> – VICTOR HUGO, LES MISÉRABLES

Let's look to a few different cultures for compelling destined partnership concepts. We've already talked about Yuanfen, the unique coincidental Destiny revered in China and Vietnam, encompassing romantic and all other relationships. Then we have the legendary *Red Thread of Fate* or *Pinyin*. According to an East Asian myth, the Moon God ties a red string of silken yarn around the ankles of two newborn babies, connecting them for their whole lives despite being hidden from mortal view. The somehow elastic red twine will ensure that even if the two intended lovers drift apart, they will always find each other again.

The Chinese folktale of the red thread explains how the Great D can lead two individuals to identify each other, no matter when, where, or how. The red thread is an unbreakable bond, symbolizing love and Destiny over time and space.

> *It is our destiny to meet across a thousand miles.*
> *A coincidence decreed or destined by heaven.*
>
> – CHINESE PROVERB

The ancient Dao system of *Bazi*—the four pillars of Destiny—allows the foretelling of the future under the guidance of *The Science of Destiny* using an eight-character system also used to determine perfect partnerships, times of luck, and gifts of life.

And, as previously mentioned, in Judaism, the romantic ideal of the Bashert, Yiddish for Destiny, encourages followers to look out for a divinely pre-chosen love partner.

In our increasingly technological and success-oriented, problem-riddled age, is the belief in a deep, destinal connection not at risk of being reduced to just wishful thinking and hope in an idea that could be too good to be true? Fortunately, falling in love does not necessarily mean we must battle against everybody and their uncle to fight for the right and freedom to feel what we feel. Destined others are said to be ready to do whatever it takes to be there for their significant person, fiercely campaigning for each other's interests, a relationship decreed to succeed by enabling us to soar.

When Destined Love Isn't in the Cards

What if we wish or have to "settle"? What if that turns out to be a necessity? Any good love is never of lesser quality than the destined variety. It's just a different path. No reason to stay single or refuse a caring relationship simply because it wasn't our turn to have that meant-to-be experience. And since so many millions of us worldwide believe in reincarnation, it may just take time before it happens.

What if we went wrong and the presumed lucky-in-love parcel from Destiny turns out to have been a tad light? When perfection begins to fade, and the attraction goes faint? Sharp disappointment can set in when relationships go south. Were we foreordained, after all, or were we just imbued in a fantasy conjured up to demand delivery from a sphere surrounding the desire for an elevated context? That makes for bitterness, but what if it is still valid anyway, and this dimmed episode turns out to be necessary?

Would that mean adopting a stiff upper lip, seeing it through, learning, and improving? Yes, it can be part of our Destiny to be a sterling partner without expecting the other to be flawless in return. It is an art to make a relationship work through loyalty, effort, and accepting enchantment, passion, laughs, and good health, as much as ailments, warts, scars, baggage, and everything else—timeless wisdom courtesy of the Bible.

A destined relationship will find itself in alliance with not just the partner but the values of the great cosmic energy. Even, if not especially, in the face of adversity and loss. A bond to master time, space, and circumstances. That is what we call love, destined or otherwise.

World-Changing Power Couples

Love, like Destiny, can enable us to plant the root of human greatness and create a legacy that will continue to inspire others to excel at being or becoming ethical individuals.

Love induces us to seek and achieve the impossible, and in some cases, it empowers bringing a much-needed change to the world.

Throughout history and steeped in literature, partners in Destiny shine from the first heartbeat they found each other.

Let us look at a few actual tales of dream teams that went on to build more than just their personal realms from the moment they found each other.

Michelle LaVaughn Robinson (born 1964) and Barack Obama (born 1961) first met in the field of corporate law. Their relationship is one of the most popular contemporary love stories. The Obamas wrote history as the first African-American couple to make it to the White House. Despite the fact they may not be to everybody's taste due to Barack Obama's actions and inactions during his time as POTUS, they still stand out as a personal example of an alliance to be reckoned with.

Cher Wang (born 1958) and Chen Wen-ch'i (born 1955), both tech entrepreneurs, reshuffled the world of the mobile phone industry when they started HTC in 1997. They proved that being united in life and business can indeed work well.

Queen Elizabeth II (1926–2022) and the Duke of Edinburgh (1921–2021) have shown the world how it's done as a loyal, disciplined, and successful par-excellence royal wife and husband. Their married journey began in 1947, and they remained a tight-knit unit of confidence.

Whatever our sentiments are about any royal house's history, these two stood the test of time.

Their son, King Charles III (born 1948), and his Queen Camilla (born 1947) tick almost all the boxes of a destined couple that patiently mastered thick and thin, no matter what.

Beyoncé (born 1981) and Jay Z (born 1969) demonstrate their might as a married couple and in business by also merging their two pop-music empires.

To be a preordained item does not guarantee or demand staying together. Destiny does not work in possessive or bourgeois ways.

Looking back at history, we have more examples:

India's Mughal Shah Jahan (1592–1666) and his queen Mumtaz Mahal's (1593–1631) union became legendary not only as exemplary royal affection. Their love produced one of the world's greatest symbolic and aesthetic wonders. When Mumtaz died in childbirth, Shah Jahan's grief led him to build the Taj Mahal near Agra as their final resting place and a symbol of his feelings for Mumtaz. Today, it is still one of the most memorable architectural masterpieces and an emblem of enduring love.

Marie Sklodowska (1867–1934) and Pierre Curie's (1859–1906) chemistry went beyond a mere relationship and the laboratory. The marriage of Madame and Monsieur Curie not only proved that compatibility exists. Together, they gave the world the X-ray and pioneered incredible advancements in physics, medicine, and microbiology.

The philosopher and writer Jean-Paul Sartre (1905–1980) and the feminist novelist Simone de Beauvoir (1908–1986) were the stars of existentialism—one of the most influential and disruptive modern schools of thought. These two lovers forged an intellectual alliance beyond physical and romantic spheres. Their respective opinions suggest the absence of divine powers and, for that matter, an impossibility of feminine biological and other destinies. However:

The cards are the cards.

— SIMONE DE BEAUVOIR

While love can guide gifted individuals to work together and alter the course of politics, science, and the arts, it can also make society change its worldviews about existing stigmas and taboos.

Novelist Gertrude Stein (1874–1946) and avant-garde personality Alice B. Toklas (1877–1967) dared to modify how same-sex relationships were viewed by becoming media darlings in the US. They were one of the most fabulous forces of the avant-garde movement, openly living as a couple. Their influential Parisian salon welcomed many important writers and artists of the time.

Mildred Jeter (1939–2008) and Richard Loving (1933–1975) created eternal footprints of freedom by falling in love as an interracial couple during American segregation. They uprooted the law preventing their marriage by reaching out to the Attorney General of the United States, Robert Kennedy. In 1967, in the landmark case Loving v. Virginia, the Supreme Court declared the ban on interracial marriages in 16 states unconstitutional.

Rachel Robinson (born 1922) and her husband Jackie suffered the pressures of living in a white-dominated society. Jackie Robinson (1919–1972) was the first African American to play Major League Baseball with the Brooklyn Dodgers. Jackie and Rachel suffered from racial prejudice and slurs while constantly receiving death threats to no avail; they stood close, strong, and tall, and their connection helped pave the path for the American Civil Rights movement.

When the going gets tough, this love will rise to fight and shine, as illustrated in the real love stories above.

While we readily use the terms soulmate or *destined other* to define an ideal love life, these mesmerizing concepts also cover the other areas of our dynamic work or creative relationships, albeit far less commonly.

Destined Synergy

There exists an already set, connective power beyond romance that produces ideal partnerships of an inventive and productive kind. These folks click, gel, and open the floodgates of congenial imagination when producing results. Some are secretive or laid back about it, while others dare to publicize and visualize their special union.

This compatibility is not defined by sensual attraction or intense romantic feelings like the lovers' soulmate or twin flame departments. Our minds meet through shared values, beliefs, dreams, and ambitions. Affinity smiles. We complement each other. We resemble Alpha and Omega, wind and fire. We are at one in a one-of-a-kind fashion. Plato, who revered an accord of verity and authenticity above the notion of happiness, would applaud. Goal-focused practical and intellectual capacity—i.e., successful and even hard work—is by no means a sinister form of doctrinal retribution (as per the Book of Genesis) or less important than romance. However, it always depends on what we want or must do and how. Sometimes, the occupational arena can be an even more attractive, comforting, and peaceful environment than the constant quest for the mirage of perfect love or saturated private life.

Some of the strongest pairings are not even romantic, whether in literature or real life.

Fictional Synergies

Huckleberry Finn and Tom Sawyer—Mark Twain's boy heroes—hail from opposite shores of the Mississippi. They do not have much in common socially but bond intensely over their shared adventurous, unconventional inclinations.

Ernie and Bert—Joan Ganz Cooney and Lloyd N. Morrisett's characters from Sesame Street—are a subtle demonstration of the values of good companionship and the ability to compromise, loved by millions of children worldwide.

Vladimir and Estragon—Samuel Beckett's tragicomical characters from his existentialist play *Waiting for Godot*—are united in their hope to be instructed in the meaning of life by the character Godot, who never shows up.

Captain Kirk and Mr. Spock—two distinctly different natures: Kirk, the emotional human, and Spock, the principled semi-Vulcan logician, connected through mutual simpatico, respect, and shared responsibilities for the USS Enterprise, and all that with an impressive portion of noble Earth-Vulcan values.

In actual life, professional synergies turn visions into flourishing careers and even modern empires that sparkle while the team phase lasts.

Business Synergies

Steve Jobs (1955–2011) and Steve Wozniak (born 1950)—co-founded Apple.

Bill Gates (born 1955) and Paul Allen (1953–2018)—co-founded Microsoft.

Larry Page (born 1973) and Sergey Brin (born 1973)—co-founded Google.

Marc Randolph (born 1958) and Reed Hastings (born 1960)—co-founded Netflix.

Music and Show Business Synergies

Paul McCartney and John Lennon—the congenial songwriters, main faces, and voices of The Beatles from 1962 to 1970—shared a musical harmony so intense and successful that McCartney described their artistic connection as "irreplaceable." In 1966, John Lennon met his future wife, Yoko Ono. In 1967, Paul McCartney found the love of his earlier life in the American photographer and animal rights activist Linda Eastman. Their happy marriage lasted twenty-nine years until Linda's death in 1998.

John and Yoko displayed an intimate union until Lennon's murder in 1980. Yoko Ono was blamed for breaking up The Beatles. But if something, anything, is meant to last, it cannot be broken easily, be it a band or any other formation.

Elaine May (born 1932) and Mike Nichols (1931–2014)—brought us smiles with their iconic improvisation comedy and unique creative relationship between 1959 and 1962. When they parted ways as a comedy duo, both went on to respective great careers as screenwriters and directors.

Robert Redford (born 1936) and Paul Newman (1925–2008)—starred with unbeatable double onscreen presence in *Butch Cassidy and the Sundance Kid* (1969) and *The Sting* (1973) and formed a lasting friendship.

Beyond Love—Transformative Synergies

Whether we call them soulmates, twin flames, destined others, synergies, or magnetic relationships—fulfilling your Destiny as a couple or dream team through the discovery of mutual goals and the will and ability to propel each other to the next level is a gift worth aspiring to, with or without romantic love, with or without success, and with or without riches.

Let us meet a few historic matches that deserve to be labeled: destined.

Roman Empress Livia Drusilla and Emperor Augustus—prime examples of female force and trust in a patriarchal world. Livia Augusta (59 BCE–29 CE) cast the cosmic continuum's mighty shadow over the once ruthless, later far more benevolent ruler Augustus (63 BCE–14 CE). Together, they transformed the Roman Empire from within.

Byzantine Imperial couple Theodora (ca. 500–548 CE) and Justinian I (482–565 CE)—a former dancer and a farmer's son—left lasting legacies in many areas and became one of the most famous married achievers in history.

American human rights activist Eleanor Roosevelt (1884–1962) and US President Franklin D. Roosevelt (1882–1945)—the quintessential unorthodox couple that left their mark on America and the world.

British tenor Peter Pears (1910–1986) and composer Benjamin Britten (1913–1976)—voice and music in the companionship of devoted love.

Rose is a rose is a rose.

– GERTRUDE STEIN, SACRED EMILY

Life continues to be an adventure, and the treasures we seek can become that one love of a lifetime. Sometimes, there may even be two loves or two or three synergies present on our journeys. Destinal relationships are by no means exhaustive of just a pairing of two. Being proverbial kindred spirits is far more impactful than often limited-term erotic attraction or the insistence on living in a romantic bubble. Moreover, it is also possible that any of these treasured relationships will only last for a while or that a mere companion or someone we cross roads with is *a* or *the* one in a different way—not through just sensual love and not by completing us, but by mutually complementing our respective uniqueness, combined yet individual personalities, unified talents, and perhaps an envisaged future.

To me, lasting, enduring, successful love in the face of whatever life throws at us seems to work best as an ethical philosophy instead of being based just on feelings. But then, I'm not all too romantically inclined, so perhaps best skip this paragraph?

Love regularly starts from an emotional and, far too often, predominantly sensual, even infatuated spark.

Our emotions can feel wonderful, just free will, yet they are in the habit of being composed of many imponderables, hormones, chemical reactions, moods, etc. They can fly too high, rooted in neediness, fear of missing out, or even personality distortions, rarely in sincerity. Feelings can be fleeting, at best just volatile by nature, with an added potential to disappoint the other(s). And then some. Our often far too many emotions aren't destined material, whereas an empathetic philosophy of love remains firmly on the cards. A philosophy, not a religion, mind you. This notion of a caring, responsible state of being with and for others does not gel with dogma and orthodoxy.

It all depends on how we, and our destinies, determine our joined voyage to unfold. Whether our alliances are romantic or not, the people who enter our world for a reason will inspire us to co-create meaning in our lives and for this world. We are here to support one another.

We meet ourselves time and again in a thousand disguises on the path of life.

– CARL JUNG

CONCLUSION

Ubiquity of a Pervasive Compass

We know for a fact that Destiny will never get old. And why is that so? No other notion has held relevance that long, impervious to the oblivion so many different concepts share when we retire them with hardcoded swansong. And that will never change. Here we all are, with the storied topic of this little book all around and within us. It is a universal, teleological principle that is as influential or magical, legitimate or invalid, or true or false as all the other worldviews, whether philosophies or religions. Destiny is matchless, nonesuch, and sans pareil because it is *the* original. The inspiration. The blueprint. The prototype. Our compass [153] rose. As mighty as it gets. Copied often, yet never equaled. Destiny is arguably the most senior and enduring spiritual phenomenon to kindle humanity's relationship with the caring or indifferent cosmos. The grand plan's often anthropomorphized representatives heralded the creation of ritualized and institutionalized faith systems, including those we revere today.

Fortunately, Destiny isn't religious since it lacks dogma and organization. It floats above and beyond any official faith system, wholly independent of anything and anyone else that may play a part in our universe, reflecting our yearning for a purposeful story. Destiny is a catalog of options, not a book of rules and laws, and offers stepping stones over the unknown depths of Nature. And it isn't decreed by anyone but Destiny. There was, is, and will be only one Big D. The rest is an echo.

Why is this popular yet polarizing concept given so much importance in the twenty-first century? Why is it omnipresent, uttered constantly, in our private circles, on the news, in movies, by leaders, lovers, and anyone aspiring to a momentous life?

This important catalyst of olde led to the rise of philosophy and the birth of religions. Seen through the sphere of classic thoughts and beliefs, Destiny is responsible for bringing order to chaos, inspiring intrinsic values and sensible virtues in whole civilizations.

It never ended up as an ancient memory, which is why it remains so active in our spirituality all over the world today.

Many belief systems offer their moral paradigms to benefit their followers. Destiny sparked many schools of metaphysics and epistemology, igniting ways of connective thinking, even if operated under different philosophical notions. That uniting, multicultural, and interspiritual factor is universal ethics.

Let's briefly return to Immanuel Kant and his Categorical Imperative, which can appear slightly rigid to a modern-minded person. It theoretically eliminates the need for religion or a government to enforce what is right or wrong. I like to go as far as to say that the Categorical Imperative, like the Golden Rule, would even solve humanity's obsession with an overload of top-down, imposed order. It is determined by a single ethos invitingly convincing us to respect one another by the simple rationale that what is bad for us is also bad for others.

Because a lot will have to change.

I don't think traditions justify atrocities for whatever reasons anyone may conjure up. What's been *okay* in the past because we didn't know better can turn out to be no longer supportable or sustainable now, let alone in the future. Continuous human slip-ups create a rift regarding the necessary degree of spirit that influences our collective future. If too many folks ignore or even reject embracing universal values, pursuing human Destiny, including a sufficient amount of self-determination, is at risk.

Both ancient philosophers and modern social scientists believe that ethically minded people would be hard-pressed to lose sight of what is right.

Let us revisit the ideas of absolute and practical free will.

Free will requires us to be able to make choices and act on our decisions under any given circumstance; in practice, it allows us to entertain choices when making decisions and consider which of these choices will let us get results that match our personal or adopted value systems. Some traditions and beliefs instilled by our environment may limit or even refuse the right to select personal choices and a self-directed future since the reigning belief or system disregards liberty and culturally unacceptable decisions. And those of us wanting to pursue a desired Destiny may find that we're still forced to make compromises or postpone, if not forgo, according to existing dogmatic norms. In light of these limitations, the necessity arises to stay keenly aware that every action we risk involves a provident analysis of how to reach our goals without upsetting the apple cart too counterproductively. Freedom of thought is an innate energy no one can easily completely rule over or take from us.

Following free choice to fulfill our Destiny may involve leaving a mark on the world. That can take place actively or invisibly. The free mind is a superpower, even if concealed and not enforced.

Every decision creates visible and invisible consequences that cause a slow but definite change in society and the universe's spheres. We can be a significant cause leading to great effect, at last. And we can, and should, stand tall, untarnished by ideology, and subtly rise against what isn't our Destiny.

Without a defined personal or general concept to measure our options and goals, neither wars nor any negative impact on or by Nature will be abolished nor prevented, nor can humanity avoid falling into brand new forms of an uncreative disorder.

One of the attractions of Destiny is that it doesn't belong to any club or worldview because it's a universal concept above and beyond cultural or historical differences, respected, celebrated, yet also dreaded throughout history. And it is honest; no excuses and no need "Destiodicy" due to the clarity that our invitation entails the dance to be likely delightful, possibly dangerous, and sometimes destructive. The choice is ours whether our own Destiny is internal, external, bi-directional, dualistic, non-dualistic, both, everything, or something else.

In concert with large parts of humanity, art, literature, music, movies, and the diverse range of perspectives of both Eastern and Western mythologies and philosophies continue to contribute to its richness and complexity; therefore, there is no end to the fascination and the scope.

Since we can, of course, view Destiny as an individual feat, it is crucial that as many of us as possible partake in creating a shared Destiny to promote the best possible, proactively forged common and individual good while inflicting the least necessary harm to other fellow beings. These are arguably the most substantial ethical obligations to pursue in realizing our united tomorrow. Above and beyond any system we live in or have to endure.

This concept has a specific name, but that is for another book. To me, Destiny is a syncretic, flexible paradigm that intersects with other phenomena such as luck, chance, serendipity, and also with necessity, determinism, and doom, the whole palette of the laws of life. Unsurprisingly, it is the vital ignitor and ongoing lead element of most religious beliefs for reasons we've discussed earlier.

We can re-spark creative cosmic harmony through spiritual determination for today and our children's tomorrow. Destiny—our secret sauce—is no longer just an external phenomenon but a human-internal awareness to guide us forward.

Together, we are the single transcendence. Democratic Destiny.

Is our consciousness of Destiny actual or just a biased illusion? Do we perceive it as a threat or a gift? Is it wishful thinking or simply an inexorable element of life? What are our most straightforward explanations for humanity's options presented by Destiny, predeterminism, and determinism?

If a theological answer is what we're after, the choice is great and offers several truths. As mentioned before, all Gods, retired and active, are stewards of Destiny to me, so all is good in my book.

And if we rather look to the horizons of free thought, we may perceive Destiny as far less elusive than in the past but neither faceless nor indifferent. Our formative paradigm is evolving beyond the spiritual phenomenon of natural law. Because we, yes we—not God(s) or any organized constructs—are the very Agents of Destiny, its rhyme and reason, intrinsically ready and more than capable of transcending arbitrary limitations.

Whether we apply faith, logical sense, Occam's Razor, or our innate knowing, all answers hinge on how every one of us questions, interprets, or accepts our Mona Lisa of spiritual marvels, forever capturing our attention with her unparalleled ability to challenge and inspire.

Endless.

Miscellany

Destiny and Co, In Other Words

Kismet

Fortune

Providence

Fortuity

Lot

Necessity

Decree

Chance

Wyd

The Way the Ball Bounces

Orlay

Joss

Predestination

Portion

Foreordination

Divine Intervention

Happenstance

Predetermination

Divine Will

Prospection

Circumstance

Serendipity

Allotment

Masir

Dharma

The Dice Have Fallen

What Is Written

The Way the Cookie Crumbles

Divine Guidance

Doom

Maktoob

Comeuppance

Luck

Wheel of Fortune

Karma

Certain Outcome

Meant to Be

Vocation

Calling

Design

Aligning Stars

The Dye Is Cast

Iacta Alea Est

Predetermination

Designation

Fortitude

Fortuity

Purpose

Ordinance

International Destinies

A few examples in Roman transliteration:

Arabic: Masir

Armenian: Chakatagir

Chinese: Mìngyùn

Filipino: Tadhana

French: Destin

Georgian: Bedi

German: Schicksal

Greek: Pepromeno

Hebrew: Ye'ood

Hindi: Bhagya, Takadeer

Indonesian: Takdir

Italian: Destino

Japanese: Unmei

Korean: Unmyeong

Latin: Fatum

Norwegian: Skjebne

Persian/Farsi: Bakht

Portuguese: Destino

Russian: Sud'ba

Sanskrit: Vidhi

Spanish: El Destino

Swahili: Hatima

Swedish: Öde

Turkish: Kısmet

Urdu: Muqaddar

Symbols of Destiny

Spindle

Sphere

Thread

Mundane Egg

Stone Tablet

Weaving shuttle

Faravahar (Zoroastrian Winged Guardian)

Cornucopia (Horn of Plenty)

Wheel of Fortune

Scroll

Dharma Wheel

Celtic Knot

Wyrd

Ming

Religions and Faith Systems

Status 2020

Buddhism—507 million.

Christianity—2.38 billion.

Folk Religions—430 million.

Hinduism—1.16 billion

Islam—1.91 billion.

Other—61 million.

Unaffiliated—1.19 billion.

Source: https://worldpopulationreview.com/country-rankings/religion-by-country

This page also offers a comprehensive overview of international religious and non-religious tendencies, developments, and specifics.

The Destinal Theme in Arts and Media

Literature

Benjamin, C. *The Immoralists*. Tinder Press, 2018.

Cornwell, B. *The Last Kingdom*. Harper Collins, 2005.

Dickens, C. *Great Expectations*. Norton & Company, 1999.

Flaubert, G. *Madame Bovary*. Wordsworth Editions Ltd, 1998.

Forster, E. M. *Howard's End*. Everyman's Library, 1991.

Frankl, V. *Trotzdem Ja zum Leben sagen—Ein Psychologe erlebt das Konzentrationslager / Man's Search for Meaning (From Death-Camp to Existentialism)*. Kösel, München, 1976.

Gaiman, N. *The Sandman*. Vertigo, 1989–1996.

Hugo, V. *Les Misérables*. A. Lacroix, Verboeckhoven & Cie, 1862.

Ishiguro, K. *Never Let Me Go*. Faber and Faber, 2005.

Ishiguro, K. *The Remains Of The Day*. Faber & Faber, 1999.

Mabinogion. ca. 1350–1410.

Malory, T. *Le Morte d'Arthur*. 1485.

Marlowe, C. *Doctor Faustus*. 1592.

Márquez, G. M. *Chronicle of a Death Foretold (Crónica de una muerte anunciada)*. La Oveja Negra, 1981.

Matheson, R. *Bid Time Return (Later: Somewhere in Time)*. Buccaneer Books, 1995.

Matheson, R. *What Dreams May Come*. Tor Books, 2004.

Ranke-Graves, R. *I, Claudius*. Penguin Books Ltd, 2001.

Sapkowski, A. *The Witcher*. Dark Horse Books, 2014.

Sophocles. *Oedipus Rex*. ca. 429 BC.

The Song of the Nibelungs. ca. 13th century.

Wachowski, L., & A. *Cloud Atlas*. Random House Trade Paperbacks, 2004.

Wilder, T. *The Bridge of San Luis Rey*. Albert & Charles Boni, 1927.

Visual Arts

Bayes, Gilbert. *Destiny (Ananke)*. 1920. Wikimedia Commons, https://commons.wikimedia.org/wiki/File:Destiny,_Gilbert_Bayes.jpg.

Capponi, Jacques-Martin. *Anankè*. 1901. Wikimedia Commons, https://commons.wikimedia.org/wiki/File:Jacques-martin_capponi,_anankè,_1901,_02.jpg.

Crane, Walter. *The Roll of Fate*. 1882. Wikimedia Commons, https://commons.wikimedia.org/wiki/File:Walter_Crane_-_The_Roll_of_Fate_(1882).jpg.

Donndorf, Karl. *Der Schicksalsbrunnen (The Well of Destiny)*. 1914. Wikipedia, https://de.wikipedia.org/wiki/Schicksalsbrunnen_(Stuttgart).

Frazier, Bernard. *Destiny*. 1966. Wikipedia, https://en.wikipedia.org/wiki/Destiny_(Frazier).

Goya, Francisco. *Atropos o Las Parcas*. *Between 1819 and 1823*. Wikimedia Commons, https://en.wikipedia.org/wiki/Atropos_(Goya)#/media/File:Atropos_o_Las_Parcas.jpg.

II Sodoma. *The Three Fates*. Ca. 1525. Wikimedia Commons, https://commons.wikimedia.org/wiki/File:Sodoma_001.jpg.

Lederer, Hugo. *The Destiny (Schicksal)*. 1905. Wikipedia, https://de.wikipedia.org/wiki/Datei:Lederer_Schicksal.jpg.

Lund, Johan Ludwig. *Nornir (The Norns)*. ca. 1844. Wikimedia Commons, https://commons.wikimedia.org/wiki/File:Nornir_by_Lund.jpg.

Mowbray, Henry Siddons. *Le Destin.* 1896. Wikimedia Commons, https://commons.wikimedia.org/wiki/File:Henry_Siddons_Mowbray_-_Le_Destin_-_1979.39_-_Museum_of_Fine_Arts.jpg.

Phyromachos. *Moira Fighting Giants.* ca. 166–156 BCE. Wikimedia Commons, https://commons.wikimedia.org/wiki/File:Pergamon-Altar_-_Moira_Giganten_1.jpg.

Shadow, Johann Gottfried. *Grabmal des Prinzen.* 1788–1789. Wikimedia Commons, https://commons.wikimedia.org/wiki/File:Schadow_Grabmal_Alexander_2.jpg.

Strudwick, John. *A Golden Thread.* 1885. Wikimedia Commons, https://commons.wikimedia.org/wiki/File:Strudwick_-_A_Golden_Thread.jpg.

Thijs, Pieter. *Time and the Three Fates.* ca. 1665. Wikimedia Commons, https://commons.wikimedia.org/wiki/File:Pieter_Thijs_-_Time_and_the_Three_Fates.jpg.

Thumann, Paul. *The Three Fates.* 19th century. Wikimedia Commons, https://commons.wikimedia.org/wiki/File:The_Three_Fates_-_Paul_Thumann.jpg.

Vedder, Elihu. *The Fates Gathering in the Stars.* 1887. Wikimedia Commons, https://commons.wikimedia.org/wiki/File:Elihu_Vedder_The_Fates_Gathering_in_the_Stars.jpg.

Wackerle, Josef. *The Three Fates Fountain.* 1956. Wikipedia, https://en.wikipedia.org/wiki/File:St_Stephens_Green_German_Gift_-_3_Fates.jpg.

Waterhouse, John William. *La Fileuse (The Spinner).* 1874. Wikimedia Commons, https://commons.wikimedia.org/wiki/File:La_Fileuse_-_John_William_Waterhouse.jpg.

Music

Almost Maybes. Davis, J., Frasure, J., Lindsey, H. Performer: Jordan Davis. 2020.

Camelot. Loewe, F. & Lerner, J. 1960.

Chances. Backstreet Boys. Tedder, R., Mendes, S., Skelton, Z., Warburton, and G. Performer: Backstreet Boys. 2019.

Definition Of Destiny. Kowalewicz, B., D'Sa, I., Gallant, J., and Solowoniuk, A. Performer: Billy Talent. 2009.

Destiny. DeRouge, C. and Rush, J. Performer: Jennifer Rush. 1985.

Detours. Davis, J., Turnbull, D., and Jenkins, J. Performer: Jordan Davis, 2020.

End Up With You. Lindsey, H., McLaughlin, B., and Rose, L. Performer: Carrie Underwood. 2018.

Falls To Climb. Berry, B., Buck, P., Mills, M., and Stipe, M. Performer: R.E.M. 1998.

Found You. Brown, K., McGinn, M., and Montgomery, C. Performer: Kane Brown. 2016.

Freewill. Lee, G., Lifeson, A., and Peart, N. Performer: Rush. 1980.

Ghost Of A Chance. Lee, G., Lifeson, A., Peart, N. Performer: Rush. 1991.

Götterdämmerung (Twilight of the Gods, Ragnarök). Wagner, Richard. 1848.

Invisible String. Swift, T., Dessner, A. Performer: Taylor Swift. 2020.

Karma Police. Yorke, T., Greenwood, J., Greenwood, C., Selway, P., O'Brien, E. Performer: Radiohead. 1997.

La Forza Del Destino (The Force of Destiny). Verdi, Giuseppe. 1861.

Magnetic. Howl, C., and Lattimer J. Performer: Chlöe Howl. 2017.

Meant to Be. Rexha, B., Hubbard, T., Garcia, D., and Miller, J. Performer: Bebe Rexha. 2017.

Moirai. Rose, L. Performer: Lucy Rose. 2017.

Que Sera, Sera (Whatever Will Be, Will Be). Livingston, J. and Evans, R. Performer: Doris Day. 1956.

Rewrite the Stars (The Greatest Showman). Pasek, B., and Paul, J. Performer: Zac Efron. 2017.

See The Sky About To Rain. Young, N. Performer: Young, N., 1974.

The Circle Game. Mitchell, J. Performer: Joni Mitchell. 1966.

The Cup Of Life. Child, D., Rosa, D., and Escolar, L. G. Performer: Ricky Martin. 1998.

The Symphony No. 5 in C minor, Op. 67. (The Fate Symphony). Beethoven, Ludwig von. 1804–1808.

The Three Fates. Emerson, K. and Lake, G. Performer: Emerson, Lake and Palmer. 1970.

There But For Fortune. Ochs, P. Performer: Joan Baez. 1989.

Tristan & Isolde. Wagner, Richard. 1859.

Wheel In The Sky. Fleischman, R., Schon, N. and Valory, D. Performer: Jouney. 1978.

When Am I Gonna Lose You. Rice, T., Ayer, K., Hahn, R., and Frazier, M. Performer: Local Natives. 2019.

Screen

12 Monkeys. Dir.: Gilliam, Terry. 1995.

Batman. The Dark Knight Trilogy. Dir.: Nolan, Christopher. 2005 – 2012.

Being There. Dir.: Ashby, Hal. 1979.

Destino. Creators: Dali, Salvador, Hench, John, Ernst, Donald W.. 1945–2004.

Eternal Sunshine of the Spotless Mind. Dir.: Gondry, Michel. 2004.

Forrest Gump. Dir.: Zemeckis, Robert. 1994.

Gladiator. Dir.: Scott, Ridley. 2000.

I am Legend. Dir.: Lawrence, Francis. 2007.

I Origins. Dir.: Cahill, Mike. 2014.

In Your Eyes. Dir: Brin, Hill. 2014.

LA Story. Dir.: Jackson, Mick. 1991.

Lost (TV series). Creators: Lieber, Jeffrey—Abrams, J. J.—Lindelof, Damon. 2004–2010.

Serendipity. Dir.: Chelsom, Peter. 2001.

Slumdog Millionaire. Dir.: Boyle, Danny. 2008.

Somewhere in Time. Dir.: Szwarc, Jeannot. 1980.

Star Wars. Creator: Lucas, George. Dir.: Various. 1977–current. (See Wikipedia: https://en.wikipedia.org/wiki/List_of_Star_Wars_films).

The Adjustment Bureau. Dir.: Nolfi, George. 2011.

The Great Gatsby. Dir.: Clayton, Jack. 1974.

The Great Gatsby. Dir.: Luhrmann, Baz. 2013.

The Lake House. Dir.: Agresti, Alejandro. 2006.

The Lord of the Rings. Dir.: Jackson, Peter. 2001–2003.

The Matrix Franchise. Dir.: Wachowski, Lana & Lilly. 1999–2021.

The Terminator. Dir.: Cameron, James. 1984.

The Wizard of Oz. Dir.: Fleming, Victor. 1939.

Bibliography & Links

Adler, A. *Der Sinn des Lebens.* Dr. Rolf Passer, 1933. Wien/Leipzig.

Aristotle. *The Works of Aristotle.* ca. 384–322 BCE. Link: http://www.gutenberg.org/ebooks/12699.

Bailey, Cyril. *The Religion of Ancient Rome.* Project Gutenberg, 2006. Link: http://www.gutenberg.org/ebooks/18564.

Bargdill, R. W. *Fate and Destiny: Some Historical Distinctions Between the Concepts. Journal of Theoretical and Philosophical Psychology,* 2006.

Berens, E. M.. *Myths and Legends of Ancient Greece and Rome.* Project Gutenberg, 2007. Link: http://www.gutenberg.org/ebooks/22381.

Bernays, E. *Crystallizing Public Opinion.* Boni and Liveright, 1923.

Bernays, E. L. *Biography of an Idea: Memoirs of Public Relations Counsel.* Simon and Schuster, 1965.

Bernays, E. *Propaganda.* Horace Liveright, 1928.

Bernays, E. *Public Relations*. University of Oklahoma Press, 1945.

Bernays, E. *The Engineering of Consent*. University of Oklahoma Press, 1955.

Bettini, M. *Weighty Words, Suspect Speech: Fari in Roman Culture. Arethusa, vol. 41, no. 2, 2008.* The Johns Hopkins University Press. Link: https://muse.jhu.edu/article/238629.

Black, J., & Green, A. *Gods, Demons and Symbols of Ancient Mesopotamia*. British Museum Press, 1992.

Brendel, Otto Johannes (1936). *Symbolism of the Sphere*. Leiden: E.J. Brill, 1977. Internet Archive. Link: https://archive.org/details/OttoBrendelSymbolismoftheSphere.

Budge, Sir E. A. Wallis. *Legends of the Gods (The Egyptian Texts, edited with Translations)*. Project Gutenberg, 2005. Link: http://www.gutenberg.org/ebooks/9411.

Bulfinch, Thomas. *Bulfinch's Mythology*. Project Gutenberg, 2004. Link: http://www.gutenberg.org/ebooks/4928.

Cassin, B., Apter, E., Lezra, J., Wood, M. *Dictionary of Untranslatables: A Philosophical Lexicon*. Princeton University Press, 2014.

Critchlow, H. *The Science of Fate: Why Your Future is More Predictable Than You Think*. Hodder & Stoughton, 2019. UK.

Dennett, D. C. *Breaking the Spell: Religion as a Natural Phenomenon*. Viking, 2006. Penguin.

Dennett, D. C. *Freedom Evolves*. Viking, 2003. New York. *Destiny*. Link: https://en.wikipedia.org/wiki/Destiny.

Duignan, B. (Editor). *The History of Philosophy, Modern Philosophy*. Britannica Educational Publishing, 2011.

Ed. Boardman, J., Griffin, Oswyn Murray, J. *The Oxford History of the Classical World*. Oxford University Press, 1986. New York / Oxford.

Eidinow, E. *Luck, Fate and Fortune: Antiquity and its Legacy*. I.B. Tauris, 2011.

Eliot, Charles. *Hinduism and Buddhism, An Historical Sketch, Vol. 1, 2, 3*. Project Gutenberg, 2005. Link: http://www.gutenberg.org/ebooks/author/4887.

Elliot, A., Menn, L. *For an Anthropology of Destiny*. HAU: Journal of Ethnographic Theory, vol. 8, no. 1/2, 2018, pp. 292-299.

Everett III, H. *Relative State—Formulation of Quantum Mechanics. Reviews of Modern Physics, vol. 29, no. 3, 1957, pp. 454.*

Frankl, V. *Trotzdem Ja zum Leben sagen—Ein Psychologe erlebt das Konzentrationslager /Man's Search for Meaning (From Death-Camp to Existentialism)*. Kösel, 1946. München, 1976.

Freud, S. *Massenpsychologie und Ich—Analyse*. Nikol, 2020. 1921.

Freud, S. *The Ego and the Id (Standard Edition of the Complete Psychological Works of Sigmund Freud)*. W. W. Norton & Co. Inc., 1962.

Giles, Herbert Allen. *Religions of Ancient China*. Project Gutenberg, 2006. Link: http://www.gutenberg.org/ebooks/2330.

Gladwell, M. Outliers: *The Story of Success*. Penguin, 2009.

Graves, R. *The Greek Myths*. Faber and Faber, 1955. London.

Greene, A. C. *The Concept of Ananke in Greek Literature Before 400 BCE*. University of Exeter, 2012. UK.

Greene, W. C. *Moira, Fate, Good and Evil in Greek Thought*. Harvard University Press, 1944. Reprint ed., 2013.

Gribbin, J. *In Search of Schrödinger's Cat: The Startling World of Quantum Physics Explained*. Wildwood House, 1984. London.

Guerber, H. A. *Myths of the Norsemen: From the Eddas and Sagas*. Project Gutenberg, 2009. Link: http://www.gutenberg.org/ebooks/28497.

Harari, Y. *Sapiens: A Brief History of Humankind*. HarperCollins, 2014.

Harris, S. *Free Will*. Free Press/Simon & Schuster, 2012.

Heisenberg, W. *Physics and Philosophy: The Revolution in Modern Science*. Harper Perennial Modern Classics, 2007. First Edition, 1958.

Hesiod. *Theogony*. ca. 700 BCE. Link: http://self.gutenberg.org/articles/hesiod%27s_theogony.

History of Art Timeline. Link: https://www.identifythisart.com/timeline-of-art-history/.

History of Literature Timeline. Link: https://www.timelineindex.com/content/select/1026/912,1,1026.

History of Movies Timeline. Link: https://www.infoplease.com/culture-entertainment/film/movie-timeline.

History of Philosophy Timeline: Link: https://www.preceden.com/timelines/47600-brief-history-of-philosophy
and https://en.wikipedia.org/wiki/Timeline_of_Western_philosophers.

History of the Free Will Problem. Link: http://www.informationphilosopher.com/freedom/history/.

History of the World Timeline. Link: https://www.infoplease.com/history/world.

Homer. *The Iliad*. ca. 7th–8th century BCE. Link: http://www.gutenberg.org/ebooks/22382.

Homer. *The Odyssey*. ca. 7th–8th century BCE. Link: http://www.gutenberg.org/ebooks/1728.

Honderich, T. *How Free Are You?: The Determinism Problem (Vol. 2)*. Oxford University Press, 1993.

Honderich, T. *On Determinism and Freedom*. Edinburgh University Press, 2005. Link: https://www.edinburghuniversitypress.com/book-determinism-and-freedom-in-the-age-of-modern-science.html.

Hughes, R. A. *The Concept of Destiny in Depth Psychology and Theology*. 2011. Link: szondiforum.org.

Hunt, M.W. *Kant and Fate*. Cosmos and History: The Journal of Natural and Social Philosophy, vol. 18, no. 1, 2022. Link: https://philarchive.org/archive/HUNKF.

Internet Encyclopedia of Philosophy Link: https://iep.utm.edu.

James, W. *The Dilemma of Determinism* (pp. 1878-1899). Kessinger Publishing, 1884.

Jung, C.G. *The Portable Jung*. Translated by R.F.C. Hull. Edited by J. Campbell. The Viking Portable Library. Viking Penguin Inc., 1971.

King, Leonard William. *The Seven Tablets of Creation* (Original: 1902). Evinity Publishing Inc, 2009. Link: https://www.sacred-texts.com/ane/stc/index.htm.

Lang, Jean. *A Book of Myths*. Project Gutenberg, 2007. Link: http://www.gutenberg.org/ebooks/22693.

Laplace, P. S. *A Philosophical Essay on Probabilities*. English edition 1951, 1900.

Lerner, G. *The Creation of Patriarchy*. Oxford University Press, 1986.

López-Ruiz, C. *Where the Gods Were Born: Greek Cosmogonies and the Near East*. Harvard University Press, 2010.

Lowen, A. *Narcissism—Denial of the True Self*. Touchstone, 1997.

Mackenzie, Donald A. *Indian Myth and Legend*. Project Gutenberg, 2014. Link: http://www.gutenberg.org/ebooks/47228.

Mackenzie, Donald A. *Myths of Babylonia and Assyria*. Project Gutenberg, 2006. Link: http://www.gutenberg.org/ebooks/16653.

Marcus Aurelius. *Meditations*. Link: https://www.gutenberg.org/ebooks/2680.

May, R. *Freedom and Destiny*. W.W. Norton & Company, 1981. United States.

May, R. *Love and Will*. W.W. Norton & Company, 1969. United States.

McLeod, S. A. *Carl Jung's Theory Of Personality: Archetypes & Collective Unconscious*. 2018. Simply Psychology. Link: https://www.simplypsychology.org/carl-jung.html.

Modupeola Ojo, Kevin Ibokanweting, Akpan Bassey Samuel. *Compatibilism as Basis for Human Freedom*. Vol.4, Issue 3, Dept. of Humanities & Social Sciences, NIT Agartala, India, 2017.

Müller, A. *Moira-Fate and Freedom in Ancient Thought*. University of Barcelona (UB) Faculty of Philosophy, Scientific Research Publishing Inc., 2016.

New Age. Link: https://en.wikipedia.org/wiki/New_Age.

Orpheus. *Orphic Mysteries*. ca. 5th–6th century BCE. Link: http://www.gutenberg.org/ebooks/12699.

Planck, M. *Über eine Verbesserung der Wien'schen Spectralgleichung*. *Verhandlungen der Deutschen Physikalischen Gesellschaft, vol. 2*. English translation by D. ter Haar, The Old Quantum Theory. Pergamon, 2013.

Plato. *The Project Gutenberg Works of Plato*. Compiled and edited by David Widger. Link: http://www.gutenberg.org/files/29441/29441-h/29441-h.htm.

Rawls, J. *Collected Papers* (1951-1998). Edited by S. Freeman, Harvard University Press, 2001. Revised edition.

Ringgren, H. *The Problem of Fatalism*. The Donner Institute, 1967. Link: https://journal.fi/scripta/article/view/67004/2730.

Rolleston, T. W.. *Myths & Legends of the Celtic Race*. Project Gutenberg, 2010. Link: http://www.gutenberg.org/ebooks/34081.

Ruiu, G. *Is Fatalism a Cultural Belief? An Empirical Analysis on the Origin of Fatalistic Tendencies*. The University of Cassino, 2012. Link: https://mpra.ub.uni-muenchen.de/41705/1/MPRA_paper_41705.pdf.

Russell, B. *On the Notion of Cause*. Proceedings of the Aristotelian Society (1912–1913, Vol. 13), Aristotelian Society, Wiley, Oxford University Press, 1912.

Sanchez, Dan. *Cosmology as Teleology*. Link: https://mises.org/wire/cosmology-teleology.

Sandowicz, M. *Luck, Fortune, and Destiny in Ancient Mesopotamia Or How the Sumerians and Babylonians Thought of Their Place in the Flow of Things*. Link: https://www.academia.edu/35603960/Luck_Fortune_and_Destiny_in_Ancient_Mesopotamia_Or_How_the_Sumerians_and_Babylonians_Thought_of_Their_Place_in_the_Flow_of_Things.

Sapolsky, R. M. Behave: *The Biology of Humans at our Best and Worse*. Penguin Press, 2017.

Schwab, G. *Die schönsten Sagen des Klassischen Altertums*. Carl Ueberreuter, 1948. Wien-Heidelberg.

Science hasn't refuted Free Will. Christian List for The Boston Review. Link: https://www.bostonreview.net/articles/christian-list-has-science-refuted-free-will.

Sophocles. *The Seven Plays*. Link: https://www.gutenberg.org/files/14484/14484-h/14484-h.htm.

Spencer, H. J. *Determinism – A Philosophical Fantasy*. Herbert James Spencer, 2012. Link: spsi@shaw.ca.

Spinoza, B. *Ethics. The Collected Works of Spinoza. Volume 1.* Ed. E. Curley, Princeton University Press, 1986.

Steinkeller, P. *Luck, Fortune and Destiny in Ancient Mesopotamia or How the Sumerians and Babylonians Thought of their Place in the Flow of Things.* Eisenbrauns, 2014.

Taylor, R. *Metaphysics.* Prentice-Hall Inc., 1963/1974. New Jersey.

The Babylonian Legends of Creation. Link: http://www.gutenberg.org/ebooks/9914.

The Determinism and Freedom Philosophy Website. Ted Honderich (Editor). Link: https://www.ucl.ac.uk.

The Epic of Gilgamesh. ca. 1800 BCE. Link: http://www.gutenberg.org/ebooks/11000.

Toy, Crawford Howell. *Introduction to the History of Religions.* Project Gutenberg, 2009. Link: http://www.gutenberg.org/ebooks/27829.

Turner, W. *History of Philosophy.* The Athenaeum Press, 1903.

Upton-Mclaughlin, S. *Are Relationships Predestined? They are in China!* 2013 Link: https://chinaculturecorner.com/2013/12/15/yuanfen-are-relationships-predestined-they-are-in-china/.

Walker, B. G. *The Woman's Encyclopedia of Myths and Secrets.* Harper Collins. Castle Books, 1996.

Wegner, D. M. *The Illusion of Conscious Will.* The MIT Press, 2002.

Werner, E. T. C. *Myths and Legends of China.* Project Gutenberg, 2005. Link: http://www.gutenberg.org/ebooks/15250.

Whitmont, E. *The Destiny Concept in Psychotherapy.* Journal of Jungian Theory and Practice, vol. 9, no. 1, 2007.

What is Destinosophy?

Destinosophy means "Wisdom of Destiny." Helena Lind coined this unique expression as a portmanteau—a fusion of the English word "Destiny" and the ancient Greek term "*sophia*," which means wisdom. Destinosophy is her modern perspective on the Mother of faiths and original order in the universe, encompassing ancient wisdom empathically reloaded with transformative insight and spiritual freedom.

Endnotes

1. Anthropomorphism (from Greek *anthrōp* for human, and *morphe* for shape) is our brain-organic tendency to assign human traits to fellow beings and supernatural entities/God(s).

2. Widengren, *History and Facets of a Religious Concept in Modern Times*. 1998. Prof. em. Dr. Lucian Hölscher, Käte Hamburg Kolleg Bochum: https://khk.ceres.rub.de/en/project/fate-history-and/ Fate

3. Ever or never?

4. Something or someone that cannot be assessed, categorized, or determined by natural or typical assessments because it exists beyond such measures/ examinations.

5. Cognitive dissonance is a form of mental discomfort caused by juxtaposition with other beliefs, even facts. The American social psychologist Prof. Leon Festinger (1919–1981) coined the term after his theory of cognitive dissonance.

6. YouGov UK poll, 2016.

7. OnePoll UK, 2018.

8. YouGov US poll, 2015.

9. Jennifer Harper, *The majority of Americans believe in Fate*. 2015. https://www.washingtontimes.com/news/2015/jul/13/poll-61-percent-republicans-believe-fate-horosocop/

10. As per Jan.1, 2023. https://www.census.gov

11. Kelsey Dallas, *When it comes to fate, even non-believers believe*. 2014. https://www.deseret.com/2014/12/5/20554139/when-it-comes-to-fate-even-non-believers-believe#believing-in-fate-or-that-everything-happens-for-a-reason-is-part-of-a-universal-human-need-to-find-purpose-in-a-chaotic-world-a-recent-study-found

12. Ozymandias is a metaphorical sonnet by Percy Bysshe Shelley (1792–1822) on former influential entities' loss of relevance exemplified by the hubristic lament of King Ozymandias's crumbling statue.

13. "And Mizpah; for he said, The Lord watch between me and thee, when we are absent one from another." Genesis 31:49-51. King James Bible (KJV)

14. Teleology (Greek telos and logos—goal and explanation) is the philosophical definition of the purpose of a phenomenon beyond its genesis or causation. Aristotle initiated the thought school of teleology. He claimed a rhyme and a reason for everything.

15. An axiom is an agreed-on premise, a widely shared notion.

16. https://en.wiktionary.org/wiki/destino

17. https://etymologeek.com/lat/destino

18. P.E. Cavendish, 75 in *The Woman's Encyclopedia of Myths and Secrets* by Barbara G. Walker. 1996. Castle Books.

19. Bargdill, R.W. *Fate and Destiny: Some historical distinctions between the concepts*. 2006. Journal of Theoretical and Philosophical Psychology

20. "A.G.I. should theoretically be able to perform any task that a human can and exhibit a range of intelligence in different areas without human intervention. Its performance should be as good as or better than humans at solving problems in most areas." https://www.techtarget.com/searchenterpriseai/definition/artificial-general-intelligence-AGI

21. https://thehill.com/opinion/technology/4003870-entering-the-singularity-has-ai-reached-the-point-of-no-return/ Entering the singularity: Has AI reached the point of no return? J. Mauricio Gaona for TheHill.

22. https://en.wikipedia.org/wiki/History_of_agriculture

23. https://www.smithsonianmag.com/history/gobekli-tepe-the-worlds-first-temple-83613665/

24. https://en.wikiquote.org/wiki/Epic_of_Gilgamesh

25. https://www.gutenberg.org/files/11000/11000-h/11000-h.htm

26. https://www.sacred-texts.com/ane/enuma.htm

27. *Ancient Mesopotamia: Portrait of a Dead Civilization* by A. Leo Oppenheim, revised edition completed by Erica Reiner, The University of Chicago Press, 1964.

28. Piotr Steinkeller, *Fortune and Misfortune in the Ancient Near East.* 2014/2017. Eisenbrauns.

29. Dianne Wolkstein and Samuel Noah Kramer, *Inanna, Queen of Heaven and Earth: Her Stories and Hymns from Sumer.* 1983. Harper Perennial. https://en.wikipedia.org/wiki/Me_(mythology)

30. Fagles translation

31. Ibid

32. J. Prescott Johnson, *The Concept of Man in Greek Thought: Individuality and Destiny.*

33. E. Cobham Brewer, *Dictionary of Phrase and Fable*, 1894.

34. https://iep.utm.edu/aristotle-ethics/

35. https://www.theoi.com/Daimon/Moirai.html

36. http://www.perseus.tufts.edu/hopper/text?doc=Perseus:text:1999.04.0104:entry=moira-bio-1

37. https://en.wikipedia.org/wiki/Ananke

38. Also referred to as early Eros.

39. E. Cobham Brewer, *Dictionary of Phrase and Fable.* 1894.

40. Bargdill, R.W. *Fate and Destiny: Some historical distinctions between the concepts.* 2006. Journal of Theoretical and Philosophical Psychology

41. Introduced by the German philosopher Gottfried Leibnitz (1646–1716).

42. Joseph Priestley (1733–1804), *The Doctrine of Philosophical Necessity*, Mill and Spencer.

43. J. Weisweiler, 1889, Gaster, 764.

44. De Divinatione.

45. Fear, Uncertainty, and Doubt.

46. Elizabeth Hill Boone, *Cycles of Time and Meaning in the Mexican Books of Fate*, University of Texas Press, 2007

47. Pew Research Center poll, 2017.

48. A. Leo Oppenheim, *Ancient Mesopotamia: Portrait of a Dead Civilization*, University of Chicago Press and https://oi.uchicago.edu/sites/oi.uchicago.edu/files/uploads/shared/docs/ois6.pdf

49. Leyden Papyrus and https://oi.uchicago.edu/sites/oi.uchicago.edu/files/uploads/shared/docs/ois6.pdf

50. Non-exhaustive examples.

51. *Fate and Destiny*, European Judaism: A Journal for the New Europe, Vol. 18, No 1, Winter 84/85.

52. Hebrew transliteration.

53. Hebrew transliteration.

54. fem. Basherte/male Basherter.

55. Hebrew transliteration.

56. It wasn't the Roman Empire, but the Armenian kingdom of originally Zoroastrian faith that first embraced Christianity as state religion at around 301 CE, a good ten years earlier than clever Constantine. It is likely the first time Rome was second to adopt something so enduringly world-shaping. The Armenian capital Yerevan was even founded before Rome: Yerevan. 782 BCE versus Rome 750 BCE.

57. https://en.m.wikipedia.org/wiki/List_of_countries_by_Zoroastrian_population

58. https://www.iranicaonline.org/articles/bakt-fate-destiny

59. India's correct name Bhārat means "descendants of King Bhārat" and goes back to the great Mahabharata epic (ca. 400 CE).

60. In 2018, the Chinese leadership introduced the Community of Common Destiny for Humanity to reflect their new attitude toward foreign politics by including the whole of mankind into their views. Considering the ancient Chinese stature of being the Middle Kingdom under heaven (i.e., the center of our planet), this notion of a shared human Destiny seems impressive, ethically endearing, and very savvy. China is the only "comeback kid" of all bygone great cultures.

61. https://en.wikipedia.org/wiki/I_Ching

62. https://americanhumanist.org/what-is-humanism/definition-of-humanism/

63. From 2019: https://www.pewresearch.org/religion/2019/10/17/in-u-s-de-cline-of-christianity-continues-at-rapid-pace/

64. The British Academy Lecture, read 2016
    https://www.thebritishacademy.ac.uk/documents/1043/11_Wood-head_1825.pdf

65. Kelsey Dallas. *When it comes to Fate even the Non-Believers believe.* 2014.
    https://www.deseret.com/2014/12/5/20554139/when-it-comes-to-fate-even-non-believers-believe#believing-in-fate-or-that-everything-happens-for-a-reason-is-part-of-a-universal-human-need-to-find-purpose-in-a-cha-otic-world-a-recent-study-found

66. Emmanuel, 62.

67. Ajai Kehinde Temitope Emmanuel et al.

68. Abiola Dopamu, *Predestination, Destiny and Faith in Yorubaland: Any Meeting Point?* 2008. Global Journal of Humanities.

69. MacDonald, 23.

70. Ajayi Kehinde Temitope Emmanuel. *African Concept of Man and His Destiny.*

    https://www.academia.edu/37179990/AFRICAN_CONCEPT_OF_MAN_AND_HIS_DESTINY_BY_AJAYI_KEHINDE_TEMITOPE_EMMANUEL

    Fasenfest, David. The Destiny of Modern Societies: the Calvinist Predestination of a New Society. 2009. Brill Academic Publishers.

    MacDonald, James. Manners, customs, superstitions, and religions of South African tribes. The Journal of the Anthropological Institute of Great Britain and Ireland, 20 (1891): 113–140.

    An Essay on African Philosophical Thought: The Akan Conceptual Scheme by Kwame Gyekye. https://www.tandfonline.com/doi/pdf/10.1080/21681392.2015.1075413?needAccess=true

71. Pascoe.

72. Wierzbicka.

73. Bruce Pascoe, *Dark Emu: Aboriginal Australia and the birth of agriculture.* 2018. Magabala Books.

Anna Wierzbicka, *Semantics, Culture, and Cognition: Universal Human Concepts in Culture-Specific Configurations*. 1992. New York: Oxford University Press.

74. David Horton, *The Pure State of Nature: The fate of Australia's environment*. 2020.

75. Anna Wierzbicka, *Semantics, Culture, and Cognition: Universal Human Concepts in Culture-Specific Configurations*. 1992. New York: Oxford University Press.

76. Brown, 76. Michael F. Brown, *The channeling zone: American spirituality in an anxious age*. 1997. Harvard University Press.

77. Siobhan Barry-Bratcher, *The Native American Church: Ancient Tradition and Modern Controversy*. 2019. https://siobhanbarry.medium.com/the-native-american-church-ancient-tradition-and-modern-controversy-ca2ed9bf879f

78. David E. Stannard, *American Holocaust: Columbus and the conquest of the New World*. 1993. Oxford University Press.

79. https://www.pewresearch.org/religion/2017/05/10/religious-beliefs/

80. Jan Hanuš Máchal: Slavic Mythology https://en.m.wikisource.org/wiki/The_Mythology_of_All_Races/Slavic_Mythology/Part_1/Chapter_4

81. Irina A. Sedakova. *The Notion of Fate in Slavonic Folk Tradition. An Ethnolinguistic Approach*. Cosmos 24, 2012. https://www.academia.edu/10810716/The_Notion_of_Fate_Russian_судьба_in_Slavonic_Folk_Tradition_An_Ethnolinguistic_Approach

82. *Humans "predisposed" to believe in Gods and the afterlife*. The Cognition, Religion and Theology Project, Prof. Dr. Justin Barrett, Centre for Anthropology and Mind at Oxford University. 2014. https://www.sciencedaily.com/releases/2011/07/110714103828.htm

83. Religious believers' and non-believers' teleological reasoning about life events. Yale Mind and Development Lab, Konika Banerjee and Paul Bloom, 2014. https://www.sciencedirect.com/science/article/abs/pii/S0010027714001358

84. Named by the author John Toland, 1670–1722.

85. Non-exhaustive examples.

86. Piotr Steinkeller, *Luck, Fortune and Destiny in Ancient Mesopotamia–Or How the Sumerians and Babylonians thought of Their Place in the Flow of Things*. 2014. Eisenbrauns, 2016

87. Here you can read more about philosophical varieties: *Moral Luck And The Unfairness Of Morality*, Robert J. Hartman, 18 September 2018: https://link.springer.com/article/10.1007/s11098-018-1169-5

88. Warren Buffett, now 89, on a lifelong success factor that few other billionaires are willing to credit. Eric Rosenbaum for CNBC: https://www.cnbc.com/2019/08/30/warren-buffett-on-a-life-success-factor-few-other-billionaires-credit.html

89. Gladwell, M. *Outliers: The Story of Success*. 2009. Penguin.

90. https://twitter.com/elonmusk/status/1450036310878478341

91. Harper, D. (n.d.). Etymology of comeuppance. Online Etymology Dictionary. https://www.etymonline.com/word/comeuppance

92. Horatio "Horace" Walpole created more than 200 specific new English words, such as souvenir, malaria, beefy and nuance: https://uselessetymology.com/2017/12/02/the-etymology-of-serendipity/

93. 2007, University of Georgia, The Terry College of Business.

94. https://en.wikipedia.org/wiki/Yuanfen

95. Author of *Comrades to Bodhisattvas: Moral Dimensions of Lay Buddhist Practice in Contemporary China*, 2014.

96. Lower case here, as revered as principles also, see chapter Principle Goddesses of Nature Philosophy.

97. https://en.wikipedia.org/wiki/Determinism

98. Believing that their God hands out predetermined life stories predicated by economic success, thus the readiness to attain salvation.

99. Specht, J. Egloff, B. Schmukle, S.C. *The Benefits of Believing in Chance or Fate: External Locus of Control as a Protective Factor for Coping with the Death of a Spouse*. 2010. Social Psychological and Personality Science. DIW Berlin. https://www.diw.de/documents/publikationen/73/diw_01.c.361905.de/diw_sp0317.pdf

100. https://plato.stanford.edu/entries/desert/

101. Gregg D. Caruso and Stephen G. Morris, *Compatibilism and Retributivist Desert Moral Responsibility: On What is of Central Philosophical and Practical Importance.*

102. Gregg D. Caruso, *Free Will Skepticism and Its Implications: An Argument for Optimism.*

103. The Information Philosopher—John Martin Fischer https://www.informationphilosopher.com/solutions/philosophers/fischer/

104. Fischer, J. M. *Problems with Actual-Sequence Incompatibilism (Comments on Robert Kane's Presentation).* 2000. The Journal of Ethics, 4(4).

105. *General Introductory Lectures*, 1916/17 and 1920 (English) *Introduction to Psychoanalysis or Introductory Lectures on Psycho-Analysis.*

106. Also influenced by Walter Lippmann's Public Opinion, 1922, his theory of Stereotypes, Wilfred Trotter's three books on *The Instinct of the Herd*, 1908–1919, and Everett Dean Martin's *The Behavior of Crowds.*

107. Despite sharing the same moniker, philosophical libertarianism should not be conflated with those Libertarians that claim interesting amounts of autonomy, individualism, and freedom garnered with anxious distrust of government power and authority, including youthful resistance to sometimes natural and necessary human, political, and economic processes.

108. James, 1884

109. Russell, 1912

110. Heisenberg, 1958

111. https://en.wikipedia.org/wiki/Uncertainty_principle

112. Honderich, 1993

113. Planck, 1900

114. Spinoza, 1930

115. Laplace, 1814; Spinoza, 1930

116. Dennett, 2003

117. Dennett, 2003

118. Robert Sapolsky is a professor of neurology, neurological sciences, neuro-surgery, and biology at Stanford University, USA.

119. Penguin Press (October 2023)

120. https://en.wikipedia.org/wiki/Gadfly_(philosophy_and_social_science)

121. El Duderino is echoing wisdom from Marcus Aurelius's *Meditations*: "Everything we hear is an opinion, not a fact; everything we see is a perspective, not the truth."

122. Coined by Speusippos (ca. 407–383), philosopher, Plato's nephew, and Aristotle.

123. Lectures collected by his pupil, Arrianus.

124. Prominently, and somehow astonishingly, quoted in the lyrics of the popular American Christmas song *Have Yourself A Merry Little Christmas*, created in 1943 by Hugh Martin and Ralph Blane.

125. Heraclitus.

126. The Enchiridion.

127. https://en.wikipedia.org/wiki/Lazy_argument

128. https://en.wikisource.org/wiki/Fragments_of_Parmenides

129. https://en.wikipedia.org/wiki/Virtue

130. The theory that moral responsibility is actually compatible with determinism, whether human free will is compatible with determinism or not.

131. https://phys.org/news/2010-03-free-illusion-biologist.html

132. Michio Kaku, *Physics of the Future: How Science Will Shape Human Destiny and Our Daily Lives by the Year 2100*, Anchor; Reprint edition, 2012.

133. Michio Kaku, *The Future of Humanity: Terraforming Mars, Interstellar Travel, Immortality, and Our Destiny Beyond Earth*, Doubleday; First edition, 2018.

134. It should be said, though, that Jung never officially supported the MBTI.

135. http://www.szondiforum.org/The%20Concept%20of%20Destiny%20in%20Depth%20Psychology%20and%20Theology.pdf

136. https://en.wikipedia.org/wiki/Maslow%27s_hierarchy_of_needs

137. Maslow added the all-important sixth top tier shortly before he died. Published in the Journal of Humanistic Psychology: https://thepsychologist.bps.org.uk/volume-27/december-2014/maslows-hierarchy-needs-sixth-level

138. https://www.statista.com/statistics/959368/belief-in-karma-in-the-us/

139. https://www.bmgresearch.co.uk/british-public-reveal-beliefs-new-survey/

140. John Rawls, *Justice as Fairness: A Restatement*. https://archive.org/details/justiceasfairnes0000rawl

141. https://en.wikipedia.org/wiki/Earning_to_give

142. https://en.wikipedia.org/wiki/Pygmalion_effect

143. https://www.heroicimagination.org

144. The unforgettable Christopher Reeve played a quintessentially democratic and humanitarian Superman in four movies between 1978 and 1987, a near perfect modern incarnation of a messianic hero seemingly sent to alleviate human insecurity.

145. *The Heroic and Exceptional Minority* by Gregory V. Diehl (2021, Identity Publications) emphasizes a mindset of believing to be different from the majority, which will open heroic avenues that enable brave actions and great leaps forward. It is an impactful, worthy book that can change the way we perceive our position in the world. Hence, I wrote the foreword to *The Heroic and Exceptional Minority: A Guide to Mythological Self-Awareness and Growth*.

146. *The Cognition, Religion and Theology Project*, Dr. Justin Barrett, Centre for Anthropology and Mind at Oxford University.

147. Non-exhaustive examples.

148. H. Oelsner, P.H. Wicksteed and T. Okey, *The Divine Comedy of Dante Alighieri, Vol I*

149. Diana Darke, *Stealing From The Saracens: How Islamic Architecture Shaped Europe*.

150. https://web.stanford.edu/group/SymCh/supplements/brahms-song-of-the-fates-text.html

151. William Park, *The Dark side of Believing in True Love*. 2019 https://www.bbc.com/future/article/20190211-the-dark-side-of-believing-in-true-love

Arthur. C. Brooks, *Stop Waiting for Your Soulmate*. 2021. https://www.theatlantic.com/family/archive/2021/09/soul-mates-love-destiny/620014/

Katie Bishop, *Why People Still believe in the "Soulmate Myth."* 2022. https://www.bbc.com/worklife/article/20220204-why-people-still-believe-in-the-soulmate-myth

152. https://www.etymonline.com/word/infatuate

153. Before conquering the field of navigation, the magnetic compass was invented as a main device for Destiny's divination under the rule of the Chinese Han Dynasty around 200 BCE. History of the Compass: https://en.m.wikipedia.org/wiki/History_of_the_compass

154. Non-exhaustive examples.

Acknowledgments

A special thank you goes to my research assistants, fact-checkers, and the expert consultant who, for the chapter Destinies, Determinisms & Co, explained several aspects of Quantum Physics and then some to a number-blind scientific dummy. And extra thanks to Gregory V. Diehl, my editor and publisher, for highlighting the destinal significance of certain video games.

Errata

Dear reader,

The author of this book has done her utmost to use accurate information and reliable sources. However, as with any human effort, errors may happen. If you come across any mistakes, we kindly ask that you bring them to our attention at contact@identitypublications.com.

This will allow us to address any points and make necessary corrections in future book editions.

Thank you for your assistance.